Mometrix
TEST PREPARATION

OSAT®

Earth Science (108) Secrets Study Guide

DEAR FUTURE EXAM SUCCESS STORY

First of all, **THANK YOU** for purchasing Mometrix study materials!

Second, congratulations! You are one of the few determined test-takers who are committed to doing whatever it takes to excel on your exam. **You have come to the right place.** We developed these study materials with one goal in mind: to deliver you the information you need in a format that's concise and easy to use.

In addition to optimizing your guide for the content of the test, we've outlined our recommended steps for breaking down the preparation process into small, attainable goals so you can make sure you stay on track.

We've also analyzed the entire test-taking process, identifying the most common pitfalls and showing how you can overcome them and be ready for any curveball the test throws you.

Standardized testing is one of the biggest obstacles on your road to success, which only increases the importance of doing well in the high-pressure, high-stakes environment of test day. Your results on this test could have a significant impact on your future, and this guide provides the information and practical advice to help you achieve your full potential on test day.

Your success is our success

We would love to hear from you! If you would like to share the story of your exam success or if you have any questions or comments in regard to our products, please contact us at **800-673-8175** or **support@mometrix.com**.

Thanks again for your business and we wish you continued success!

Sincerely,
The Mometrix Test Preparation Team

Written and edited by the Mometrix Exam Secrets Test Prep Team
Printed in the United States of America

TABLE OF CONTENTS

Introduction

Thank you for purchasing this resource! You have made the choice to prepare yourself for a test that could have a huge impact on your future, and this guide is designed to help you be fully ready for test day. Obviously, it's important to have a solid understanding of the test material, but you also need to be prepared for the unique environment and stressors of the test, so that you can perform to the best of your abilities.

For this purpose, the first section that appears in this guide is the **Secret Keys**. We've devoted countless hours to meticulously researching what works and what doesn't, and we've boiled down our findings to the five most impactful steps you can take to improve your performance on the test. We start at the beginning with study planning and move through the preparation process, all the way to the testing strategies that will help you get the most out of what you know when you're finally sitting in front of the test.

We recommend that you start preparing for your test as far in advance as possible. However, if you've bought this guide as a last-minute study resource and only have a few days before your test, we recommend that you skip over the first two Secret Keys since they address a long-term study plan.

If you struggle with **test anxiety**, we strongly encourage you to check out our recommendations for how you can overcome it. Test anxiety is a formidable foe, but it can be beaten, and we want to make sure you have the tools you need to defeat it.

Secret Key #1 – Plan Big, Study Small

There's a lot riding on your performance. If you want to ace this test, you're going to need to keep your skills sharp and the material fresh in your mind. You need a plan that lets you review everything you need to know while still fitting in your schedule. We'll break this strategy down into three categories.

Information Organization

Start with the information you already have: the official test outline. From this, you can make a complete list of all the concepts you need to cover before the test. Organize these concepts into groups that can be studied together, and create a list of any related vocabulary you need to learn so you can brush up on any difficult terms. You'll want to keep this vocabulary list handy once you actually start studying since you may need to add to it along the way.

Time Management

Once you have your set of study concepts, decide how to spread them out over the time you have left before the test. Break your study plan into small, clear goals so you have a manageable task for each day and know exactly what you're doing. Then just focus on one small step at a time. When you manage your time this way, you don't need to spend hours at a time studying. Studying a small block of content for a short period each day helps you retain information better and avoid stressing over how much you have left to do. You can relax knowing that you have a plan to cover everything in time. In order for this strategy to be effective though, you have to start studying early and stick to your schedule. Avoid the exhaustion and futility that comes from last-minute cramming!

Study Environment

The environment you study in has a big impact on your learning. Studying in a coffee shop, while probably more enjoyable, is not likely to be as fruitful as studying in a quiet room. It's important to keep distractions to a minimum. You're only planning to study for a short block of time, so make the most of it. Don't pause to check your phone or get up to find a snack. It's also important to **avoid multitasking**. Research has consistently shown that multitasking will make your studying dramatically less effective. Your study area should also be comfortable and well-lit so you don't have the distraction of straining your eyes or sitting on an uncomfortable chair.

The time of day you study is also important. You want to be rested and alert. Don't wait until just before bedtime. Study when you'll be most likely to comprehend and remember. Even better, if you know what time of day your test will be, set that time aside for study. That way your brain will be used to working on that subject at that specific time and you'll have a better chance of recalling information.

Finally, it can be helpful to team up with others who are studying for the same test. Your actual studying should be done in as isolated an environment as possible, but the work of organizing the information and setting up the study plan can be divided up. In between study sessions, you can discuss with your teammates the concepts that you're all studying and quiz each other on the details. Just be sure that your teammates are as serious about the test as you are. If you find that your study time is being replaced with social time, you might need to find a new team.

Secret Key #2 – Make Your Studying Count

You're devoting a lot of time and effort to preparing for this test, so you want to be absolutely certain it will pay off. This means doing more than just reading the content and hoping you can remember it on test day. It's important to make every minute of study count. There are two main areas you can focus on to make your studying count.

Retention

It doesn't matter how much time you study if you can't remember the material. You need to make sure you are retaining the concepts. To check your retention of the information you're learning, try recalling it at later times with minimal prompting. Try carrying around flashcards and glance at one or two from time to time or ask a friend who's also studying for the test to quiz you.

To enhance your retention, look for ways to put the information into practice so that you can apply it rather than simply recalling it. If you're using the information in practical ways, it will be much easier to remember. Similarly, it helps to solidify a concept in your mind if you're not only reading it to yourself but also explaining it to someone else. Ask a friend to let you teach them about a concept you're a little shaky on (or speak aloud to an imaginary audience if necessary). As you try to summarize, define, give examples, and answer your friend's questions, you'll understand the concepts better and they will stay with you longer. Finally, step back for a big picture view and ask yourself how each piece of information fits with the whole subject. When you link the different concepts together and see them working together as a whole, it's easier to remember the individual components.

Finally, practice showing your work on any multi-step problems, even if you're just studying. Writing out each step you take to solve a problem will help solidify the process in your mind, and you'll be more likely to remember it during the test.

Modality

Modality simply refers to the means or method by which you study. Choosing a study modality that fits your own individual learning style is crucial. No two people learn best in exactly the same way, so it's important to know your strengths and use them to your advantage.

For example, if you learn best by visualization, focus on visualizing a concept in your mind and draw an image or a diagram. Try color-coding your notes, illustrating them, or creating symbols that will trigger your mind to recall a learned concept. If you learn best by hearing or discussing information, find a study partner who learns the same way or read aloud to yourself. Think about how to put the information in your own words. Imagine that you are giving a lecture on the topic and record yourself so you can listen to it later.

For any learning style, flashcards can be helpful. Organize the information so you can take advantage of spare moments to review. Underline key words or phrases. Use different colors for different categories. Mnemonic devices (such as creating a short list in which every item starts with the same letter) can also help with retention. Find what works best for you and use it to store the information in your mind most effectively and easily.

Secret Key #3 – Practice the Right Way

Your success on test day depends not only on how many hours you put into preparing, but also on whether you prepared the right way. It's good to check along the way to see if your studying is paying off. One of the most effective ways to do this is by taking practice tests to evaluate your progress. Practice tests are useful because they show exactly where you need to improve. Every time you take a practice test, pay special attention to these three groups of questions:

- The questions you got wrong
- The questions you had to guess on, even if you guessed right
- The questions you found difficult or slow to work through

This will show you exactly what your weak areas are, and where you need to devote more study time. Ask yourself why each of these questions gave you trouble. Was it because you didn't understand the material? Was it because you didn't remember the vocabulary? Do you need more repetitions on this type of question to build speed and confidence? Dig into those questions and figure out how you can strengthen your weak areas as you go back to review the material.

Additionally, many practice tests have a section explaining the answer choices. It can be tempting to read the explanation and think that you now have a good understanding of the concept. However, an explanation likely only covers part of the question's broader context. Even if the explanation makes perfect sense, **go back and investigate** every concept related to the question until you're positive you have a thorough understanding.

As you go along, keep in mind that the practice test is just that: practice. Memorizing these questions and answers will not be very helpful on the actual test because it is unlikely to have any of the same exact questions. If you only know the right answers to the sample questions, you won't be prepared for the real thing. **Study the concepts** until you understand them fully, and then you'll be able to answer any question that shows up on the test.

It's important to wait on the practice tests until you're ready. If you take a test on your first day of study, you may be overwhelmed by the amount of material covered and how much you need to learn. Work up to it gradually.

On test day, you'll need to be prepared for answering questions, managing your time, and using the test-taking strategies you've learned. It's a lot to balance, like a mental marathon that will have a big impact on your future. Like training for a marathon, you'll need to start slowly and work your way up. When test day arrives, you'll be ready.

Start with the strategies you've read in the first two Secret Keys—plan your course and study in the way that works best for you. If you have time, consider using multiple study resources to get different approaches to the same concepts. It can be helpful to see difficult concepts from more than one angle. Then find a good source for practice tests. Many times, the test website will suggest potential study resources or provide sample tests.

Practice Test Strategy

If you're able to find at least three practice tests, we recommend this strategy:

Untimed and Open-Book Practice

Take the first test with no time constraints and with your notes and study guide handy. Take your time and focus on applying the strategies you've learned.

Timed and Open-Book Practice

Take the second practice test open-book as well, but set a timer and practice pacing yourself to finish in time.

Timed and Closed-Book Practice

Take any other practice tests as if it were test day. Set a timer and put away your study materials. Sit at a table or desk in a quiet room, imagine yourself at the testing center, and answer questions as quickly and accurately as possible.

Keep repeating timed and closed-book tests on a regular basis until you run out of practice tests or it's time for the actual test. Your mind will be ready for the schedule and stress of test day, and you'll be able to focus on recalling the material you've learned.

Secret Key #4 – Pace Yourself

Once you're fully prepared for the material on the test, your biggest challenge on test day will be managing your time. Just knowing that the clock is ticking can make you panic even if you have plenty of time left. Work on pacing yourself so you can build confidence against the time constraints of the exam. Pacing is a difficult skill to master, especially in a high-pressure environment, so **practice is vital**.

Set time expectations for your pace based on how much time is available. For example, if a section has 60 questions and the time limit is 30 minutes, you know you have to average 30 seconds or less per question in order to answer them all. Although 30 seconds is the hard limit, set 25 seconds per question as your goal, so you reserve extra time to spend on harder questions. When you budget extra time for the harder questions, you no longer have any reason to stress when those questions take longer to answer.

Don't let this time expectation distract you from working through the test at a calm, steady pace, but keep it in mind so you don't spend too much time on any one question. Recognize that taking extra time on one question you don't understand may keep you from answering two that you do understand later in the test. If your time limit for a question is up and you're still not sure of the answer, mark it and move on, and come back to it later if the time and the test format allow. If the testing format doesn't allow you to return to earlier questions, just make an educated guess; then put it out of your mind and move on.

On the easier questions, be careful not to rush. It may seem wise to hurry through them so you have more time for the challenging ones, but it's not worth missing one if you know the concept and just didn't take the time to read the question fully. Work efficiently but make sure you understand the question and have looked at all of the answer choices, since more than one may seem right at first.

Even if you're paying attention to the time, you may find yourself a little behind at some point. You should speed up to get back on track, but do so wisely. Don't panic; just take a few seconds less on each question until you're caught up. Don't guess without thinking, but do look through the answer choices and eliminate any you know are wrong. If you can get down to two choices, it is often worthwhile to guess from those. Once you've chosen an answer, move on and don't dwell on any that you skipped or had to hurry through. If a question was taking too long, chances are it was one of the harder ones, so you weren't as likely to get it right anyway.

On the other hand, if you find yourself getting ahead of schedule, it may be beneficial to slow down a little. The more quickly you work, the more likely you are to make a careless mistake that will affect your score. You've budgeted time for each question, so don't be afraid to spend that time. Practice an efficient but careful pace to get the most out of the time you have.

Secret Key #5 – Have a Plan for Guessing

When you're taking the test, you may find yourself stuck on a question. Some of the answer choices seem better than others, but you don't see the one answer choice that is obviously correct. What do you do?

The scenario described above is very common, yet most test takers have not effectively prepared for it. Developing and practicing a plan for guessing may be one of the single most effective uses of your time as you get ready for the exam.

In developing your plan for guessing, there are three questions to address:

- When should you start the guessing process?
- How should you narrow down the choices?
- Which answer should you choose?

When to Start the Guessing Process

Unless your plan for guessing is to select C every time (which, despite its merits, is not what we recommend), you need to leave yourself enough time to apply your answer elimination strategies. Since you have a limited amount of time for each question, that means that if you're going to give yourself the best shot at guessing correctly, you have to decide quickly whether or not you will guess.

Of course, the best-case scenario is that you don't have to guess at all, so first, see if you can answer the question based on your knowledge of the subject and basic reasoning skills. Focus on the key words in the question and try to jog your memory of related topics. Give yourself a chance to bring the knowledge to mind, but once you realize that you don't have (or you can't access) the knowledge you need to answer the question, it's time to start the guessing process.

It's almost always better to start the guessing process too early than too late. It only takes a few seconds to remember something and answer the question from knowledge. Carefully eliminating wrong answer choices takes longer. Plus, going through the process of eliminating answer choices can actually help jog your memory.

Summary: Start the guessing process as soon as you decide that you can't answer the question based on your knowledge.

How to Narrow Down the Choices

The next chapter in this book (**Test-Taking Strategies**) includes a wide range of strategies for how to approach questions and how to look for answer choices to eliminate. You will definitely want to read those carefully, practice them, and figure out which ones work best for you. Here though, we're going to address a mindset rather than a particular strategy.

Your odds of guessing an answer correctly depend on how many options you are choosing from.

Number of options left	5	4	3	2	1
Odds of guessing correctly	20%	25%	33%	50%	100%

You can see from this chart just how valuable it is to be able to eliminate incorrect answers and make an educated guess, but there are two things that many test takers do that cause them to miss out on the benefits of guessing:

- Accidentally eliminating the correct answer
- Selecting an answer based on an impression

We'll look at the first one here, and the second one in the next section.

To avoid accidentally eliminating the correct answer, we recommend a thought exercise called **the $5 challenge**. In this challenge, you only eliminate an answer choice from contention if you are willing to bet $5 on it being wrong. Why $5? Five dollars is a small but not insignificant amount of money. It's an amount you could afford to lose but wouldn't want to throw away. And while losing $5 once might not hurt too much, doing it twenty times will set you back $100. In the same way, each small decision you make—eliminating a choice here, guessing on a question there—won't by itself impact your score very much, but when you put them all together, they can make a big difference. By holding each answer choice elimination decision to a higher standard, you can reduce the risk of accidentally eliminating the correct answer.

The $5 challenge can also be applied in a positive sense: If you are willing to bet $5 that an answer choice *is* correct, go ahead and mark it as correct.

Summary: Only eliminate an answer choice if you are willing to bet $5 that it is wrong.

Which Answer to Choose

You're taking the test. You've run into a hard question and decided you'll have to guess. You've eliminated all the answer choices you're willing to bet $5 on. Now you have to pick an answer. Why do we even need to talk about this? Why can't you just pick whichever one you feel like when the time comes?

The answer to these questions is that if you don't come into the test with a plan, you'll rely on your impression to select an answer choice, and if you do that, you risk falling into a trap. The test writers know that everyone who takes their test will be guessing on some of the questions, so they intentionally write wrong answer choices to seem plausible. You still have to pick an answer though, and if the wrong answer choices are designed to look right, how can you ever be sure that you're not falling for their trap? The best solution we've found to this dilemma is to take the decision out of your hands entirely. Here is the process we recommend:

Once you've eliminated any choices that you are confident (willing to bet $5) are wrong, select the first remaining choice as your answer.

Whether you choose to select the first remaining choice, the second, or the last, the important thing is that you use some preselected standard. Using this approach guarantees that you will not be enticed into selecting an answer choice that looks right, because you are not basing your decision on how the answer choices look.

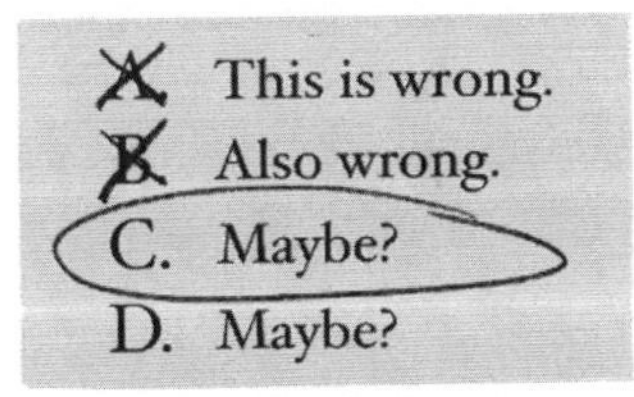

This is not meant to make you question your knowledge. Instead, it is to help you recognize the difference between your knowledge and your impressions. There's a huge difference between thinking an answer is right because of what you know, and thinking an answer is right because it looks or sounds like it should be right.

Summary: To ensure that your selection is appropriately random, make a predetermined selection from among all answer choices you have not eliminated.

Test-Taking Strategies

This section contains a list of test-taking strategies that you may find helpful as you work through the test. By taking what you know and applying logical thought, you can maximize your chances of answering any question correctly!

It is very important to realize that every question is different and every person is different: no single strategy will work on every question, and no single strategy will work for every person. That's why we've included all of them here, so you can try them out and determine which ones work best for different types of questions and which ones work best for you.

Question Strategies

✓ Read Carefully

Read the question and the answer choices carefully. Don't miss the question because you misread the terms. You have plenty of time to read each question thoroughly and make sure you understand what is being asked. Yet a happy medium must be attained, so don't waste too much time. You must read carefully and efficiently.

✓ Contextual Clues

Look for contextual clues. If the question includes a word you are not familiar with, look at the immediate context for some indication of what the word might mean. Contextual clues can often give you all the information you need to decipher the meaning of an unfamiliar word. Even if you can't determine the meaning, you may be able to narrow down the possibilities enough to make a solid guess at the answer to the question.

✓ Prefixes

If you're having trouble with a word in the question or answer choices, try dissecting it. Take advantage of every clue that the word might include. Prefixes can be a huge help. Usually, they allow you to determine a basic meaning. *Pre-* means before, *post-* means after, *pro-* is positive, *de-* is negative. From prefixes, you can get an idea of the general meaning of the word and try to put it into context.

✓ Hedge Words

Watch out for critical hedge words, such as *likely, may, can, often, almost, mostly, usually, generally, rarely,* and *sometimes.* Question writers insert these hedge phrases to cover every possibility. Often an answer choice will be wrong simply because it leaves no room for exception. Be on guard for answer choices that have definitive words such as *exactly* and *always.*

✓ Switchback Words

Stay alert for *switchbacks.* These are the words and phrases frequently used to alert you to shifts in thought. The most common switchback words are *but, although,* and *however.* Others include *nevertheless, on the other hand, even though, while, in spite of, despite,* and *regardless of.* Switchback words are important to catch because they can change the direction of the question or an answer choice.

⊘ FACE VALUE

When in doubt, use common sense. Accept the situation in the problem at face value. Don't read too much into it. These problems will not require you to make wild assumptions. If you have to go beyond creativity and warp time or space in order to have an answer choice fit the question, then you should move on and consider the other answer choices. These are normal problems rooted in reality. The applicable relationship or explanation may not be readily apparent, but it is there for you to figure out. Use your common sense to interpret anything that isn't clear.

Answer Choice Strategies

⊘ ANSWER SELECTION

The most thorough way to pick an answer choice is to identify and eliminate wrong answers until only one is left, then confirm it is the correct answer. Sometimes an answer choice may immediately seem right, but be careful. The test writers will usually put more than one reasonable answer choice on each question, so take a second to read all of them and make sure that the other choices are not equally obvious. As long as you have time left, it is better to read every answer choice than to pick the first one that looks right without checking the others.

⊘ ANSWER CHOICE FAMILIES

An answer choice family consists of two (in rare cases, three) answer choices that are very similar in construction and cannot all be true at the same time. If you see two answer choices that are direct opposites or parallels, one of them is usually the correct answer. For instance, if one answer choice says that quantity *x* increases and another either says that quantity *x* decreases (opposite) or says that quantity *y* increases (parallel), then those answer choices would fall into the same family. An answer choice that doesn't match the construction of the answer choice family is more likely to be incorrect. Most questions will not have answer choice families, but when they do appear, you should be prepared to recognize them.

⊘ ELIMINATE ANSWERS

Eliminate answer choices as soon as you realize they are wrong, but make sure you consider all possibilities. If you are eliminating answer choices and realize that the last one you are left with is also wrong, don't panic. Start over and consider each choice again. There may be something you missed the first time that you will realize on the second pass.

⊘ AVOID FACT TRAPS

Don't be distracted by an answer choice that is factually true but doesn't answer the question. You are looking for the choice that answers the question. Stay focused on what the question is asking for so you don't accidentally pick an answer that is true but incorrect. Always go back to the question and make sure the answer choice you've selected actually answers the question and is not merely a true statement.

⊘ EXTREME STATEMENTS

In general, you should avoid answers that put forth extreme actions as standard practice or proclaim controversial ideas as established fact. An answer choice that states the "process should be used in certain situations, if..." is much more likely to be correct than one that states the "process should be discontinued completely." The first is a calm rational statement and doesn't even make a definitive, uncompromising stance, using a hedge word *if* to provide wiggle room, whereas the second choice is far more extreme.

⊘ BENCHMARK

As you read through the answer choices and you come across one that seems to answer the question well, mentally select that answer choice. This is not your final answer, but it's the one that will help you evaluate the other answer choices. The one that you selected is your benchmark or standard for judging each of the other answer choices. Every other answer choice must be compared to your benchmark. That choice is correct until proven otherwise by another answer choice beating it. If you find a better answer, then that one becomes your new benchmark. Once you've decided that no other choice answers the question as well as your benchmark, you have your final answer.

⊘ PREDICT THE ANSWER

Before you even start looking at the answer choices, it is often best to try to predict the answer. When you come up with the answer on your own, it is easier to avoid distractions and traps because you will know exactly what to look for. The right answer choice is unlikely to be word-for-word what you came up with, but it should be a close match. Even if you are confident that you have the right answer, you should still take the time to read each option before moving on.

General Strategies

⊘ TOUGH QUESTIONS

If you are stumped on a problem or it appears too hard or too difficult, don't waste time. Move on! Remember though, if you can quickly check for obviously incorrect answer choices, your chances of guessing correctly are greatly improved. Before you completely give up, at least try to knock out a couple of possible answers. Eliminate what you can and then guess at the remaining answer choices before moving on.

⊘ CHECK YOUR WORK

Since you will probably not know every term listed and the answer to every question, it is important that you get credit for the ones that you do know. Don't miss any questions through careless mistakes. If at all possible, try to take a second to look back over your answer selection and make sure you've selected the correct answer choice and haven't made a costly careless mistake (such as marking an answer choice that you didn't mean to mark). This quick double check should more than pay for itself in caught mistakes for the time it costs.

⊘ PACE YOURSELF

It's easy to be overwhelmed when you're looking at a page full of questions; your mind is confused and full of random thoughts, and the clock is ticking down faster than you would like. Calm down and maintain the pace that you have set for yourself. Especially as you get down to the last few minutes of the test, don't let the small numbers on the clock make you panic. As long as you are on track by monitoring your pace, you are guaranteed to have time for each question.

⊘ DON'T RUSH

It is very easy to make errors when you are in a hurry. Maintaining a fast pace in answering questions is pointless if it makes you miss questions that you would have gotten right otherwise. Test writers like to include distracting information and wrong answers that seem right. Taking a little extra time to avoid careless mistakes can make all the difference in your test score. Find a pace that allows you to be confident in the answers that you select.

⊘ Keep Moving

Panicking will not help you pass the test, so do your best to stay calm and keep moving. Taking deep breaths and going through the answer elimination steps you practiced can help to break through a stress barrier and keep your pace.

Final Notes

The combination of a solid foundation of content knowledge and the confidence that comes from practicing your plan for applying that knowledge is the key to maximizing your performance on test day. As your foundation of content knowledge is built up and strengthened, you'll find that the strategies included in this chapter become more and more effective in helping you quickly sift through the distractions and traps of the test to isolate the correct answer.

Now that you're preparing to move forward into the test content chapters of this book, be sure to keep your goal in mind. As you read, think about how you will be able to apply this information on the test. If you've already seen sample questions for the test and you have an idea of the question format and style, try to come up with questions of your own that you can answer based on what you're reading. This will give you valuable practice applying your knowledge in the same ways you can expect to on test day.

Good luck and good studying!

Science Practices and the Engineering Process

Safety and Equipment

Laboratory Accidents

Any spills or accidents should be **reported** to the teacher so that the teacher can determine the safest clean-up method. The student should start to wash off a **chemical** spilled on the skin while reporting the incident. Some spills may require removal of contaminated clothing and use of the **safety shower**. Broken glass should be disposed of in a designated container. If someone's clothing catches fire they should walk to the safety shower and use it to extinguish the flames. A fire blanket may be used to smother a **lab fire**. A fire extinguisher, phone, spill neutralizers, and a first aid box are other types of **safety equipment** found in the lab. Students should be familiar with **routes** out of the room and the building in case of fire. Students should use the **eye wash station** if a chemical gets in the eyes.

Safety Procedures

Students should wear a **lab apron** and **safety goggles**. Loose or dangling clothing and jewelry, necklaces, and earrings should not be worn. Those with long hair should tie it back. Care should always be taken not to splash chemicals. Open-toed shoes such as sandals and flip-flops should not be worn, nor should wrist watches. Glasses are preferable to contact lenses since the latter carry a risk of chemicals getting caught between the lens and the eye. Students should always be supervised. The area where the experiment is taking place and the surrounding floor should be free of clutter. Only the lab book and the items necessary for the experiment should be present. Smoking, eating, and chewing gum are not permitted in the lab. Cords should not be allowed to dangle from work stations. There should be no rough-housing in the lab. Hands should be washed after the lab is complete.

Fume Hoods

Because of the potential safety hazards associated with chemistry lab experiments, such as fire from vapors and the inhalation of toxic fumes, a **fume hood** should be used in many instances. A fume hood carries away vapors from reagents or reactions. Equipment or reactions are placed as far back in the hood as practical to help enhance the collection of the fumes. The **glass safety shield** automatically closes to the appropriate height, and it should be low enough to protect the face and body. The safety shield should only be raised to move equipment in and out of the hood. One should not climb inside a hood or stick one's head inside. All spills should be wiped up immediately, and the glass should be cleaned if a splash occurs.

Common Safety Hazards

Some specific safety hazards possible in a chemistry lab include:

- **Fire**: Fire can be caused by volatile solvents such as ether, acetone, or benzene being kept in an open beaker or Erlenmeyer flask. Vapors can creep along the table and ignite if they reach a flame or spark. Solvents should be heated in a hood with a steam bath, not on a hot plate.
- **Explosion**: Heating or creating a reaction in a closed system can cause an explosion, resulting in flying glass and chemical splashes. The system should be vented to prevent this.

- **Chemical and thermal burns**: Many chemicals are corrosive to the skin and eyes.
- **Inhalation of toxic fumes**: Some compounds severely irritate membranes in the eyes, nose, throat, and lungs.
- **Absorption** of toxic chemicals such as dimethyl sulfoxide (DMSO) and nitrobenzene through the skin.
- **Ingestion** of toxic chemicals.

Safety Gloves

There are many types of **gloves** available to help protect the skin from cuts, burns, and chemical splashes. There are many considerations when choosing a glove. For example, gloves that are highly protective may limit dexterity. Some gloves may not offer appropriate protection against a specific chemical. Other considerations include degradation rating, which indicates how effective a glove is when exposed to chemicals; breakthrough time, which indicates how quickly a chemical can break through the surface of the glove; and permeation rate, which indicates how quickly chemicals seep through after the initial breakthrough. Disposable latex, vinyl, or nitrile gloves are usually appropriate for most circumstances, and offer protection from incidental splashes and contact. Other types of gloves include butyl, neoprene, PVC, PVA, Viton, Silver Shield, and natural rubber. Each offers its own type of protection but may have drawbacks as well.

Proper Handling and Storage of Chemicals

Students should take care when **carrying chemicals** from one place to another. Chemicals should never be taken from the room, tasted, or touched with bare hands. **Safety gloves** should be worn when appropriate and glove/chemical interactions and glove deterioration should be considered. Hands should always be **washed** thoroughly after a lab. Potentially hazardous materials intended for use in chemistry, biology, or other science labs should be secured in a safe area where relevant **Safety Data Sheets (SDS)** can be accessed. Chemicals and solutions should be used as directed and labels should be read before handling solutions and chemicals. Extra chemicals should not be returned to their original containers, but should be disposed of as directed by the school district's rules or local ordinances. Local municipalities often have hazardous waste disposal programs. Acids should be stored separately from other chemicals. Flammable liquids should be stored away from acids, bases, and oxidizers.

Bunsen Burners

When using a **Bunsen burner**, loose clothing should be tucked in, long hair should be tied back, and safety goggles and aprons should be worn. Students should know what to do in case of a fire or accident. When lighting the burner, strikers should always be used instead of matches. Do not touch the hot barrel. Tongs (never fingers) should be used to hold the material in the flame. To heat liquid, a flask may be set upon wire gauze on a tripod and secured with an iron ring or clamp on a stand. The flame is extinguished by turning off the gas at the source.

Safety Procedures Related to Animals

Animals to be used for **dissections** should be obtained from a company that provides animals for this purpose. Road kill or decaying animals that a student brings in should not be used. It is possible that such an animal may have a pathogen or a virus, such as rabies, which can be transmitted via the saliva of even a dead animal. Students should use gloves and should not participate if they have open sores or moral objections to dissections. It is generally accepted that biological experiments may be performed on lower-order life forms and invertebrates, but not on mammalian vertebrates and birds. No animals should be harmed physiologically. Experimental animals should be kept, cared for, and handled in a safe manner and with compassion. Pathogenic (anything able to cause a disease) substances should not be used in lab experiments.

Lab Notebooks

A **lab notebook** is a record of all pre-lab work and lab work. It differs from a lab report, which is prepared after lab work is completed. A lab notebook is a formal record of lab preparations and what was done. **Observational recordings** should not be altered, erased, or whited-out to make corrections. Drawing a single line through an entry is sufficient to make changes. Pages should be numbered and should not be torn out. Entries should be made neatly, but don't necessarily have to be complete sentences. **Entries** should provide detailed information and be recorded in such a way that another person could use them to replicate the experiment. **Quantitative data** may be recorded in tabular form, and may include calculations made during an experiment. Lab book entries can also include references and research performed before the experiment. Entries may also consist of information about a lab experiment, including the objective or purpose, the procedures, data collected, and the results.

Lab Reports

A **lab report** is an item developed after an experiment that is intended to present the results of a lab experiment. Generally, it should be prepared using a word processor, not hand-written or recorded in a notebook. A lab report should be formally presented. It is intended to persuade others to accept or reject a hypothesis. It should include a brief but descriptive **title** and an **abstract**. The abstract is a summary of the report. It should include a purpose that states the problem that was explored or the question that was answered. It should also include a **hypothesis** that describes the anticipated results of the experiment. The experiment should include a **control** and one **variable** to ensure that the results can be interpreted correctly. Observations and results can be presented using written narratives, tables, graphs, and illustrations. The report should also include a **summation** or **conclusion** explaining whether the results supported the hypothesis.

Types of Laboratory Glassware

Two types of flasks are Erlenmeyer flasks and volumetric flasks. **Volumetric flasks** are used to accurately prepare a specific volume and concentration of a solution. **Erlenmeyer flasks** can be used for mixing, transporting, and reacting, but are not appropriate for accurate measurements.

A **pipette** can be used to accurately measure small amounts of liquid. Liquid is drawn into the pipette through a bulb. The liquid measurement is read at the **meniscus**. There are also plastic disposable pipettes. A **repipette** is a hand-operated pump that dispenses solutions.

Beakers can be used to measure mass or dissolve a solvent into a solute. They do not measure volume as accurately as a volumetric flask, pipette, graduated cylinder, or burette.

Graduated cylinders are used for precise measurements and are considered more accurate than Erlenmeyer flasks or beakers. To read a graduated cylinder, it should be placed on a flat surface and read at eye level. The surface of a liquid in a graduated cylinder forms a lens-shaped curve. The measurement should be taken from the bottom of the curve. A ring may be placed at the top of tall, narrow cylinders to help avoid breakage if they are tipped over.

A **burette**, or buret, is a piece of lab glassware used to accurately dispense liquid. It looks similar to a narrow graduated cylinder, but it includes a stopcock and tip. It may be filled with a funnel or pipette.

Microscopes

There are different kinds of microscopes, but **optical** or **light microscopes** are the most commonly used in lab settings. Light and lenses are used to magnify and view samples. A specimen or sample is placed on a slide, and the slide is placed on a stage with a hole in it. Light passes through the hole and illuminates the sample. The sample is magnified by lenses and viewed through the eyepiece. A simple microscope has one lens, while a typical compound microscope has three lenses. The light source can be room light redirected by a mirror, or the microscope can have its own independent light source that passes through a condenser. In this case, there are diaphragms and filters to allow light intensity to be controlled. Optical microscopes also have coarse and fine adjustment knobs.

Other types of microscopes include **digital microscopes**, which use a camera and a monitor to allow viewing of the sample. **Scanning electron microscopes (SEMs)** provide greater detail in terms of a sample's surface topography and can produce magnifications much greater than those possible with optical microscopes. The technology of an SEM is quite different from an optical microscope in that it does not rely on lenses to magnify objects, but uses samples placed in a chamber. In one type of SEM, a beam of electrons from an electron gun scans and actually interacts with the sample to produce an image.

Wet mount slides designed for use with a light microscope typically require a thin portion of the specimen to be placed on a standard glass slide. A drop of water is added, and a cover slip or cover glass is placed on top. Air bubbles and fingerprints can make viewing difficult. Placing the cover slip at a 45-degree angle and allowing it to drop into place can help avoid the problem of air bubbles. A **cover slip** should always be used when viewing wet mount slides. The viewer should start with the objective in its lowest position and then fine-focus. The microscope should be carried with two hands and stored with the low-power objective in the down position. **Lenses** should be cleaned with lens paper only. A **graticule slide** is marked with a grid line, and is useful for counting or estimating a quantity.

Balances

Balances such as triple-beam balances, spring balances, and electronic balances measure mass and force. An **electronic balance** is the most accurate, followed by a **triple-beam balance** and then a **spring balance**. One part of a **triple-beam balance** is the plate, which is where the item to be weighed is placed. There are also three beams, which have hash marks indicating amounts and which hold the weights that rest in the notches. The front beam measures weights between 0 and 10 grams, the middle beam measures weights in 100-gram increments, and the far beam measures weights in 10-gram increments. The sum of the weight of each beam is the total weight of the object. A triple beam balance also includes a set screw to calibrate the equipment, as well as a mark indicating that the object and counterweights are in balance.

Chromatography

Chromatography refers to a set of laboratory techniques used to separate or analyze **mixtures**. Mixtures are dissolved in their mobile phases. In the stationary or bonded phase, the desired component is separated from other molecules in the mixture. In chromatography, the analyte is the substance to be separated. **Preparative chromatography** refers to the type of chromatography that involves purifying a substance for further use rather than further analysis. **Analytical chromatography** involves analyzing the isolated substance. Other types of chromatography include column, planar, paper, thin layer, displacement, supercritical fluid, affinity, ion exchange, and size exclusion chromatography. Reversed phase, two-dimensional, simulated moving bed, pyrolysis, fast protein, counter current, and chiral are also types of chromatography. **Gas**

chromatography refers to the separation technique in which the mobile phase of a substance is in gas form.

Review Video: Paper Chromatography Visit mometrix.com/academy and enter code: 543963

Reagents and Reactants

A **reagent** or **reactant** is a chemical agent for use in chemical reactions. When preparing for a lab, it should be confirmed that glassware and other equipment have been cleaned and/or sterilized. There should be enough materials, reagents, or other solutions needed for the lab for every group of students completing the experiment. Distilled water should be used instead of tap water when performing lab experiments because distilled water has most of its impurities removed. Other needed apparatus such as funnels, filter paper, balances, Bunsen burners, ring stands, and/or microscopes should also be set up. After the lab, it should be confirmed that sinks, workstations, and any equipment used have been cleaned. If chemicals or specimens need to be kept at a certain temperature by refrigerating them or using another storage method, the temperature should be checked periodically to ensure the sample does not spoil.

Diluting Acids

When preparing a solution of **dilute acid**, always add the concentrated acid solution to water, not water to concentrated acid. Start by adding approximately $\frac{2}{3}$ of the total volume of water to the graduated cylinder or volumetric flask. Next, add the concentrated acid to the water. Add additional water to the diluted acid to bring the solution to the final desired volume.

Cleaning After Acid Spills

In the event of an **acid spill**, any clothes that have come into contact with the acid should be removed and any skin contacted with acid must be rinsed with clean water. To the extent a window can be opened or a fume hood can be turned on, do so. Do not try to force air circulation, such as by adding a fan, as acid fumes can be harmful if spread.

Next, pour one of the following over the spill area: sodium bicarbonate, baking soda, soda ash, or cat litter. Start from the outside of the spill and then move towards the center, in order to prevent splashing. When the clumps have thoroughly dried, sweep up the clumps and dispose of them as chemical waste.

Centrifuges

A centrifuge is used to separate the components of a heterogeneous mixture (consisting of two or more compounds) by spinning it. The solid precipitate settles in the bottom of the container, and the liquid component of the solution, called the **centrifugate**, is at the top. A well-known application of this process is using a centrifuge to separate blood cells and plasma. The heavier cells settle on the bottom of the test tube, and the lighter plasma stays on top. Another example is using a salad spinner to help dry lettuce.

ELECTROPHORESIS, CALORIMETRY, AND TITRATION

- **Electrophoresis** is the separation of molecules based on electrical charge. This is possible because particles dispersed in a fluid usually carry electric charges on their surfaces. Molecules are pulled through the fluid toward the positive end if the molecules have a negative charge and are pulled through the fluid toward the negative end if the molecules have a positive charge.
- **Calorimetry** is used to determine the heat released or absorbed in a chemical reaction.
- **Titration** helps determine the precise endpoint of a reaction. With this information, the precise quantity of reactant in the titration flask can be determined. A burette is used to deliver the second reactant to the flask and an indicator or pH meter is used to detect the endpoint of the reaction.

FIELD STUDIES AND RESEARCH PROJECTS

Field studies may facilitate scientific inquiry in a manner similar to indoor lab experiments. Field studies can be interdisciplinary in nature and can help students learn and apply scientific concepts and processes. **Research projects** can be conducted in any number of locations, including school campuses, local parks, national parks, beaches, or mountains. Students can practice the general techniques of observation, data collection, collaborative planning, and analysis of experiments. Field studies give students the chance to learn through hands-on applications of scientific processes, such as map making in geography, observation of stratification in geology, observation of life cycles of plants and animals, and analysis of water quality.

Students should watch out for obvious outdoor **hazards**. These include poisonous flora and fauna such as poison ivy, poison oak, and sumac. Depending on the region of the United States in which the field study is being conducted, hazards may also include rattlesnakes and black widow or brown recluse spiders. Students should also be made aware of potentially hazardous situations specific to **geographic locales** and the possibility of coming into contact with **pathogens**.

Field studies allow for great flexibility in the use of traditional and technological methods for **making observations** and **collecting data**. For example, a nature study could consist of a simple survey of bird species within a given area. Information could be recorded using still photography or a video camera. This type of activity gives students the chance to use technologies other than computers. Computers could still be used to create a slide show of transferred images or a digital lab report. If a quantitative study of birds was being performed, the simple technique of using a pencil and paper to tabulate the number of birds counted in the field could also be used. Other techniques used during field studies could include collecting specimens for lab study, observing coastal ecosystems and tides, and collecting weather data such as temperature, precipitation amounts, and air pressure in a particular locale.

Scientific Inquiry and Reasoning

Scientific Inquiry

The concept of **scientific inquiry** refers to the idea of how one thinks and asks questions in a logical way to gain trustworthy information. The underlying motivation of science is to try to understand the natural world. Much of human thought is based on assumptions about how things work that may or may not be true. The goal of scientific inquiry is to test those assumptions to gain a greater understanding of the world with good questions and objective tests, and then re-use what was learned to ask better questions. The more we understand about the natural world, the better the questions we can ask, and that is the general idea behind scientific inquiry. The applied practice of scientific inquiry is to ask questions in a systematic method, called the scientific method.

Scientific Knowledge

Scientific knowledge refers to any topic that is studied **empirically**, meaning that it is based on observation of a **phenomenon** in an objective way. The body of **scientific knowledge** is often broken down into several domains including biology, ecology, Earth science, space science, physics, and chemistry. These each have further subdomains and are overlapping in many ways. For instance, ecology is the study of ecosystems, which are made up of biological factors and geological factors, so it contains elements of both biology and Earth science. Each of these domains is subject to the concepts of scientific inquiry, such as the scientific method, scientific facts, hypotheses, and scientific laws.

Important Terminology

- A **phenomenon** is an event or effect that is observed.
- A **scientific fact** is considered an objective and verifiable observation. Usually, a fact can be repeated or demonstrated to others.
- A **scientific theory** is a proposition explaining why or how something happens and is built on scientific facts and laws. Scientific theories can be tested, but are not fully proven. If new evidence is found that disproves the theory, it is no longer considered true.
- A **hypothesis** is an educated guess that is not yet proven. It is used to predict the outcome of an experiment in an attempt to solve a problem or answer a question.
- A **law** is an explanation of events that always leads to the same outcome. It is a fact that an object falls. The law of gravity explains why an object falls. The theory of relativity, although generally accepted, has been neither proven nor disproved.
- A **model** is used to explain something on a smaller scale or in simpler terms to provide an example. It is a representation of an idea that can be used to explain events or applied to new situations to predict outcomes or determine results.

History of Scientific Knowledge

When one examines the history of **scientific knowledge**, it is clear that it is constantly **evolving**. The body of facts, models, theories, and laws grows and changes over time. In other words, one scientific discovery leads to the next. Some advances in science and technology have important and long-lasting effects on science and society. Some discoveries were so alien to the accepted beliefs of the time that not only were they rejected as wrong, but were also considered outright blasphemy. Today, however, many beliefs once considered incorrect have become an ingrained part of scientific knowledge, and have also been the basis of new advances. Examples of advances include: Copernicus's heliocentric view of the universe, Newton's laws of motion and planetary orbits, relativity, geologic time scale, plate tectonics, atomic theory, nuclear physics, biological evolution, germ theory, industrial revolution, molecular biology, information and communication, quantum theory, galactic universe, and medical and health technology.

Scientific Inquiry and Scientific Method

Scientists use a number of generally accepted techniques collectively known as the **scientific method**. The scientific method generally involves carrying out the following steps:

- Identifying a problem or posing a question
- Formulating a hypothesis or an educated guess
- Conducting experiments or tests that will provide a basis to solve the problem or answer the question
- Observing the results of the test
- Drawing conclusions

An important part of the scientific method is using acceptable experimental techniques. Objectivity is also important if valid results are to be obtained. Another important part of the scientific method is peer review. It is essential that experiments be performed and data be recorded in such a way that experiments can be reproduced to verify results. Historically, the scientific method has been taught with a more linear approach, but it is important to recognize that the scientific method should be a cyclical or **recursive process**. This means that as hypotheses are tested and more is learned, the questions should continue to change to reflect the changing body of knowledge. One cycle of experimentation is not enough.

Review Video: The Scientific Method
Visit mometrix.com/academy and enter code: 191386

Metric and International System of Units

The **metric system** is the accepted standard of measurement in the scientific community. The **International System of Units (SI)** is a set of measurements (including the metric system) that is almost globally accepted. The United States, Liberia, and Myanmar have not accepted this system. **Standardization** is important because it allows the results of experiments to be compared and reproduced without the need to laboriously convert measurements. The SI is based partially on the **meter-kilogram-second (MKS) system** rather than the **centimeter-gram-second (CGS) system**. The MKS system considers meters, kilograms, and seconds to be the basic units of measurement, while the CGS system considers centimeters, grams, and seconds to be the basic units of measurement. Under the MKS system, the length of an object would be expressed as 1 meter instead of 100 centimeters, which is how it would be described under the CGS system.

Review Video: Metric System Conversions
Visit mometrix.com/academy and enter code: 163709

Basic Units of Measurement

Using the **metric system** is generally accepted as the preferred method for taking measurements. Having a **universal standard** allows individuals to interpret measurements more easily, regardless of where they are located. The basic units of measurement are: the **meter**, which measures length; the **liter**, which measures volume; and the **gram**, which measures mass. The metric system starts with a base unit and increases or decreases in units of 10. The prefix and the base unit combined are used to indicate an amount. For example, deka- is 10 times the base unit. A dekameter is 10 meters; a dekaliter is 10 liters; and a dekagram is 10 grams. The prefix hecto- refers to 100 times the base amount; kilo- is 1,000 times the base amount. The prefixes that indicate a fraction of the base unit are deci-, which is $\frac{1}{10}$ of the base unit; centi-, which is $\frac{1}{100}$ of the base unit; and milli-, which is $\frac{1}{1,000}$ of the base unit.

Common Prefixes

The prefixes for multiples are as follows:

Deka	(da)	$\mathbf{10^1}$ (deka is the American spelling, but deca is also used)
Hecto	(h)	10^2
Kilo	(k)	10^3
Mega	(M)	10^6
Giga	(G)	10^9
Tera	(T)	10^{12}

The prefixes for subdivisions are as follows:

Deci	(d)	$\mathbf{10^{-1}}$
Centi	(c)	10^{-2}
Milli	(m)	10^{-3}
Micro	(μ)	10^{-6}
Nano	(n)	10^{-9}
Pico	(p)	10^{-12}

The rule of thumb is that prefixes greater than 10^3 are capitalized when abbreviating. Abbreviations do not need a period after them. A decimeter (dm) is a tenth of a meter, a deciliter (dL) is a tenth of a liter, and a decigram (dg) is a tenth of a gram. Pluralization is understood. For example, when referring to 5 mL of water, no "s" needs to be added to the abbreviation.

Basic SI Units of Measurement

SI uses **second(s)** to measure time. Fractions of seconds are usually measured in metric terms using prefixes such as millisecond ($\frac{1}{1,000}$ of a second) or nanosecond ($\frac{1}{1,000,000,000}$ of a second). Increments of time larger than a second are measured in **minutes** and **hours**, which are multiples of 60 and 24. An example of this is a swimmer's time in the 800-meter freestyle being described as 7:32.67, meaning 7 minutes, 32 seconds, and 67 one-hundredths of a second. One second is equal to $\frac{1}{60}$ of a minute, $\frac{1}{3,600}$ of an hour, and $\frac{1}{86,400}$ of a day. Other SI base units are the **ampere** (A) (used to measure electric current), the **kelvin** (K) (used to measure thermodynamic temperature), the **candela** (cd) (used to measure luminous intensity), and the **mole** (mol) (used to measure the amount of a substance at a molecular level). **Meter** (m) is used to measure length and **kilogram** (kg) is used to measure mass.

Significant Figures

The mathematical concept of **significant figures** or **significant digits** is often used to determine the accuracy of measurements or the level of confidence one has in a specific measurement. The significant figures of a measurement include all the digits known with certainty plus one estimated or uncertain digit. There are a number of rules for determining which digits are considered "important" or "interesting." They are:

- All non-zero digits are *significant*.
- Zeros between digits are *significant*.
- Leading and trailing zeros are *not significant* unless they appear to the right of the non-zero digits in a decimal.

For example, in 0.01230, the significant digits are 1230, and this number would be said to be accurate to the hundred-thousandths place. The zero indicates that the amount has actually been measured as 0. Other zeros are considered placeholders and are not important. A decimal point may be placed after zeros to indicate their importance (in "100." for example).

Graphs and Charts

Graphs and charts are effective ways to present scientific data such as observations, statistical analyses, and comparisons between dependent variables and independent variables. On a line chart, the **independent variable** (the one that is being manipulated for the experiment) is represented on the horizontal axis (the x-axis). Any **dependent variables** (the ones that may change as the independent variable changes) are represented on the y-axis. An **XY** or **scatter plot** is often used to plot many points. A "best fit" line is drawn, which allows outliers to be identified more easily. Charts and their axes should have titles. The x and y interval units should be evenly spaced and labeled. Other types of charts are **bar charts** and **histograms**, which can be used to compare differences between the data collected for two variables. A **pie chart** can graphically show the relation of parts to a whole.

Review Video: Identifying Variables
Visit mometrix.com/academy and enter code: 627181

Review Video: Data Interpretation of Graphs
Visit mometrix.com/academy and enter code: 200439

Data Presentation

Data collected during a science lab can be organized and **presented** in any number of ways. While **straight narrative** is a suitable method for presenting some lab results, it is not a suitable way to present numbers and quantitative measurements. These types of observations can often be better presented with **tables** and **graphs**. Data that is presented in tables and organized in rows and columns may also be used to make graphs quite easily. Other methods of presenting data include illustrations, photographs, video, and even audio formats. In a **formal report**, tables and figures are labeled and referred to by their labels. For example, a picture of a bubbly solution might be labeled Figure 1, Bubbly Solution. It would be referred to in the text in the following way: "The reaction created bubbles 10 mm in size, as shown in Figure 1, Bubbly Solution." Graphs are also labeled as figures. Tables are labeled in a different way. Examples include: Table 1, Results of Statistical Analysis, or Table 2, Data from Lab 2.

Statistical Precision and Errors

Errors that occur during an experiment can be classified into two categories: random errors and systematic errors. **Random errors** can result in collected data that is wildly different from the rest of the data, or they may result in data that is indistinguishable from the rest. Random errors are not consistent across the data set. In large data sets, random errors may contribute to the variability of data, but they will not affect the average. Random errors are sometimes referred to as noise. They may be caused by a student's inability to take the same measurement in exactly the same way or by outside factors that are not considered variables, but influence the data. A **systematic error** will show up consistently across a sample or data set, and may be the result of a flaw in the experimental design. This type of error affects the average, and is also known as bias.

Scientific Notation

Scientific notation is used because values in science can be very large or very small, which makes them unwieldy. A number in **decimal notation** is 93,000,000. In **scientific notation**, it is 9.3×10^7. The first number, 9.3, is the **coefficient**. It is always greater than or equal to 1 and less than 10. This number is followed by a multiplication sign. The base is always 10 in scientific notation. If the number is greater than ten, the exponent is positive. If the number is between zero and one, the exponent is negative. The first digit of the number is followed by a decimal point and then the rest of the number. In this case, the number is 9.3, and the decimal point was moved seven places to the right from the end of the number to get 93,000,000. The number of places moved, seven, is the exponent.

Statistical Terminology

- **Mean**—The average, found by taking the sum of a set of numbers and dividing by the number of numbers in the set.
- **Median**—The middle number in a set of numbers sorted from least to greatest. If the set has an even number of entries, the median is the average of the two in the middle.
- **Mode**—The value that appears most frequently in a data set. There may be more than one mode. If no value appears more than once, there is no mode.
- **Range**—The difference between the highest and lowest numbers in a data set.
- **Standard deviation**—Measures the dispersion of a data set, or how far from the mean a single data point is likely to be.
- **Regression analysis**—A method of analyzing sets of data and sets of variables. It involves studying how the typical value of the dependent variable changes when any one of the independent variables is varied and the other independent variables remain fixed.

Review Video: Mean, Median, and Mode
Visit mometrix.com/academy and enter code: 286207

Review Video: Standard Deviation
Visit mometrix.com/academy and enter code: 419469

Chapter Quiz

Ready to see how well you retained what you just read? Scan the QR code to go directly to the chapter quiz interface for this study guide. If you're using a computer, simply visit the online resources page at **mometrix.com/resources719/osatearsci108** and click the Chapter Quizzes link.

Space Systems

Earth-Moon-Sun System

Earth's Rotation

The **Earth rotates** west to east about its axis, an imaginary straight line that runs nearly vertically through the center of the planet. This rotation (which takes 23 hours, 56 minutes, and 5 seconds) places each section of the Earth's surface in a position facing the Sun for a period of time, thus creating the alternating periods of light and darkness we experience as **day and night**. This rotation constitutes a sidereal day; it is measured as the amount of time required for a reference star to cross the meridian (an imaginary north-south line above an observer). Each star crosses the meridian once every (sidereal) day. Since the speed at which Earth rotates is not exactly constant, we use the mean solar day (a 24-hour period) in timekeeping rather than the slightly variable sidereal day.

Sun

The **Sun** is the vital force of life on Earth; it is also the central component of our solar system. It is basically a sphere of extremely hot gases (close to 15 million degrees at the core) held together by gravity. Some of these gaseous molecules are ionized due to the high temperatures. The balance between its gravitational force and the pressure produced by the hot gases is called **hydrostatic equilibrium**. The source of the solar energy that keeps the Sun alive and plays a key role in the perpetuation of life on Earth is located in the Sun's core, where nucleosynthesis produces heat energy and photons. The Sun's atmosphere consists of the photosphere, the surface visible from Earth, the chromosphere, a layer outside of and hotter than the photosphere, the transition zone (the region where temperatures rise between the chromosphere and the corona), and the corona, which is best viewed at x-ray wavelengths. A solar flare is an explosive emission of ionized particles from the Sun's surface.

Review Video: The Sun
Visit mometrix.com/academy and enter code: 699233

Earth's Revolution Around the Sun

Like all celestial objects in our solar system, planet Earth revolves around the Sun. This process takes approximately 365 1/4 days, the period of time that constitutes a calendar year. The path of the orbit of Earth around the Sun is not circular but **elliptical**. Therefore, the distances between the Earth and the Sun at points on either extreme of this counterclockwise orbit are not equal. In other words, the distance between the two objects varies over the course of a year. At **perihelion**, the minimum heliocentric distance, Earth is 147 million kilometers from the Sun. At **aphelion**, the maximum heliocentric distance, Earth is 152 million kilometers from the Sun. This movement of the Earth is responsible for the apparent annual motions of the Sun (in a path referred to as the ecliptic) and other celestial objects visible from Earth's surface.

Review Video: Astronomy
Visit mometrix.com/academy and enter code: 640556

Review Video: The Solar System
Visit mometrix.com/academy and enter code: 273231

Seasons

The combined effects of Earth's revolution around the Sun and the tilt of the planet's rotational axis create the **seasons**. Earth's axis is not perfectly perpendicular to its orbital plane; rather, it is **tilted** about 23.5 degrees. Thus, at different times of the year, certain areas of the surface receive different amounts of sunlight. For example, during the period of time in Earth's orbit when the Northern Hemisphere is tipped toward the Sun, it is exposed to higher amounts of nearly direct sunlight than at any other time of year (days are longer, and the direction of Sun's rays striking the surface is nearly perpendicular). This period of time is summer in the Northern Hemisphere and winter in the Southern Hemisphere; on the opposite side of the orbit, the seasons are reversed in each hemisphere.

Review Video: Earth's Tilt and Seasons
Visit mometrix.com/academy and enter code: 602892

Summer and Winter Solstices

The **summer solstice** occurs when Earth's orbital position and axial tilt point the North Pole most directly toward the Sun. This happens on or near June 21 each year. On this day in the Northern Hemisphere, the Sun appears to be directly overhead (at its zenith) at 12:00 noon. The entire Arctic Circle (the north polar region above approximately 66.5 degrees north latitude) is bathed in sunlight for a complete solar day. The North Pole itself experiences constant daylight for six full months. Conversely, the **winter solstice** occurs when the South Pole is oriented most directly toward the Sun. This phenomenon, which falls on or near December 22 each year, orients the Sun as viewed from the Northern Hemisphere at its lowest point above the horizon.

Equinoxes

The **ecliptic** (the Sun's apparent path through the sky) crosses Earth's equatorial plane twice during the year; these intersections occur when the North Pole is at a right angle from the line connecting the Earth and the Sun. At these times, the two hemispheres experience equal periods of light and dark. These two points in time are respectively referred to as the vernal (spring) equinox (on or about March 21) and the autumnal (fall) equinox (on or about September 23). A calendar year is measured as the length of time between vernal equinoxes.

Moon

Earth's Moon is historically one of the most studied celestial bodies. Its mass is approximately 1.2% of the Earth's mass, and its radius is just over one-fourth of the size of the Earth's radius. Measurements of the Moon's density suggest that its characteristics are similar to those of the rocks that make up Earth's crust. The **landscape** of the Moon consists mostly of mountains and craters formed by collisions of this surface with meteors and other interplanetary materials. The Moon's crust (estimated to be 50 to 100 kilometers in thickness) is made up of a layer of regolith (lunar soil) supported by a layer of loose rocks and gravel. Beneath the crust is a mantle made up of a solid lithosphere and a semiliquid asthenosphere. The Moon's **core** (the innermost 500 kilometers of the body) is not as dense as that of the Earth. The Moon is made up mostly of refractory elements with high melting and boiling points with low levels of heavy elements such as iron.

Formation Theories

The **fission model** of Moon origin suggests that the Moon is actually a piece of the Earth that split off early during the planet's formation. In this model, a portion of the Earth's mantle fissioned off during a liquid stage in its formation, creating the Moon. According to the **capture model**, the Moon formed elsewhere in the solar system and was subsequently captured by the Earth's gravitational field. The **double-impact model** states that the Earth and the Moon formed during the same period of time from the same accretion material. Each of these theories has its strengths, but none of them can explain all of the properties of the Moon and its relationship to the Earth. Recently, a fourth (widely accepted) hypothesis has been suggested, which involves the **collision** between the Earth and a large asteroid. This hypothetical collision is said to have released a large amount of Earth's crustal material into its orbit; the Moon accreted from that material and the material displaced from the asteroid due to the collision.

Earth-Moon System

While the Moon is commonly referred to as a satellite of the Earth, this is not entirely accurate. The ratio of the masses of the two bodies is much larger than that of any other planet-satellite system. Also, the Moon does not truly **revolve** around the Earth. Rather, the two bodies revolve around a common center of mass beneath the surface of the Earth (approximately 4,800 kilometers from Earth's core). The **orbital planes** of the Moon and the Earth are nearly aligned; therefore, the Moon moves close to the ecliptic, as seen from Earth. Due to the Moon's synchronous rotation (its rotation period and orbital period are equal); the same side of the Moon is always facing Earth. This occurs because of the **mutual gravitational** pull between the two bodies.

Phases

The **sidereal period** of the Moon (the time it takes the Moon to orbit the Earth with the fixed stars as reference points) is about 27 days. The **lunar month** (or synodic period) is the period of time required for the Moon to return to a given alignment as observed from the Earth with the Sun as a reference point; this takes 29 days, 12 hours, 44 minutes, and 28 seconds. A discrepancy exists between the two periods of time because the Earth and the Moon move at the same time. Sunlight reflected off of the Moon's surface at different times during the lunar month causes its apparent shape to change. The sequence of the Moon's shapes is referred to as the **phases of the Moon**. The full Moon can be viewed when the body is directly opposite from the Sun. The opposite end of the cycle, the new Moon, occurs when the Moon is not visible from Earth because it is situated between the Earth and the Sun.

Configurations

The **configurations of the Moon** describe its position with respect to the Earth and the Sun. We can thus observe a correlation between the phases of the Moon and its configuration. The Moon is at **conjunction** at the time of the new Moon—it is situated in the same direction as the Sun. **Quadrature** (which signals the first quarter phase) is the position of the Moon at a right angle between the Earth-Sun line; we see exactly half of the Moon's sunlit hemisphere. This is the **waxing crescent phase**, in which we see more of the Moon each night. Then comes opposition (which occurs when the Moon lies in the direction opposite the Sun)—we see the full Moon. After this point, the Moon enters its **waning gibbons phase** as it travels back toward quadrature. When it reaches that point again, it has entered the third-quarter phase. Finally, as the Moon circles back toward conjunction, it is in its waning crescent phase.

Review Video: Moon
Visit mometrix.com/academy and enter code: 880415

The Solar System

Terrestrial Planets

The term **terrestrial planets** refers to the four planets closest to the Sun (Mercury, Venus, Earth, and Mars). They are classified together because they share many similarities that distinguish them from the giant planets. The terrestrial planets have **high densities and atmospheres** that constitute a small percentage of their total masses. These atmospheres consist mostly of heavy elements, such as carbon dioxide, nitrogen, and water, and are maintained by the gravitational field of the planets (which could not prevent hydrogen from escaping). These planets exhibit magnetic fields of varying intensity. An important characteristic that distinguishes the terrestrial planets from the giant planets is the evidence of various levels of internally generated activity, which caused these planets to evolve from their original states. These processes are thought to have been caused by constant meteoritic impacts during the first few hundred million years of the planets' existence. Radioactive decay of certain isotopes increased the internal temperatures of these planets, leading to volcanic activity on all of the terrestrial planets except Venus.

Review Video: Terrestrial Planets
Visit mometrix.com/academy and enter code: 100346

Mercury

Mercury, the smallest interior planet, is the least well known of the four. This is due to its close proximity to the Sun and high temperatures. Mercury's atmosphere is not very dense; this means that the planet's surface experiences wide temperature differentials from day to night. Mercury's density is close to that of Earth. As the smallest planet known to have experienced planetary evolution, Mercury's internal activity ceased (it became extinct) thousands of millions of years ago. The size of the planet is relevant because less massive bodies cool more quickly than larger ones after cessation of radioactivity. Mercury's surface is characterized by craters produced by meteoritic impact.

Venus

Venus is comparable to Earth in both size and mass. Venus is the brightest planet in the sky, partially due to the fact that it is proximate to the Sun. This proximity to the Sun makes exploration of its surface difficult. This planet's atmosphere consists mainly of carbon dioxide, with trace amounts of water and carbon oxide molecules, as well as high levels of sulfuric, nitric, and hydrofluoric acids in the clouds that characterize this atmosphere. The concentration of clouds, coupled with the chemical makeup of Venus's atmosphere, result in a strong greenhouse effect at the planet's surface. This surface consists of large plains (thought to be created by either volcanic activity or by meteoritic impacts) and large impact craters. The materials that compose Venus's surface are highly radioactive. Some astronomers have suggested past single-plate tectonic activity; again, however, the planet's dense atmosphere makes valid surface observation quite difficult. Recent evidence points to the likelihood of current volcanic activity.

MARS

Mars and Earth exhibit many similarities. For example, Mars has an internal structure that includes a central metallic core, a mantle rich in olivine and iron oxide, and a crust of hydrated silicates. Martian soil consists largely of basalts and clay silicate, with elements of sulfur, silicon oxide, and iron oxide. The planet's surface belies high levels of past volcanic activity (though, due to its relatively small mass, it is probably extinct). In fact, Mars is home to the largest known volcano in the solar system. The Martian landscape also includes two major basins, ridges and plateaus, and, most notably, apparent evidence of fluvial (water-based) erosion landforms, such as canyons and canals. It is possible that the past pressures and temperatures on Mars allowed water to exist on the red planet. Some have gone so far as to suggest that this planet was a site of biochemical evolution. So far, however, no evidence of life has been found.

MARS'S SATELLITES

Two Martian satellites have been observed: **Phobos** and **Deimos**. Each of these bodies is ellipsoidal; the circular orbits of the two satellites lie in Mars's equatorial plane. The gravitational forces between this planet and Phobos and Deimos have caused both satellites to settle into synchronous rotation (the same parts of their surfaces are always facing Mars). This feature exerts a braking force on Phobos's orbit. In other words, its orbit is decreasing in size. The relationship between Deimos and Mars is similar to the Earth-Moon system, in which the radius of the satellite's orbit is gradually growing. The differential compositions and densities of Mars and its satellites indicate that Phobos and Deimos probably did not break off from Mars.

GIANT PLANETS

The **large diameters** of Jupiter, Saturn, Uranus, and Neptune gave rise to the name of the category into which they fall. The **hypothetical icy cores** of these planets cause them to exhibit primary atmospheres, because the large levels of mass they accreted prevented even the lightest elements from escaping their gravitational pulls. The atmospheres of the giant planets thus consist mostly of hydrogen and helium. The giant planets do not have solid surfaces like those of the terrestrial planets. Jupiter probably consists of a core (made of ice and rock) surrounded by a layer of metallic hydrogen, which is covered by a convective atmosphere of hydrogen and helium. Saturn is believed to have the same type of core and hydrogen mantle, enriched by the helium missing from the atmosphere, surrounded by a differentiation zone and a hydrogenic atmosphere. Uranus and Neptune probably have the same type of core, surrounded by ionic materials, bounded by methane-rich molecular envelopes. Uranus is the only giant planet that exhibits no evidence of internal activity.

Review Video: Giant Planets
Visit mometrix.com/academy and enter code: 563115

RINGS

Each of the four giant planets exhibits **rings**. These are flat disks of fragmented material that orbit just next to their respective planets. Many of the giant planets' smaller satellites are embedded in these rings. There are two main hypotheses regarding the formation of such rings. One theory suggests that the tidal force exerted on a satellite by its planet may surpass the **Roche limit** (the point at which particle cohesion is no longer possible) and break the satellite into fragments, which then collide and become smaller. This material then spreads out and forms a ring. An alternate theory of the formation of the rings of the giant planets suggests that there was unaccreted material left over after the formation of these planets. Below the Roche limit (within a certain vicinity to the planet), these particles could not join together to form satellites and would consequently settle into orbital rings.

Satellites

Each of the giant planets possesses a number of **satellites. Jupiter** has over 50 known satellites—they are grouped according to size. Each of the four largest satellites of Jupiter exhibits evidence of internal activity at some point in their evolutions. In fact, Io, the densest satellite and the one closest to Jupiter, is the only celestial body besides Earth known to be currently volcanically active. **Saturn** has 21 satellites. Titan, the second-largest known satellite, has its own atmosphere. The other six largest of Saturn's satellites all have icy surfaces; some of these show evidence of past internal activity. The smaller 14 are relatively unknown. **Uranus** has five satellites. Each of them displays evidence of geological activity, in the form of valleys, smoothed surfaces, cliffs, mountains, and depressions. **Neptune** has eight known satellites. The larger, Triton, is similar to Titan in that it has an atmosphere. The other seven satellites of Neptune are relatively unknown.

Pluto and Charon

Though Charon was originally considered a satellite of Pluto, it now appears that the two are more accurately described as a double dwarf planet system (largely because of the similarity in the sizes of the two and the recurring debate over how Pluto should be classified). It is believed that these bodies formed from the solar nebula like most other objects in the solar system. Pluto has a highly irregular orbit, which places it closer to the Sun than Neptune for periods of time. In sharp contrast to its giant neighbors, this planet's density is higher than that of water ice. The surface of Pluto consists of high levels of methane absorbed into ice, with trace amounts of carbon oxide and nitrogen. Charon resembles the major Uranian satellites more so than it does Pluto. It consists of water ice with a siliceous or hydrocarbonate contaminant.

Review Video: Pluto and Charon
Visit mometrix.com/academy and enter code: 426296

Kepler's Laws

Kepler's laws are a collection of observations about the motion of planets in the solar system. Formulated by Johannes Kepler in the 1600s, these laws are still vital to our understanding of the way the universe works. **Kepler's first law** states that each planet moves in its own elliptical path and that all of these orbits have the Sun as their singular focal point. Before Kepler's discovery, astronomers had assumed that planetary orbits were circular (because the heavens were assumed to be geometrically perfect). **Kepler's second law** says that a straight line between a planet and the Sun sweeps out equal areas in equal time. In other words, planets move quickest in the part of their orbit that is closest to the Sun, and vice versa. **Kepler's third law** states that the further a planet is from the Sun, the longer its orbital period will be. In mathematical terms, the square of a planet's period is directly proportional to the cube of the radius of its orbit.

Stars and Other Objects in Space

Stellar Observation

The observation of stars relates to one of three stellar properties: position, brightness, and spectra. **Positional stellar observation** is principally performed through study of the positions of stars on multiple photographic plates. Historically, this type of analysis was done through measurement of the angular positions of the stars in the sky. **Parallax** of a star is its apparent shift in position due to the revolution of the Earth about the Sun; this property can be used to establish the distance to a star. Observation of the **brightness** of a star involves the categorization of stars according to their magnitudes. There is a fixed intensity ratio between each of the six magnitudes. Since stars emit light over a range of wavelengths, viewing a star at different wavelengths can give an indication of its temperature. The analysis of stars' **spectra** provides information about the temperatures of stars—the higher a star's temperature, the more ionized the gas in its outer layer. A star's spectrum also relates to its chemical composition.

Binary Star

Binary star systems, of which about fifty percent of the stars in the sky are members, consist of two stars that orbit each other. The orbits of and distances between members of a binary system vary. A **visual binary** is a pair of stars that can be visually observed. Positional measurements of a visual binary reveal the orbital paths of the two stars. Astronomers can identify astrometric binaries through long-term observation of a visible star—if the star appears to wobble, it may be inferred that it is orbiting a companion star that is not visible. An **eclipsing binary** can be identified through observation of the brightness of a star. Variations in the visual brightness of a star can occur when one star in a binary system passes in front of the other. Sometimes, variations in the spectral lines of a star occur because it is in a binary system. This type of binary is a spectroscopic binary.

Review Video: Types of Stars
Visit mometrix.com/academy and enter code: 831934

Hertzsprung-Russell Diagram

The **Hertzsprung-Russell (H-R) diagram** was developed to explore the relationships between the luminosities and spectral qualities of stars. This diagram involves plotting these qualities on a graph, with absolute magnitude (luminosity) on the vertical and spectral class on the horizontal. Plotting a number of stars on the H-R diagram demonstrates that stars fall into narrowly defined regions, which correspond to stages in stellar evolution. Most stars are situated in a diagonal strip that runs from the top-left (high temperature, high luminosity) to the lower-right (low temperature, low luminosity). This diagonal line shows stars in the main sequence of evolution (often called dwarfs). Stars that fall above this line on the diagram (low temperature, high luminosity) are believed to be much larger than the stars on the main sequence (because their high luminosities are not due to higher temperatures than main sequence stars); they are termed giants and supergiants. Stars below the main sequence (high temperature, low luminosity) are called white dwarfs. The H-R diagram is useful in calculating distances to stars.

Stellar Evolution

The life cycle of a star is closely related to its **mass**—low-mass stars become white dwarfs, while high-mass stars become **supernovae**. A star is born when a **protostar** is formed from a **collapsing interstellar cloud**. The temperature at the center of the protostar rises, allowing nucleosynthesis to begin. **Nucleosynthesis**, or hydrogen-burning through fusion, entails a release of energy.

Eventually, the star runs out of fuel (hydrogen). If the star is relatively low mass, the disruption of hydrostatic equilibrium allows the star to contract due to gravity. This raises the temperature just outside the core to a point at which nucleosynthesis and a different kind of fusion (with helium as fuel) that produces a carbon nucleus can occur. The star swells with greater energy, becoming a red giant. Once this phase is over, gravity becomes active again, shrinking the star until the degeneracy pressure of electrons begins to operate, creating a white dwarf that will eventually burn out. If the star has a high mass, the depletion of hydrogen creates a supernova.

SUPERNOVA

When a star on the main sequence runs out of hydrogen fuel, it begins to burn helium (the by-product of nucleosynthesis). Once helium-burning is complete in a massive star, the mass causes the core temperature to rise, enabling the fusion of carbon, then silicon, and a succession of other atomic nuclei, each of which takes place in a new shell further out of the core. When the fusion cycle reaches iron (which cannot serve as fuel for a nuclear reaction), an iron core begins to form, which accumulates over time. Eventually, the temperature and pressure in the core become high enough for electrons to interact with protons in the iron nuclei to produce neutrons. In a matter of moments, this reaction is complete. The core falls and collides with the star's outer envelope, causing a massive explosion (a supernova). This continues until the neutrons exert degeneracy pressure; this creates a pulsar. In more massive stars, nothing can stop the collapse, which ends in the creation of a black hole.

METEOROID

A **meteoroid** is a small, solid fragment of material in the solar system. An enormous number of these objects are present in the system. The term meteor is used to refer to such a body when it enters the Earth's atmosphere. Interaction (friction) between meteors and the upper levels of the atmosphere cause them to break up; most disintegrate before they reach the surface. The heat associated with frictional forces causes meteors to glow, creating the phenomena of shooting stars. The meteors that are large enough to avoid complete disintegration, and can therefore travel all the way down through the atmosphere to Earth's surface, are termed meteorites. Analysis of these fragments indicates that these bodies originate from the Moon, Mars, comets, and small asteroids that cross Earth's orbital path. The forceful impacts of meteorites on Earth's surface compress, heat, and vaporize some of the materials of the meteorite as well as crustal materials, producing gases and water vapor.

ASTEROID

An **asteroid** is a small, solid planet (planetoid) that orbits the Sun. The orbital paths of most asteroids are between the orbits of Jupiter and Mars. Many of these bodies have been studied extensively and given names; those in the main belt (which tend to be carbonaceous) are classified into subgroups based on their distance from a large, named asteroid (for example, Floras, Hildas, Cybeles). **Atens** are asteroids whose orbits lie between the Earth and the Sun, and Apollos are asteroids with orbits that mimic Earth's. Asteroids may also be classified based on their composition. **C-type asteroids are similar in composition to the non-volatile elements of the sun. The sun is composed of about 74% hydrogen, 24% helium, and about 2% heavier elements**. S-type asteroids are made up of nickel-iron and iron- and magnesium-silicates; these are relatively bright. **Bright asteroids** made up exclusively of nickel-iron are classified as M-type. Observation of the relative brightness of an asteroid allows astronomers to estimate its size.

Review Video: Comets, Asteroids, and Meteoroids
Visit mometrix.com/academy and enter code: 100347

Interstellar Medium

The **interstellar**, or interplanetary, **medium** (the space between planets and stars) is populated by comets, asteroids, and meteoroids. However, particles exist in this medium on an even smaller scale. Tiny solid bodies (close to a millionth of a meter in diameter) are called **interplanetary dust**. The accumulation of this material in arctic lakes, for example, allows scientists to study it. Such analysis has revealed that these grains are most likely miniscule fragments of the **nuclei of dead comets**. They possess low density, for they are really many microscopic particles stuck together. The interplanetary dust refracts sunlight, which produces a visible (but faint) glow in parts of the sky populated by clouds of this dust. The interstellar medium also contains particle remnants of **dead stars** and **gases** (such as hydrogen molecules ionized by ultraviolet photons). **Black holes** (objects that collapse under their own gravitational forces), which trap photons, are also believed to populate the interstellar medium. Black holes are a form of dark matter.

Dark Matter

Observations of the **gravitational force** in the solar system (based on Kepler's laws) have indicated for years that there are bodies in the system that we cannot see. **Dark matter** (sometimes called missing matter) is thought to account for the unseen masses, though its exact nature is unknown. Some dark matter may simply be **ordinary celestial bodies** too small to be observed from Earth, even with technology such as high-powered telescopes. The presence of MACHOs (massive compact halo objects) has been noted through observation of distant galaxies—at certain times astronomers can discern dips in the brightness of these galaxies, thought to be caused by a large object (a MACHO) passing between Earth and the galaxy under observation. Some have postulated that dark matter is made up of **WIMPs** (weakly interacting massive particles), which do not interact with photons or other forms of electromagnetic radiation; these particles are hypothetical, because astronomers cannot detect or study them.

> **Review Video: Dark Matter**
> Visit mometrix.com/academy and enter code: 251909

Eclipses

Eclipses occur when one celestial body obscures the view of another, either partially or completely. A **solar eclipse**, or eclipse of the Sun by the Moon, happens when the Moon passes directly in front of the Sun (as observed from Earth). Alternately, a **lunar eclipse** occurs when the Moon is situated in the Earth's shadow and is therefore completely invisible. These events do not happen every month because of the differential between the orbital planes of the Moon and the Earth—the Moon's orbit is about five degrees off from the ecliptic. The Moon's orbital path is subject to the same precession that occurs in the Earth's rotational axis; this causes the occasional intersection of the orbital planes of the two bodies. Therefore, eclipses are produced by a combination of the effects of the precession of the Moon's orbit, the orbit itself, and the Earth's orbit.

> **Review Video: Eclipses**
> Visit mometrix.com/academy and enter code: 691598

Newton's Law of Gravitation

Newton's law of gravitation (sometimes referred to as the law of universal gravitation) states that the force of gravity operates as an attractive force between all bodies in the universe. Prior to Newton's formulation of this law, scientists believed that two gravitational forces were at work in the universe—that gravity operated differently on Earth than it did in space. Newton's discovery served to unify these two conceptions of gravity. This law is expressed as a mathematical formula:

$F = \frac{GMm}{D^2}$, in which F is the gravitational force, M and m are the masses of two bodies, D is the distance between them, and G is the gravitational constant $(6.67 \times 10^{-11} \frac{\text{m}^3}{\text{kg s}^2})$. The gravitational attraction between two objects, therefore, depends on the distance between them and their relative masses. Newton's law of gravitation served to clarify the mechanisms by which Kepler's laws operated. In effect, Newton proved Kepler's laws to be true through the development of this law.

Review Video: Newton's Law of Gravitation
Visit mometrix.com/academy and enter code: 709086

Characteristics of the Milky Way and Other Galaxies

Milky Way

The **Milky Way**, which houses the Earth's solar system, is a spiral galaxy. It consists of a central bulging disk, the center of which is referred to as a **nucleus**. Most of a galaxy's visible light comes from stars in this region. The disk is surrounded by a halo of stars and star clusters that spread above, next to, and beneath the nucleus. **Globular clusters** (dense, spherical clusters of ancient stars) are often found in the halo. Spiral arms of high-luminosity stars (from which this type of galaxy gets its name) fan out from the nucleus as well, with stars that are less bright in between. Interstellar dust populates the entire galaxy between celestial bodies. The entire galaxy rotates about the center. While Earth, the Sun, and its solar system are located on the disk, we are far from the center of the Milky Way. The galaxy's mass is about 1.5 trillion solar masses.

Structures of Galaxies

Elliptical galaxies are roughly spherical. Within this category, subgroups based on the degree of flattening exhibited in the galaxy's shape range from E0 (spherical) to E7 (flat). A dwarf elliptical galaxy has a spheroidal shape, with low mass and low luminosity. An S0 galaxy is similar in shape to a spiral galaxy, but lacks spiral arms. Spiral galaxies such as the Milky Way are characterized by disk-like nuclei with spiral arms. Subtypes of this category are determined by the tightness of the spiral arms and the size of the nucleus; a spiral galaxy of Sa type has a large nucleus and tightly wound arms, and an Sc-type galaxy consists of a small nucleus with open spiral arms. A barred spiral galaxy exhibits an elongated nucleus. The subtypes of barred spiral galaxies are determined like those of spiral galaxies. Some irregular galaxies (type I) display a loose spiral structure with high levels of disorganization. Other irregular galaxies (type II) can be of any shape.

Review Video: Galaxies
Visit mometrix.com/academy and enter code: 226539

Theories Relating to the Origin of the Universe

Model of the Inflationary Universe

Hubble's law states that the speed at which a galaxy appears to be moving away from the Earth is proportional to its distance from Earth. This relatively simple formula ($v = Hr$, where v is the **velocity of a receding galaxy**, r is its distance from Earth, and H is the Hubble constant) had an important implication at the time that it was developed—the universe is expanding. This fact, in turn, implies that the universe began at a **specific point** in the past. This model suggests that a random conglomeration of quarks and leptons, along with the strong force (all the forces in the universe unified as one), existed in the very dense, very hot, early universe. When the universe was a certain age (about 10–35 seconds old), the strong force separated out from the mass. This enabled the rapid expansion of the particles that formed the universe.

Big Bang Theory

The **theory of the big bang** expands upon the model of the **inflationary universe**. This theory hypothesizes that the early universe consisted of elementary particles, high energy density and high levels of pressure and heat. This single mass experienced a **phase change** (similar to that of freezing water) when it cooled and expanded. This transition caused the early universe to expand exponentially; this period of growth is called **cosmic inflation**. As it continued to grow, the temperature continued to fall. At some point, **baryogenesis** (an unknown process in which quarks and gluons become baryons, such as protons and neutrons) occurred, somehow creating the distinction between matter and antimatter. As the universe continued to cool, the **elementary forces** reached their present form, and **elementary particles** engaged in big bang **nucleosynthesis** (a process that produced helium and deuterium nuclei). **Gravity** became the predominant force governing interactions between particles; this enabled increasing accretion of particles of matter, which eventually formed the universal constituents as we recognize them today.

Chapter Quiz

Ready to see how well you retained what you just read? Scan the QR code to go directly to the chapter quiz interface for this study guide. If you're using a computer, simply visit the online resources page at **mometrix.com/resources719/osatearsci108** and click the Chapter Quizzes link.

Geological Systems

Theory of Plate Tectonics

PLATE TECTONICS

MAIN CONCEPTS

Plate tectonics is a geological theory that was developed to explain the process of continental drift. The theoretical separation of the Earth's lithosphere and asthenosphere is based upon the mechanical properties of the materials in the two respective layers and is distinct from the chemical separation of Earth's crust, mantle, and core. According to the theory of plate tectonics, the Earth's lithosphere is divided into **ten major plates**: African, Antarctic, Australian, Eurasian, North American, South American, Pacific, Cocos, Nazca, and Indian; it floats atop the asthenosphere. The plates of the lithosphere abut one another at plate boundaries (divergent, convergent, or transform fault), where the formation of topological features of Earth's surface begins.

THEORY

This theory of plate tectonics arose from the fusion of **continental drift** (first proposed in 1915 by Alfred Wegener) and **seafloor spreading** (first observed by Icelandic fishermen in the 1800s and later refined by Harry Hess and Robert Dietz in the early 1960s) in the late 1960s and early 1970s. Prior to this time, the generally accepted explanation for continental drift was that the continents were floating on the Earth's oceans. The discovery that mountains have "roots" (proved by George Airy in the early 1950s) did not categorically disprove the concept of floating continents; scientists were still uncertain as to where those mountainous roots were attached. It was not until the identification and study of the Mid-Atlantic Ridge and magnetic striping in the 1960s that plate tectonics became accepted as a scientific theory. Its conception was a landmark event in the field of Earth sciences—it provided an explanation for the empirical observations of continental drift and seafloor spreading.

TECTONIC PLATE MOTION

The two main sources of **tectonic plate motion** are **gravity** and **friction**. The energy driving tectonic plate motion comes from the dissipation of heat from the mantle in the relatively weak asthenosphere. This energy is converted into gravity or friction to incite the motion of plates. Gravity is subdivided by geologists into ridge-push and slab-pull. In the phenomenon of **ridge-push**, the motion of plates is instigated by the energy that causes low-density material from the mantle to rise at an oceanic ridge. This leads to the situation of certain plates at higher elevations; gravity causes material to slide downhill. In **slab-pull**, plate motion is thought to be caused by cold, heavy plates at oceanic trenches sinking back into the mantle, providing fuel for future convection. Friction is subdivided into mantle drag and trench suction. Mantle drag suggests that plates move due to the friction between the lithosphere and the asthenosphere. Trench suction involves a downward frictional pull on oceanic plates in subduction zones due to convection currents.

> **Review Video: Plate Tectonic Theory**
> Visit mometrix.com/academy and enter code: 535013

CONVERGENT PLATE BOUNDARIES

A **convergent** (destructive) **plate boundary** occurs when adjacent plats move toward one another. The Earth's diameter remains constant over time. Therefore, the formation of new plate material at diverging plate boundaries necessitates the destruction of plate material elsewhere. This process occurs at convergent (destructive) plate boundaries. One plate slips underneath the other at a subduction zone. The results of converging plates vary, depending on the nature of the lithosphere in said plates. When two oceanic plates converge, they form a deep underwater trench. If each of the converging plates at a destructive boundary carries a continent, the light materials of the continental lithosphere enables both plates to float above the subduction area. They crumple and compress, creating a mid-continent mountain range. When a continental plate converges with an oceanic plate, the denser oceanic lithosphere slides beneath the continental lithosphere. The result of such convergence is an oceanic trench on one side and a mountain range on the other.

Divergent Plate Boundary

A **divergent**, or constructive, **plate boundary** exists when two adjacent plates move away from one another. Observation of activity at diverging boundaries provided unquestionable proof of the seafloor-spreading hypothesis. At this type of plate boundary, kinetic energy generated by asthenospheric convection cells cracks the lithosphere and pushes molten magma through the space left by separating tectonic plates. This magma cools and hardens, creating a new piece of the Earth's crust. In the oceanic lithosphere, diverging plate boundaries form a series of rifts known as the oceanic ridge system. The Mid-Atlantic Ridge is a consequence of undersea diverging boundaries. At divergent boundaries on the continental lithosphere, plate movement results in rift valleys, typified by the East African Rift Valley.

Transform Plate Boundary

A **transform** (conservative) **plate boundary** exists when two tectonic plates slide past each other laterally and in opposite directions. Due to the rocky composition of lithospheric plates, this motion causes the plates to grind against each other. Friction causes stress to build when the plates stick; this potential energy is finally released when the built-up pressure exceeds the slipping point of the rocks on the two plates. This sudden release of energy causes earthquakes. This type of plate boundary is also referred to as a **strike-slip fault**. The San Andreas Fault in California is the most famous example of such a boundary.

Geologic Faults

A **geologic fault** is a fracture in the Earth's surface created by movement of the crust. The majority of faults are found along **tectonic plate boundaries**; however, smaller faults have been identified at locations far from these boundaries. There are three types of geologic faults, which are named for the original direction of movement along the active fault line. The landforms on either side of a fault are called the footwall and the hanging wall, respectively. In a **normal fault**, the hanging wall moves downward relative to the footwall. A **reverse fault** is the opposite of a normal fault: The hanging wall moves upward relative to the footwall. The dip of a reverse fault is usually quite steep; when the dip is less than 45 degrees, the fault is called a thrust fault. In the third type of geologic fault, the **strike-slip fault**, the dip is virtually nonexistent, and the footwall moves vertically left (sinistral) or right (dextral). A transform plate boundary is a specific instance of a strike-slip fault.

Features of the Earth's Crust

Geologic Folding

A **geologic fold** is a region of curved or deformed stratified rocks. Folding is one process by which Earth's crust is deformed. Rock strata are normally formed horizontally; however, geologists have identified areas where these strata arc upwards or downwards. **Anticlines** are upfolded areas of rock; downfolds are called synclines. In anticlines, the rocks are oldest along the axis (a horizontal line drawn through the point of the fold's maximum curvature), and in synclines, the youngest rocks are at the axis. **Monoclines**, or flextures, are rock structures that slope in one direction only, and often pass into geologic fault lines. The process of folding usually occurs underneath the Earth's surface, but surface erosion eventually exposes these formations. Folding is generally thought to be caused by the horizontal compression of the Earth's surface, which is related to the movement of tectonic plates and fault activity.

Orogenesis

Orogenesis refers to mountain-building processes, specifically as they relate to the movement of tectonic plates. An individual orogeny can take millions of years. Generally, mountains are created when compressional forces push surface rock upward, resulting in a landform that is higher than the land around it. There are four broad categories of mountains (which are not mutually exclusive); these categories are based on the mountain's formative origin. **Folded mountains**, formed from the long-term deformation and metamorphosis of sedimentary and igneous rocks, usually occur in chains. This type of mountain often forms at convergent plate boundaries. **Fault-block mountains** occur at normal or reverse faults with high dips. Portions of Earth's crust are vertically displaced along the faults. **Oceanic ridges** are formed at divergent boundaries beneath the ocean. When plates move apart, material from the mantle rises up and creates long mountain chains. **Volcanic mountains** form from the accumulation of products of volcanic eruptions, such as ash and lava. They often occur singularly, unlike other mountain types that usually exist in chains.

Continental Drift

Continental drift is a theory that explains the separation and movement of the continents based on shifts in a plastic layer of Earth's interior caused by the planet's rotation (seafloor spreading). Continental drift is part of the larger theory of plate tectonics. In the early twentieth century, many scientists and scholars noted that the edges of certain continents seemed to look like connecting pieces of a puzzle. Due to this observation, as well as the fact that similar geologic features, fossils, fauna, and flora existed on the Atlantic coasts of continents like South America and Africa, these observers theorized the previous existence of a supercontinent (referred to as Pangaea), in which all of the discrete continents identifiable today were joined together.

Continental Crust

The **continental crust** (sial) is 10–50 kilometers thick. It is more complex and locally variable than the oceanic crust. There is a correlation between the thickness of the sial and the age of the last orogenic (mountain-forming) event recorded at the surface: The thinnest crust occurs in areas of the oldest orogenic activity, and the thickest crust is located near present-day mountain chains. The continental crust consists of two layers separated by a seismic velocity discontinuity located 8–10 kilometers below the surface. The upper layer has an average density of 2,670 $\frac{\text{kg}}{\text{m}^3}$ and is composed mainly of granite. This layer exhibits thermal energy related to the activity of radioactive elements. The lower layer has gabbroic properties and an average density of 3,000 $\frac{\text{kg}}{\text{m}^3}$. The temperature of this layer is thought to be below the melting point of its component rocks and minerals and is extremely variable, depending on the presence of volatiles (elements such as water, carbon dioxide, and sulfur).

OCEANIC CRUST

The **oceanic crust** (sima) is 5–10 kilometers thick. It is remarkably uniform in composition and thickness and consists of a layer of sediments (fossils of marine life and continental debris) that overlies three distinct layers of igneous rock. The first of these is 1–2.5 kilometers thick and is made up of basaltic lavas. The second, main igneous layer is 5 kilometers thick and is of coarse-grained gabbroic composition. The third layer is very thin (less than half a kilometer thick) and possesses a density of 3,000 $\frac{\text{kg}}{\text{m}^3}$; this layer is made up of basalts. The temperature of the sima is very high along seismically active ridges and lower near oceanic basins. Based on dating of the fossils present in its sediments, scientists estimate that the oceanic crust is only 200 million years old (in comparison, the continental crust is estimated to be several billion years old). The relatively young age of the oceanic crust provides support for theories of the creative/destructive processes of seafloor spreading.

MAGNETIC STRIPING

Magnetic striping is a manifestation of the magnetic properties of the oceanic lithosphere. In general, the mineral composition of rocks has one of two magnetic orientations: normal polarity, which roughly corresponds with the polarity of the Earth's magnetic north, or reversed polarity, which is basically the opposite of the Earth's magnetic field. Cooled magma, which makes up the basalt of the ocean floor, aligns itself with Earth's current magnetic orientation during the cooling process. While the Earth's magnetic field normally shifts very slowly, it undergoes radical changes, called magnetic reversals, over long periods of time. Diverging plate boundaries on the ocean floor have been forming new crust material for tens of thousands of years, creating new midocean ridges throughout multiple reversals of Earth's magnetic field. Consequently, the ocean floor displays stripes of rocks with opposing polarities. The discovery of magnetic striping in the oceanic crust contributed to widespread acceptance of the seafloor-spreading hypothesis.

SEAFLOOR SPREADING

Seafloor spreading was originally put forth as an explanation for the existence of midocean ridges such as the Mid-Atlantic Ridge. These ridges were identified as features of a vast undersea mountain system that spans the globe. Seafloor spreading postulates that the ocean floor expands outward from these ridges. The process occurs when the upper mantle layer of the Earth (the asthenosphere), just beneath the planet's crust, is heated through convection. The heat causes the asthenosphere to become more elastic and less dense. This heated material causes the crust to bow outward and eventually separate. The lighter material then flows out through the resultant rift and hardens, forming new oceanic crust. If a rift opens completely into an ocean, the basin will be flooded with seawater and create a new sea. Often, the process results in failed rifts, rifts that stopped opening before complete separation is achieved.

Earthquakes

An **earthquake** is a sudden movement of a portion of the Earth's crust. Strain energy, built up in the lithosphere, is swiftly released in the form of seismic waves which, among other things, cause vibratory ground motion. The majority of these events occur at high-stress tectonic plate boundaries. The **rupture zone** is the total size of the fault that slips; the larger the rupture zone, the greater the effects of the earthquake. The **focus**, or hypocenter, of an earthquake is the location from which the seismic waves seem to emanate. The **epicenter** is the location on the Earth's crust above an earthquake's hypocenter. Earthquakes are classified according to their focus depths: shallow (0–70 kilometers below the surface), intermediate (70–300 kilometers below the surface), or deep (below 300 kilometers deep).

Review Video: Earthquakes
Visit mometrix.com/academy and enter code: 252531

Elastic Rebound Theory

In periods between seismic events, tectonic plates move relative to one another except at their boundaries, where the rocks are locked together. The differential movement of the plates causes the rocks near the plate boundaries to undergo elastic deformation and build up a level of strain. This process occurs slowly and for long periods of time. When the strain along the fault becomes powerful enough to overcome the strength of the rocks, they snap or rebound into place, aligning themselves in seconds with the plates, which have been moving slowly but steadily for tens or hundreds of years. According to **elastic rebound theory**, this release of strain energy constitutes an earthquake.

Interplate and Intraplate Earthquakes

An **interplate earthquake** occurs at a boundary between two tectonic plates. The slippage of rocks on either side of the boundary results in deformation of the surrounding land and the release of seismic waves. Interplate earthquakes are more common than intraplate earthquakes. Although plate tectonics envisions the Earth's surface as a series of plates moving past one another, we must remember that those plates are fractured aspects of the ancient crust. **Intraplate earthquakes** occur along highly stressed fault lines on the interior of tectonic plates. Because the faults that cause these earthquakes are often below the surface, they are difficult to predict or study.

Teleseism, Deep-Focus Earthquake, and Blind Thrust Earthquake

A **teleseism** is measurable movement of a location on the Earth's surface caused by a large earthquake in a distant location. Generally, earthquakes of magnitude 5.3 or higher at any location cause these tremors (discernible through the use of modern seismic-detection equipment) in any part of the world. A **deep-focus earthquake** originates 600–700 kilometers beneath the Earth's surface. Scientists believe that deep-focus earthquakes are related to catastrophic phase changes in the Earth's interior. A **blind thrust earthquake** occurs along a previously undetected thrust fault. Blind thrust faults usually form in high-stress zones near large plate boundaries. This type of earthquake can be the most deadly, due to the fact that city planners cannot take the location of an unknown fault line into consideration during new construction and earthquake preparedness planning.

Foreshocks and Aftershocks

A **foreshock** is a small earthquake that occasionally precedes a larger, principal earthquake. Foreshocks can potentially be used to aid in the prediction of larger, more-dangerous events. They occur less often than **aftershocks**, which are small tremors following a principal earthquake.

According to Omori's law, the rate of aftershocks is proportional to the inverse of the time lapse since the main earthquake. Some aftershocks last longer than others: In the New Madrid Seismic Zone, the effects of huge earthquakes in 1811–1812 are still being felt. Aftershocks have the potential to exponentially increase the damage caused by a large earthquake. For example, an aftershock can level buildings that have already suffered damage during the main event. The unpredictability of aftershocks makes them especially dangerous.

Damage

The following are earthquake-damage–related terms:

- A **tsunami** is a series of waves created by sudden, large-scale displacement of water in a large body of water. Tsunamis are not tidal waves (though many use the terms interchangeably), but strong, seemingly endless tides originating in the depths of the body of water (rather than on the surface). The height of a tsunami and its energy increase as it nears a shoreline; a powerful tsunami has the strength to flatten a coastline.
- A **seiche** is a related phenomenon: It is a standing wave generated by a disturbance (usually seismic or wind-related) in a body of water. A seiche moves vertically as gravity attempts to restore horizontal equilibrium on the water's surface.
- **Liquefaction** basically refers to the suspension of soil particles in water. Earthquakes increase water pressure, which increases the potential mobility of soil particles. This, in turn, significantly decreases the ability of said soil to support building foundations and upper layers of soil.
- A **landslide** is an effect of liquefaction in which portions of the Earth's surface are rapidly displaced.

Preparation

Earthquakes cannot be prevented, and techniques that have been suggested to predict earthquakes are unreliable and yet unproven. Therefore, the best way to prevent property damage and harm to humans during an earthquake is to lessen their effects through engineering. For example, selecting a building site atop a **formation of solid rock** can lessen earthquake damage because such sites are more stable than unconsolidated or water-laden ground. Obviously, knowledge of fault lines can also aid in the selection of optimal building sites. The type of buildings we construct can also affect the amount of damages endured during an earthquake. For instance, the use of **reinforcing rods** and construction of buildings that are **capable of oscillating as a unit** can prevent serious damage to such structures during an earthquake. A **suspension bridge** is an example of a structure that can flex during earthquakes, lessening its potential to be damaged during a seismic event.

Prediction

Many different theories have been put forth regarding the methodology of **earthquake prediction**. These ideas have ranged from analysis of the behavior of animals to observation of changes in the electrical conductivity of granite in a quake zone. Hypotheses suggesting that earthquakes can be predicted through, for example, measurement of variations in the gravitational pull of the Sun, planets, and Moon have not been verified. Other theories, such as analysis of the time and space patterns created by past earthquakes in a certain area to predict an upcoming quake, have experienced some validation. An increase in the radon levels in an area, the appearance of strange clouds, foreshocks, and the detection of strain in crustal rocks have all been suggested as possible indicators of a looming earthquake. Ultimately however, there is no method of earthquake prediction that is consistently and reliably accurate.

SEISMIC WAVES

Seismic waves are mechanical disturbances that transfer energy. These waves are created by earthquakes or explosions. **Body waves** travel within the Earth's interior on curved pathways due to the various densities of the Earth's composite materials. The category of body waves is further subdivided into **primary** (P) waves and **secondary** (S) waves. **P waves** can travel through any material (although they move fastest in a solid), alternately compressing and dilating such materials in the direction of wave movement. They are similar to sound waves and move more quickly than S waves. **S waves** (or transverse waves) can only travel through solids. They displace the ground perpendicularly to the direction of wave movement to one side and then to the other. **Surface waves**, similar to water waves, travel above the Earth's surface and cause more damage than body waves due to their low frequencies. **Rayleigh waves** perpetuate ground roll during earthquakes: The Earth's surface ripples like the surface of water. **Love waves** move marginally more quickly than Rayleigh waves and cause horizontal shearing of the Earth's crust.

The study of seismic waves reveals the magnitude of and distance to a seismic disturbance. **Seismology** can also provide valuable information about inaccessible parts of the Earth's interior. Seismic waves radiate outward in all directions from such a disturbance, and therefore travel through the depths of the Earth before arrival at distant seismograph stations. Understanding the properties of body waves (for instance, the materials they can travel through and the effects of density, pressure, and temperature upon the velocities at which they can travel through those materials) enables seismologists to make reasonable inferences about the composition of the inner Earth, based upon seismographic data collected from all over the world.

SEISMIC DATA AND INNER EARTH

Based upon information about the **variations in the velocities** of primary (P) and secondary (S) waves at different locations on the surface, scientists have created a hypothetical structure of the outermost 700 kilometers of the Earth (which expands accepted theories about the crust, mantle, and core layers). Body waves travel at high velocities through the strong, solid lithosphere. Waves moving through the asthenosphere travel more slowly, suggesting that this layer is 1–10% molten and relatively weak. The presence of the Mohorovičić discontinuity (the crust-mantle boundary), also known as the Moho boundary, is demonstrated by a sharp increase in the velocity of body waves at a depth of 6–70 kilometers. The mesosphere is the mantle zone beneath the asthenosphere, where increased pressure strengthens the rock again. Extreme increases in wave velocity occur at 350–400 kilometers and at 650–700 kilometers below the surface, suggesting phase transitions at these depths, in which the density of the materials becomes much higher due to increased pressure. At these stages, iron and magnesium are thought to break down (due to extreme pressure) into silicates.

Generally, wave velocities increase steadily from 700–2,900 kilometers below the surface, indicating increasing pressure and the presence of increasingly dense mantle material in the form of iron and magnesium silicates. At 2,900 kilometers, primary (P) wave velocities experience a drastic drop, and secondary (S) waves disappear completely. This data indicates that the rock at 2,900 kilometers changes abruptly from a solid to a liquid state (since S waves cannot travel through liquid and P waves move through liquid very slowly). Thus, 2,900 kilometers below surface level is believed to be the boundary between the mesosphere and the liquid outer core. At a depth of 5,100 kilometers, observed P wave velocities rise sharply once again, and S waves are faintly detectable. This change in body wave velocities provides strong evidence for the presence of a final phase change between the liquid outer core and the inner core, which is thought to be solid and composed mainly of iron.

SEISMOGRAPH

The **seismograph**, or seismometer, is an instrument used to record the waves released during an earthquake or other seismic event. This instrument, originally constructed by Zhang Heng in 132 AD, has evolved into a sophisticated machine capable of measuring waves of different types, sizes, and directions. Seismologists study and compare these records to shed light on the processes that occur during an earthquake and to discover information about the inner Earth. The seismograph consists of a large mass suspended from a frame, which is secured to the Earth. Gravity holds the massive object in a reference position while seismic waves initiate movement of the Earth's surface and the seismograph's foundation. The instrument then records the relative motion between the suspended object and the frame. Advances in physics and electronics have aided in the process of perfecting the seismograph. Modern instruments are capable of recording and differentiating north-south, east-west, and up-down dimensions of ground movement.

Review Video: Measuring Earthquakes
Visit mometrix.com/academy and enter code: 393730

IMPORTANT TERMS

- **Slip** - Slip is a measurement of the net relative displacement of structural surfaces along a fault.
- **Dip** - Dip is the angle that a rock body or structural rock surface makes with the horizontal surface plane. True dip is quantified through downward measurement of the angle in the direction of greatest inclination; apparent dip is the measurement of dip in any direction. Dip is equal to zero in the direction of strike and has its maximum measurement in the direction of true dip.
- **Strike** - Strike is the direction of a line of intersection drawn between the horizontal surface plane and the surface of an uptilted rock structure.
- **Hot spot** - A hot spot is an area of the Earth's surface that experiences high levels of volcanic activity, created by hypothetical phenomena called mantle plumes. Mantle plumes are exceptionally hot portions of the Earth's mantle that rise (through convection) to the crust. Hot spots are responsible for the formation of volcanic chains such as the Hawaiian Islands.
- **Fracture zone** - A fracture zone is an area surrounding a transform fault, created by inconsistent rates of seafloor spreading.
- **Subsidence** - Subsidence is the downward motion of the Earth's crust. This process occurs when the lithosphere is stretched and cracked, and hot portions of the asthenosphere rise to fill the resultant void. Consequently, the crust and upper mantle heat up. This heat energy is later released from the surface as radiation; the lithosphere then cools and contracts.
- **Elastic deformation** - Elastic, or brittle, deformation refers to the change in the shape of a material under a load when the material can return to its original shape after the removal of the load.
- **Plastic deformation** - Plastic, or ductile, deformation is permanent deformation—a material cannot recover after the introduction and subsequent removal of a load.
- **Proportional elastic limit** - The proportional elastic limit of a substance is the maximum level of stress that a material can endure and still be able to recover to its original shape with the release of stress.
- **Rupture strength** - Rupture strength refers to the amount of stress a material can withstand (for a period of time, at a certain temperature) before it ruptures.

- **Ultimate strength** - Ultimate strength is the greatest level of stress a material can endure before or during rupture; this can be tensional strength (resistance to lengthwise deformation), compressional strength (resistance to rupture under compression), or shear strength (resistance to a tangential force).
- **Graben**: A graben is a depressed portion of land between two parallel, normal geologic faults.
- **Horst** - A horst is a raised portion of land (a ridge) between two parallel, normal geologic faults.
- **Magnitude** - Magnitude refers to the strength of an earthquake, and it is observed quantitatively through measurement of the strain energy released during such an event. Charles Richter formulated a scale to describe relative magnitudes of earthquakes based on a progression of logarithmic values of magnitude.
- **Intensity** - Intensity is a measure of the effects of an earthquake on a particular area and its human inhabitants. This measurement is more subjective, and thus less scientifically reliable, than the measurement of magnitude because measurement is usually taken in the area with the most damage, and it can be affected by localized factors such as building design. The intensity of earthquakes is measured on the Mercalli (or Modified Mercalli) scale in the United States and on the European Macroseismic Scale in the European Union.
- **Ionosphere** - The ionosphere is the inner layer of Earth's magnetosphere. Consisting of a plasma made up of nitrogen and oxygen ionized by X-rays and ultraviolet radiation from the Sun, the Earth's ionosphere enables the use of radio waves for communication around the globe.
- **Solar variation** - Solar variation refers to changes in the amount of energy emitted by the Sun. Higher levels of solar radiation can contribute to the visual phenomena of polar aura (caused by interaction between Earth's magnetosphere, magnetic field, and atmosphere and a solar wind).
- **Solar wind** - Solar winds are made up of hydrogen and helium ions (protons and electrons) in the form of plasma. These particles are able to escape the Sun's surface due to their high levels of thermal energy. They flow through space like a wind. This solar wind is deflected around the Earth by the magnetosphere like air around the nose of a jet.

Earth's Layers and Processes

Earth's Layers

Chemical Layers

The **crust** is the outermost layer of the Earth. It is located 0–35 kilometers below the surface. Earth's crust is composed mainly of basalt and granite. The crust is less dense, cooler, and more rigid than the planet's internal layers. This layer floats on top of the **mantle**. Located 35–2,890 kilometers below the Earth's surface, the mantle is separated from the crust by the **Mohorovicic discontinuity**, or Moho (which occurs at 30–70 kilometers below the continental crust and at 6–8 kilometers beneath the oceanic crust). The mantle is made up of rocks such as peridotite and eclogite; its temperature varies from 100 to 3,500 degrees Celsius. Material in the mantle cycles due to convection. The innermost layer of the Earth is the core, which consists of a liquid outer layer and a solid inner layer. It is located 2,890–6,378 kilometers below the surface. The core is thought to be composed of iron and nickel and is the densest layer of the Earth.

Sublayers

The **lithosphere** consists of the crust and the uppermost portion of the mantle of the Earth. It is located 0–60 kilometers below the surface. The lithosphere is the cooling layer of the planet's convection cycle and thickens over time. This solid shell is fragmented into pieces called tectonic plates. The oceanic lithosphere is made up of mafic basaltic rocks and is thinner and generally more dense than the continental lithosphere (composed of granite and sedimentary rock); the lithosphere floats atop Earth's mantle. The **asthenosphere** is the soft, topmost layer of the mantle. It is located 100–700 kilometers below the surface. A combination of heat and pressure keeps the asthenosphere's composite material plastic. The **mesosphere** is located 900–2,800 kilometers below the surface; it therefore spans from the lower part of the mantle to the mantle-core boundary. The liquid **outer core** exists at 2,890–5,100 kilometers below surface level, and the solid inner core exists at depths of 5,100–6,378 kilometers.

Review Video: Earth's Structure
Visit mometrix.com/academy and enter code: 713016

Volcanoes

Volcanic Eruption

A **volcanic eruption** generally entails a build-up of magma (a silicate solution formed of melted rocks) in a magma chamber. **Gases** present in the magma, such as water vapor, carbon dioxide, and sulfur dioxide, cause increasing pressure in the material. Often, the vent that would enable release of the built-up pressure is blocked by solidified magma. The viscosity of the magma also affects the release of gas pressure; the more viscous the magma, the more pressure will build up. A volcano erupts when the pressure becomes too great to be contained and the gases are suddenly and violently released. The freed gases expand, forcing magma and solid materials upward. The products of a volcanic eruption include ash, lava, and solid igneous rocks.

Eruption Types

Volcanic eruptions are classified by their degree of **explosivity**. Explosive eruptions expel gases, ash, and rocks (such as pumice) to incredible heights; these products affect areas miles away. An explosive eruption can affect atmospheric pressure and increase the electricity of the surrounding air. Eruptions of intermediate explosivity often occur in stratovolcanoes. They are similar to explosive eruptions but their effects are smaller in scale. **Quiet eruptions**, consistent with shield volcanoes, exhibit virtually no explosivity. Lava flows from the volcano instead of shooting out of it vertically. This type of eruption is often powered by the release of steam rather than the release of magmatic gases. **Fissure eruptions** are those during which lava flows from a series of small fissures, or fractures, in the Earth's crust instead of from a single volcanic vent. This type of eruption is usually accompanied by flood lava.

Shape Categories

All volcanoes are formed from the accumulation of erupted materials into a **volcanic cone landform.** The majority of volcanoes also exhibit **craters**, which are depressions at the top of volcanic cones that mark the location of the vent through which eruptive materials are expelled. Stratovolcanoes, or composite cones, are characterized by different kinds of material in their constitution. This type of volcano erupts lava as well as large amounts of pyroclastic material (ash, solid rocks, and so on); all of this material piles up to form a tall, steep volcanic cone. Shield volcanoes erupt only fluid lava, which flows for long distances prior to solidification. Consequently, shield volcanoes are relatively wide and flat. Cinder cones are small, short-lived volcanoes whose eruptive products are almost exclusively solid materials. These materials pile up and create a volcano-shaped hill.

Activity Level

Due to the life spans of volcanoes (from a few months to millions of years), it is difficult to develop a standardized system to classify their activity levels. However, scientists have attempted to create a broad classification system. Generally, a volcano is considered active if it is presently erupting or showing signs of unrest, such as **gas emission** or **seismic activity**. Also, volcanoes are usually considered active if they have erupted in historic time. A dormant volcano is one that is not currently active but possesses the potential to become active in the future. A volcano is considered extinct when it is unlikely to erupt ever again. The classification of extinct is usually the most problematic to determine.

Volcanic Activity at Different Plate Boundaries

Volcanic activity occurs at divergent plate boundaries most often under the ocean. Divergent plate boundaries are also known as constructive plate boundaries because new crustal material must be formed to fill the void created by the separation of tectonic plates. As oceanic lithospheric plates pull apart, magma rises from beneath to fill the gap; the increased temperature and magma concentration breeds volcanic activity. At convergent, or destructive, plate margins, friction creates the heat energy necessary to melt crustal rocks into magma. Also, the subduction of one plate under another pushes crustal material into the mantle, where temperatures are higher. The presence of volatiles (such as water and carbon dioxide) at subduction zones can force magma out through vents in the Earth's surface. Occasionally, volcanic activity occurs at locations far from any plate boundary. These locations, called hotspots, are thought to exist over particularly active mantle zones which shoot "plumes" of molten material up toward the crust.

Pyroclastic Materials

Pyroclastic materials are those expelled from a volcano during eruption separate from the flowing molten rock. They have been found to exist in all types of composition. Clots of lava that cool while they are airborne are called volcanic bombs. Due to the rapid cooling processes they undergo, volcanic bombs usually exhibit aphanitic or glassy textures. Lapilli are small pieces of chilled lava expelled during a volcanic eruption; lapilli tuffs are rocks composed of lapilli. Exploding volcanoes also spew ash into the atmosphere. Rocks composed of volcanic ash are called ash-fall tuffs. Sedimentary processes can act on the layers of volcanic residue surrounding a volcano to form rocks.

Minerals

A **mineral** is a naturally occurring, inorganic, solid physical substance. Minerals have **regular atomic structures** (crystallizations) and definite **homogenous** chemical compositions. Some minerals are elements, but many are chemical compounds. These materials are formed through the cooling and hardening of magma, sublimation of a gas (especially near volcanic vents), precipitation (parsing out of solids from a solution), or through metamorphism. **Metamorphism** is the process whereby a rock experiences changes in characteristics while remaining in a solid state. This occurs due to the presence of one or more of these agents: heat, stress, pressure, or chemically active fluids. This chemical reaction can produce minerals as byproducts. Minerals are identified and classified based on certain physical characteristics; the study of minerals is called mineralogy.

Classification

Color

When light waves act upon minerals, certain wavelengths **reflect** off of the material into an observer's eye, while others are absorbed by the mineral's component atoms. The reflected light waves establish the mineral's **color**. An **idiochromatic mineral** is a substance whose color is indicative of its chemical composition, so color is thus a characteristic that can be used to validly classify minerals. Ions of particular elements, such as copper, iron, and cobalt, are extremely absorptive of certain light wavelengths. These elements are called **chromophores**. The presence of chromophores in minerals often gives those substances vivid and distinctive coloration. Minerals whose chemical compositions do not contain chromophores possess color properties due to the presence of impurities; this phenomenon is called **allochromatism**. The impurities are often chromophore mixtures that are not part of the mineral's chemical composition. In these cases, color is not helpful in classifying the mineral.

LUSTER

Luster in mineralogy and petrography is the relative difference in **opacity** and **translucency** of minerals (in other words, luster refers to the quality and quantity of light reflected off of minerals' exterior surfaces). This property depends on the type of atomic bonds present in the mineral and thus demonstrates characteristics about the mineral's structure and texture. Minerals with **metallic** luster (and therefore metallic atomic bonds) are relatively opaque, which means they reflect many light waves and appear to sparkle. Minerals with **nonmetallic** luster are those whose surfaces are highly absorptive; they usually exhibit ionic bonding in their atomic structures. Various adjectives are used to describe the qualities of nonmetallic minerals (e.g., pearly, resinous, silky, dull). Hematite is an example of a mineral with **submetallic** luster; this classification falls just short of metallic luster.

STREAK

The observation of **streak** is similar to the observation of color in a mineral—the mineral's color is evaluated after it has been crushed into powder. The term streak comes from the practice of **smearing** a crushed mineral across a plate in a line. The **color of a streak sample** results from the random arrangement of the substance's component crystals rather than from the substance's crystalline structure (as in the observation of color). The property of streak is a better basis for classification than color because the presence of impurities in a mineral is relevant only when the material's crystals are organized into a regular structure. In streak, the jumble of crushed crystals negates the possibility of discoloration due to the presence of an impurity. Observation of a mineral's streak can also aid in determination of the mineral's luster quality: Minerals with metallic luster tend to be dark and thick because they do not transmit light, while nonmetallic minerals (which do transmit light) appear light and thin.

HARDNESS

Hardness in mineral classification refers to the level of a mineral's resistance to **scratching**. A mineral's hardness provides evidence of the strength of the bonds composing its crystal structure. Hardness is quantified through the use of either the **Mohs' scratch test** or the **diamond indentation method**. The Mohs' test is based on a scale populated by ten reference minerals arranged in ascending order from softest (talc) to hardest (diamond). In this system, a mineral that can scratch and be scratched by a particular reference mineral has a hardness number equal to that of the reference mineral. The Mohs' scale is accurate to the half-increment. In the diamond indentation method, the point of a diamond is pressed into the surface of a mineral under a specific load; the indentation left by the diamond is then measured under a microscope. The units of hardness attained from this method of measurement are kilograms per millimeter squared (the weight of the load divided by the surface area of the resultant indentation).

Cleavage

Cleavage refers to the ability of a mineral to split along closely spaced parallel planes called cleavage planes. The presence and identification of these planes in a mineral reveal areas of weak atomic bonds and/or wide lattice spacing in the mineral's atomic organization. In mineral identification, geologists observe the ease with which a mineral cleaves and the characteristics of the cleavage surface. A mineral's cleavage is said to be perfect when it splits easily and exhibits smooth, unblemished cleavage surfaces. Distinct cleavage occurs easily but results in marred, imperfect surfaces. Other classifications of mineral cleavage are good, indistinct, difficult, and so on. The direction of cleavage tends to be parallel to crystal planes with high concentrations of ions. Observation of cleavage thus contributes to identification of the atomic structure of a mineral.

Fracture

Fracture is a characteristic usually exhibited by minerals with imperfect or nonexistent cleavage. The term refers to the **breaking** or **crushing** of a mineral's surface (as opposed to the clear splitting associated with cleavage). There are three types of fracture patterns that can be used in mineral identification. **Conchoidal fracture** refers to a shell-like pattern of fracture, characterized by a series of concentric rings spreading outward from the point of the break. **Irregular fracture** is simply a rough, uneven surface. Hackly fracture refers to a line of fracture with sharp, jagged edges. Like the property of cleavage, the property of fracture can be used as an indicator of a mineral's crystalline structure.

Specific Gravity

Specific gravity in mineral identification expresses how much denser a mineral is than water. This property is usually defined as the weight of a specified volume of a mineral divided by the weight of an equal volume of water in its densest state (at 4 degrees Celsius). The density of a mineral can also be measured through the creation of a solution made up of a dense liquid and a miscible (mixable), lower-density liquid. The ratio of the two liquids in the solution is adjusted until a specific mineral is able to achieve suspension in the solution. The weight of a specified volume of the solution is then measured and used to calculate the density of the solution and thus the mineral. The measurement of the density or specific gravity of a mineral is useful in its identification because density is determined by the chemical composition of the mineral (the weight of its component atoms) as well as by the mineral's crystal structure (the spacing of its component atoms).

Tenacity

Tenacity in mineral identification refers to the way a mineral responds to the application of deformative forces such as cutting, bending, or crushing. A mineral exhibits **brittle** tenacity when it fractures under a forceful blow. A mineral that deforms temporarily due to deformative stresses but reverts to its original state with the removal of pressure possesses **elastic tenacity**. A **flexible** mineral will bend rather than break under external stresses but will not return to its original shape. Minerals with **malleable** tenacities can be reshaped without fracturing (gold, for example, can be flattened into thin sheets). **Ductile** minerals can be drawn into thin strands without breaking. Rare **sectile** minerals exist that can be sliced into thin sheets through the use of a sharp instrument but cannot withstand the force of a blow.

Habit

Crystal habit refers to the favored crystal growth pattern of a mineral species. Atomic structure is a defining characteristic of minerals; the observation of habit is thus very important in the process of mineral identification (although crystal formation is rarely perfect). The growth pattern of a mineral crystal is closely related to the environmental conditions under which it forms. Pressure, temperature, and the chemical conditions of precipitation are all factors that influence the shape of a forming crystal. A **crystal** is said to have an equant habit when its sides are of nearly equal length in all directions. **Bladed** crystals exhibit long, flat areas that are reminiscent of knife blades. A plumose crystal has a series of feathery scales. Minerals of **micaceous** habit consist of thin, flat sheets that can be easily flaked or peeled from the larger mineral mass. **Prismatic** crystals are elongated. Other adjectives used for the description of crystal habit are capillary, fibrous, striated, columnar, and mammillary.

Review Video: Rocks vs. Minerals
Visit mometrix.com/academy and enter code: 947587

Crystallization

Speed of Cooling

Nucleation is the process whereby clusters of atoms in a liquid arrange themselves in a solid configuration. At lower temperatures, these nuclei become stable. When this process occurs slowly (when the rate of growth is greater than the rate of nucleation), large, stable crystals form. When the rate of **nucleation** is greater than the **rate of growth** (during rapid cooling), the process results in the formation of many small crystals. Minerals with this crystalline composition are inherently unstable and will aggregate into a large, solid crystal over time. Rapid cooling usually produces **anhedral crystals** (crystals with internal regularity but without external crystal faces). Slower cooling processes generally result in the formation of **euhedral crystals** (those with well-formed faces) or **subhedral crystals** (which exhibit intermediate, rounded outlines).

Types of Crystal Growth

The ideal type of crystal growth is **two-dimensional nucleation**. In this process, crystals are formed in separate layers. The crystal faces are built up through accumulation of these layers, as the mineral's atoms arrange themselves in the configuration of highest stability (that with the lowest energy). Two-dimensional nucleation occurs slowly and necessitates high supersaturation. **Spiral growth**, on the other hand, is a quick process. Also called screw dislocation, spiral growth is the continuous growth of a single layer in the form of a spiral. This type of growth occurs in regions of low saturation. **Branching growth** is the rapid growth of a crystal in limited directions, resulting in a treelike structure. Heat transfer halts favorable growth and causes growth in an unfavorable direction. This process creates dendrites, formed from a single nucleus and with a single crystallographic orientation.

Modes of Crystal Aggregation

Crystal aggregates are more common than single crystals. An **oriented overgrowth** is one form of crystal aggregate. This type of aggregate is formed by parallel deposits of one mineral on the surface of another. The surface atoms of the host mineral exert organizational forces on the atoms of the overgrowing crystal, orienting the latter's nuclei into the same crystal structure as the former. This process occurs most often between mineral species with dissimilar chemical compositions. **Cavernous crystals** are formed when atoms rapidly assimilate on the edges of a crystal instead of growing in complete layers across the crystal's face. This growth process produces a crystal with deep depressions in the centers of its faces. A cavernous crystal grows when supersaturation exists at high levels along the edges of a forming crystal. A **phantom crystal** occurs when impurities are present in the material of a growing crystal. The impurities form along the inner faces of a crystallizing mineral and result in an outline of a crystal within a crystal.

Cycling of Earth's Materials

Rock Cycle

The **rock cycle** is the process whereby the materials that make up the Earth transition through the three types of rock: igneous, sedimentary, and metamorphic. Rocks, like all matter, cannot be created or destroyed; rather, they undergo a series of changes and adopt different forms through the functions of the rock cycle. Plate tectonics and the water cycle are the driving forces behind the rock cycle; they force rocks and minerals out of equilibrium and force them to adjust to different external conditions. Viewed in a generalized, cyclical fashion, the rock cycle operates as follows: rocks beneath Earth's surface melt into magma. This **magma** either erupts through volcanoes or remains inside the Earth. Regardless, the magma cools, forming igneous rocks. On the surface, these rocks experience **weathering** and **erosion**, which break them down and distribute the fragments across the surface. These fragments form layers and eventually become **sedimentary rocks**. Sedimentary rocks are then either transformed to **metamorphic rocks** (which will become magma inside the Earth) or melted down into magma.

Rock Formation

Igneous Rocks: Igneous rocks can be formed from sedimentary rocks, metamorphic rocks, or other igneous rocks. Rocks that are pushed under the Earth's surface (usually due to plate subduction) are exposed to high mantle temperatures, which cause the rocks to melt into magma. The magma then rises to the surface through volcanic processes. The lower atmospheric temperature causes the magma to cool, forming grainy, extrusive igneous rocks. The creation of extrusive, or volcanic, rocks is quite rapid. The cooling process can occur so rapidly that crystals do not form; in this case, the result is a glass, such as obsidian. It is also possible for magma to cool down inside the Earth's interior; this type of igneous rock is called intrusive. Intrusive, or plutonic, rocks cool more slowly, resulting in a coarse-grained texture.

Sedimentary Rocks: Sedimentary rocks are formed when rocks at the Earth's surface experience weathering and erosion, which break them down and distribute the fragments across the surface. Fragmented material (small pieces of rock, organic debris, and the chemical products of mineral sublimation) is deposited and accumulates in layers, with top layers burying the materials beneath. The pressure exerted by the topmost layers causes the lower layers to compact, creating solid sedimentary rock in a process called lithification.

Metamorphic Rocks: Metamorphic rocks are igneous or sedimentary rocks that have "morphed" into another kind of rock. In metamorphism, high temperatures and levels of pressure change preexisting rocks physically and/or chemically, which produces different species of rocks. In the rock cycle, this process generally occurs in materials that have been thrust back into the Earth's mantle by plate subduction. Regional metamorphism refers to a large band of metamorphic activity; this often occurs near areas of high orogenic (mountain-building) activity. Contact metamorphism refers to metamorphism that occurs when "country rock" (that is, rock native to an area) comes into contact with high-heat igneous intrusions (magma).

Plate Tectonics Rock Cycle

The plate tectonics rock cycle expands the concept of the traditional rock cycle to include more specific information about the tectonic processes that propel the rock cycle, as well as an evolutionary component. Earth's materials do not cycle endlessly through the different rock forms; rather, these transitive processes cause, for example, increasing diversification of the rock types found in the crust. Also, the cycling of rock increases the masses of continents by increasing the volume of granite. Thus, the **tectonic rock cycle** is a model of an evolutionary rock cycle. In this model, new oceanic lithosphere is created at divergent plate boundaries. This new crust spreads outward until it reaches a **subduction zone**, where it is pushed back into the mantle, becomes magma, and is thrust out into the **atmosphere**. It experiences erosion and becomes **sedimentary rock**. At convergent continental plate boundaries, this crust is involved in mountain building and the associated metamorphic pressures. It is **eroded** again, and returns to the lithosphere.

Role of Water

Water plays an important role in the rock cycle through its roles in **erosion** and **weathering**: it wears down rocks; it contributes to the dissolution of rocks and minerals as acidic soil water; and it carries ions and rock fragments (sediments) to basins where they will be compressed into **sedimentary rock**. Water also plays a role in the **metamorphic processes** that occur underwater in newly-formed igneous rock at mid-ocean ridges. The presence of water (and other volatiles) is a vital component in the melting of rocky crust into magma above subduction zones.

Metamorphism

Metamorphism is the process whereby existing sedimentary, igneous, or metamorphic rocks (protoliths) are transformed due to a change in their original physiochemical environment, where they were mineralogically stable. This generally happens alongside sedimentation, orogenesis, or the movement of tectonic plates. Between the Earth's surface and a depth of 20 kilometers, there exists a wide range of temperatures, pressure levels, and chemical activity. Metamorphism is generally an **isochemical process**, which means that it does not alter the initial chemical composition of a rock. The changes a rock undergoes in metamorphism are usually physical. Neither a metamorphosing rock nor its component minerals are melted during this process—they remain almost exclusively in a solid state. Metamorphism, like the formation of plutonic rock bodies, can be studied only after metamorphic rocks have been exposed by weathering and erosion of the crustal rocks above.

Factors

Heat is a primary factor in metamorphism. When extreme heat is applied to existing rocks, their component minerals are able to recrystallize (which entails a reorganization of the grains or molecules of a mineral, resulting in increased density, as well as the possible expulsion of volatiles such as water and carbon dioxide). High levels of thermal energy may also cause rocks to contort and deform. **Pressure** is another factor affecting the metamorphism of rocks. Increased pressure can initiate recrystallization through compression. Pressure forces can also lead to spot-melting at individual grain boundaries. Lithostatic, or confining, pressure is created by the load of rocks above a metamorphosing rock. Pore-fluid pressure results from the release of volatiles due to thermal energy. Directed pressure is enforced in a certain direction due to orogenesis: This type of pressure is responsible for foliation, or layering, which entails parallel alignment of mineral particles in a rock, characteristic of metamorphism. **Chemical activity** affects metamorphism due to the presence of volatiles in pore fluids.

Biogeochemical Cycle

The term biogeochemical cycle refers to one of several chemical processes in which chemical elements are (re)cycled among **biotic** (living) and **abiotic** (nonliving) constituents of an ecosystem. The theory of relativity necessitates the presence of such cycles in nature by virtue of its supposition that energy and matter are not created or destroyed in a closed system such as Earth's ecosystem. Generally, a **biogeochemical cycle** operates as follows: inorganic compounds, such as carbon, are converted from water, air, and soil to organic molecules by organisms called **autotrophs**. **Heterotrophs** (organisms that cannot independently produce their own food) consume the autotrophs; some of the newly formed organic molecules are transferred. Finally, the organic molecules are broken down and processed once again into inorganic compounds by secondary and tertiary consumers and replaced within water, air, and soil. Carbon, nitrogen, and phosphorus provide examples of nutrients that are recycled in the Earth's ecosystem.

Rock Types and Formation

Rock

A **rock** is a naturally formed inorganic object composed of one or more of the minerals found in the Earth's crust. The term usually refers to hard, compact, coherent materials. While **minerals** are homogenous substances, rocks are **heterogeneous**. There are three main types of processes through which rocks are formed: sedimentary, igneous, and metamorphic. In **petrogenesis**, rocks are classified according to their origin. In **petrography**, rocks are described and identified based on several physical characteristics. **Petrology**, the general study of rocks, contributed to the formation of plate tectonics as a coherent theory; it also plays an important role in studies of Earth's interior. Due to the (sometimes numerous) different physical properties of a rock's component materials, petrogenesis is usually a more favorable rock-identification technique than petrography; therefore, the former is more generally practiced and accepted.

Review Video: Igneous, Sedimentary, and Metamorphic Rocks
Visit mometrix.com/academy and enter code: 689294

Sedimentary Rocks

Sediments

Sediments are the materials that make up sedimentary rocks. They are **deposited** in layers through erosion and fall into four general categories. Solid particles are fragmented byproducts of weathering. This type of sediment consists of fragmented rocks produced by mechanical weathering, as well as materials such as sand, gravel, and silt, which are produced in chemical weathering. **Solid-particle sediments** provide clues as to their source areas. Fine-grained clay minerals are formed in surface areas of low temperatures, such as soil. This type of sediment also has the potential to reveal information about its source. **Chemical weathering** produces ion and salt byproducts that can be deposited as sediments. These materials form minerals when precipitated from a solution due to rapid evaporation. Sediments can also be organic in origin. For example, the shells of organisms may be deposited as sediments.

Conversion into Solid Rock

The consolidation of sediments into solid rock is called **lithification**. Deposition of sediments in layers leads to the increase of overburdening pressure on the lower strata. This pressure compresses the particles in a sediment and expels the connate fluids (water and ionic solutions) that occupy pore space in the sediment. This process, called **compaction**, is followed by cementation. In **cementation**, precipitated minerals, such as calcite, are deposited as a film atop layers of compacted sediment. The cementing material moves into the pore space previously held by the connate fluids, creating solid rock. After lithification, any further change (physical, chemical, or biological) in the rock's component sediments, other than weathering, is referred to as **diagenesis**.

Clastic Sedimentary Rocks

Clastic sedimentary rocks are formed exclusively from fragments of other rocks. These fragments vary greatly in composition; therefore, analysis of the sizes of the particles that make up a clastic rock is used as an identification technique more often than analysis of the rock's composition. The sizes of the particles deposited in sediments are related to the energy of the medium that transports them. **Conglomerates** are clastic rocks formed from the compaction and cementation of gravels. The component gravel fragments may range from a few millimeters to several meters in diameter. **Sandstones** are clastic rocks formed from particles with diameters of 0.0625 mm to 2 mm. The identity of the cementing materials determines the strength of the various varieties of sandstone. Clastic rocks formed from **silt** and **clay** grains with diameters less than 0.0625 mm are called shale. Almost half of all sedimentary rocks are shale.

Precipitated Rocks

Precipitated, or chemical, rocks are sedimentary rocks formed from the byproducts of chemical reactions. **Evaporites** are minerals or rocks created through the evaporation of the liquid in a solution. Ions precipitate from the solution and form crystalline mineral residues. Halite (table salt) is an example of an evaporite mineral. **Carbonate rocks** are sedimentary rocks made up of carbonate compounds, usually calcite or dolomite. Calcite often forms due to temperature changes in seawater, which causes precipitation. If a carbonate rock contains mostly calcite, it is considered limestone (though limestone is largely organic in origin). If dolomite predominates, the rock is simply called dolomite or dolostone.

Organic Rock

An **organic**, or biogenic, rock is a type of sedimentary rock formed from the remains of plant and animal organisms. The bones and shells of animals contain minerals (such as calcite) that can become cemented together after soft tissues decay, forming fossils that make up organic rocks. This type of rock also contains lithified plant remains. Limestone is the most abundant organic sedimentary rock; it makes up, for example, coral reefs, which are formed of fossils, corals, and algae. Coal is a good example of an organic sedimentary rock formed from cemented plant remains. Plants become so compacted over time, squeezing out volatiles and impurities, that coal, a fossil fuel, consists mainly of organic carbon.

Stratification

Stratification is a feature of sedimentary rocks that distinguishes them from other rock types. Sedimentary rocks are made up of usually horizontal layers of sediment (called strata) of various thickness. When a stratum is thicker than 1 centimeter, it is called a **bed**. **Laminae** are strata with thicknesses less than 1 centimeter. Sediment in a particular stratum is usually evenly distributed. However, graded bedding (a bed with larger particles at the bottom) is formed when sediment is rapidly expelled into a calm body of water. Stratification occurs due to variations in the volume, mineral composition, or color of sediment in transport; the energy of the transporting medium can also affect this process. **Varves** are sediments (common in glacier-fed lakes) characterized by the repetition of two layers: a lower layer of coarse silt and an upper layer made up of fine-grained silt and clay, each deposited seasonally. One varve therefore represents one year of a lake's development, not unlike the rings of a tree.

Continental Sediment Deposition

Sediments, and thus sedimentary rocks, are usually found in the lower areas of a landscape. **Floodplains** are the flat areas adjacent to rivers over which water flows during flooding. Each flood brings with it a new layer of sediment that is deposited on the floodplain. **Alluvial** fans form when a rapidly flowing river or stream carrying sediment abruptly reaches a basin. The sediment is quickly dumped and spreads out in the shape of a fan on the basin floor. Sediments are often deposited at the junctions of rivers and large water bodies such as gulfs. Loads of sediment are deposited on top of each other, creating a delta. Wind plays an important role in continental sediment deposition, forming, for example, well-sorted sand dunes. Wind is most effective in sediment deposition in regions with little stabilizing vegetation and plentiful sand.

Zones of Marine Sediment Deposition

The distribution of sediment in oceanic bodies is related to distance from land, water depth, the physical and chemical properties of the water itself, and the local plant and animal life. **Tidal activity** deposits coarse materials, such as sand and gravel, at the shore zone (the area where waves break against the shore). Sediment from land, such as clay and silts, is usually deposited on the continental shelf, which is much broader than the shore zone. In this area, algae and coral, which excrete carbonate, play active roles in the formation of sedimentary rocks. The continental slope is the downward incline from the continental shelf to the ocean floor. The ocean floor (termed the abyss in discussion of marine deposition zones) is where the finest sediments accumulate.

Color, Ripple Marks, and Roundness

The color of sedimentary rocks can be used to distinguish them from other rock types. Sedimentary rocks are generally multicolored by their cementing materials. Red is a common pigment in sedimentary rocks—it indicates the presence of weathered and eroded fragments of **oxidized**, iron-bearing minerals. **Organic** rocks, such as coal, usually exhibit gray or black coloration.

Ripple marks are distinguishable in sedimentary rocks that experienced strong wind, water, or gravitational forces during their formation. **Roundness** is a property of the grains that make up clastic sedimentary rocks. The roundness of a sediment's grains can provide clues about the distance a sediment was transported before deposition.

Identification

Concretions are solid bodies of near-spherical shape that are sometimes found in sedimentary rock. They are formed when a cementing material forms around a nucleus, such as a shell fragment or a grain of sand. The cement binds all the particles together and enlarges the object like a snowball. The sorting property of sedimentary rocks is defined as the degree of similarity among the particle sizes in a sediment. Sediments are described as having poor, moderate, or good sorting depending on the level of consistency of the sizes of their component particles. When sediment strata are oriented in steep inclines, rather than in nearly uniform horizontal layers, they are said to be cross-bedded. Sand dunes (formed by wind and gravity) often exhibit cross-bedding, as do deltas. **Fossils** are the remains of organisms that are preserved in sedimentary rock in a process similar to the petrifaction of wood. Remains high in the mineral calcite (such as teeth, bones, and shells) are fossilized more often than soft tissues.

Igneous Rocks

Formation

Igneous rocks are formed by the **crystallization** of minerals due to the cooling of molten rock (called magma or melt). **Magma** can come from the Earth's mantle; it can also be formed when existing rocks melt because of high temperature and pressure levels in magma chambers (pools surrounded by solid rock). Igneous rocks formed on Earth's surface from cooling magma after a volcano erupts are called **volcanic** or **extrusive rocks**. Not all magma is expelled from a magma chamber during a volcano eruption. The magma left behind cools and crystallizes beneath the Earth's surface. The rocks formed from this process are called **plutonic** or **intrusive**. The mineral composition of igneous rocks depends on the initial composition of the melt from which they were formed. All magmas contain high levels of oxygen and silica. Igneous rocks make up 95% of the upper crust; however, a thin, widespread layer of sedimentary and metamorphic rocks blankets the abundant igneous rocks.

CATEGORIES OF MAGMA

Magmas are generated 100–300 kilometers below the Earth's surface. Several different types of rock are present in this area; the following terms can be used to describe the parent rocks that melt to form magmas as well as the magmas themselves. **Mafic magmas** are those containing high levels of iron, calcium, and magnesium. The parent materials from which mafic magmas are formed are commonly found beneath oceanic and continental crusts. **Felsic magmas** are rich in potassium, sodium, and silicon. This type of magma forms from parent rocks within the continental crust. **Intermediate magmas** are those with compositions in transition between the compositions of mafic and felsic magmas. Intermediate magmas form when mafic and felsic parent materials melt at depth at the margins of continents. **Ultramafic magmas** display large amounts of iron and magnesium in their composition. Like mafic magma, ultramafic magma originates beneath the crust of oceans and continents.

CREATION OF MAGMA FROM PARENT ROCKS

The various melting points of the minerals that make up a parent rock affect the composition of the magmas they form. Obviously, the minerals with lower melting points will melt before those with higher melting points as temperatures rise. Sometimes, the heat energy exerted on a rock is limited. This results in **partial melting**; the resultant magma will contain only the minerals with lower melting points. The melting of parent rocks to create magma is also affected by the presence of volatiles such as water and carbon dioxide. Water, for example, can act as a catalyst in the melting of silicate materials, sometimes reducing the melting point of a mineral by 200 degrees Celsius. Water is thought to increase magma generation in many areas.

MAGMA CRYSTALLIZATION

Magma crystallizes when it is erupted to Earth's surface and exposed to the cooling atmosphere or when it stops moving underneath the surface. The crystallization process is the opposite of melting. Temperatures fall until the movement of mineral particles becomes slow enough for ionic bonds to form and stabilize to create **crystals**. Minerals with the highest melting points (1,050–950 °C), such as olivine and calcic plagioclase, crystallize first. Minerals with intermediate melting points (900–750 °C), such as augite and hornblende, crystallize next, followed by those with the lowest melting points (750–600 °C), such as feldspar and quartz. The order of the minerals that form from magma crystallization is obviously dependent on the initial composition of the magma as well as the ambient temperature.

MAGMATIC DIFFERENTIATION

Magmatic differentiation refers to the processes by which the composition of magma is altered during cooling and crystallization. Magmatic differentiation may occur due to compositional zonation within a magma chamber. In some magma chambers, the material in the top of the chamber (which erupts first) is cooler and more felsic than that at the bottom of the chamber. Thus, the minerals crystallized from magma expelled at the beginning of an eruption may contain higher levels of feldspar and silicon than those formed from magma erupted at the end of the volcanic event. Crystal fractionation is another type of magmatic differentiation. Crystals formed early in the cooling process are differentiated from the remaining magma when certain ions become concentrated in those crystals, leaving lower levels of those elements in the magma. This process leads to the production of starting and secondary magmas (and thus igneous rocks) that differ in mineral composition. Hybrid magma is produced when magma of the original composition is introduced to the chamber after crystal fractionation has begun.

Texture

Texture is one of the most important distinguishing characteristics of igneous rocks because it gives indications of the speed at which the formative magma cooled and where the crystallization process occurred. Volcanic rocks generally form quickly when magma is exposed to the atmosphere above the surface; they have fine-grained textures. Plutonic rocks, on the other hand, undergo slow cooling processes that result in coarse-grained textures. Observation of a glassy texture in an igneous rock (such as obsidian) indicates that it cooled so rapidly that the ions in the magma had no time to arrange themselves in a crystalline pattern. A porphyritic texture is common in plutonic rocks formed in small bodies at shallow depths. This texture suggests that the formative magma underwent two stages of cooling, which produced crystals of two different sizes. Large, well-formed crystals begin to solidify in magma in a deep chamber. The magma then moves upward to a shallower location, causing the remaining liquid magma to cool quickly, forming smaller crystals around the large crystals that were formed first.

Felsic Igneous Rocks

Granite, a common form of **felsic igneous rock**, is composed mainly of coarse- to fine-grained potassium feldspar and sodic plagioclase and is generally light in color. Quartz is also present in granite; it is the last mineral to crystallize during the cooling process. Granite is often used in the construction of buildings and monuments. Rhyolite is the volcanic complement to plutonic granite. The two rocks exhibit similar constitutions but different textures. Rhyolite is usually fine grained, glassy, or porphyritic. Pumice is a form of rhyolitic volcanic glass. It forms when there is a high concentration of gases in the original magma. Pumice has been described as petrified froth.

Mafic Igneous Rocks

Gabbro, a common form of **mafic igneous rock**, is generally coarse grained and dark colored. It is composed of pyroxene and calcic plagioclase crystals with traces of olivine. It contains higher levels of ferromagnesian (internally magnetic) materials than felsic rocks. Basalt is the most common volcanic rock. It is very similar to gabbro in composition; however, its texture is very fine grained or even aphanitic (composed of crystals too small to be seen by the naked eye). Basalt is similar to pumice in that it is formed from magma with a high concentration of gases, which results in vesicles (small holes caused by gas bubbles in cooling magma). Basaltic melts flow more quickly than felsic melts. This causes them to cool from a thin outer layer inward. The associated compaction and stress cause fractures called columnar jointing, which are common in basaltic rocks.

Intermediate Rocks

Diorite, an **intermediate rock**, exhibits textures from fine to coarse grained; it possesses a mineral composition halfway between those of granite and gabbro. Plagioclase feldspar is diorite's main component; it also contains a generous proportion of hornblende. Diorite is normally a somber gray color. Andesite, a volcanic rock, is a common type of intermediate rock. It is fine grained and exhibits gray or black coloration. Andesite often manifests a porphyritic texture. Its composition is similar to that of diorite. This type of rock is more common on the Earth's surface than rhyolites, but less common than basalts.

Metamorphic Rocks

Contact Metamorphic Rocks

Contact metamorphic rocks are those created by the movements of magma near the margins of plutonic rock bodies such as dikes or batholiths. The thermal energy associated with magma initiates recrystallization of the surrounding country rocks. The formation of contact metamorphic rocks (or hornfels) is, therefore, a localized process. The region where contact metamorphism is possible is called an aureole; aureoles vary from a few centimeters to more than 1 meter. Hornfels may consist simply of reoriented mineral grains, or they may be formed from the products of chemical reactions between two or more mineral species.

Hydrothermal Metamorphic Rocks

Hydrothermal metamorphic rocks are another form of localized metamorphic rocks. Hydrothermal solutions are released due to the movement of magma near batholiths. These solutions (liquid or gas) are rich in water and magmatic ions. Their influence creates chemical reactions with the minerals in the ambient country rock. These reactions include catalyzation of the recrystallization process as well as the addition or removal of chemical elements of certain minerals in the country rocks. Serpentinization, the change in the mineral olivine that produces serpentine rocks, is a common hydrothermal reaction in metamorphosing rocks.

Cataclastic Metamorphic Rocks

Pressure is the primary factor in the formation of **cataclastic metamorphic rocks**, which, like hydrothermal and contact rocks, exist locally. In **cataclastic metamorphism**, the movement of tectonic plates causes stress to build up. This stress (and its associated pressure) has a grinding effect on local rocks. At greater depths, the higher temperatures allow the granulated rocks to recrystallize. The products of these processes are termed cataclastic rocks. The malleability of the metamorphosing rocks affects the way they are shaped by cataclastic metamorphism. Mica, for example, is stretched into parallel layers, while more brittle minerals, such as feldspar, are easily crushed.

Dynamothermal Metamorphic Rocks

Dynamothermal metamorphic rocks occur regionally, probably near converging plate boundaries. They usually exist in shields, which are large sections (sometimes covering thousands of square kilometers) of crystalline rock exposed by weathering and erosion. These rock bodies generally form near large plutons, such as batholiths and stocks. Mineral composition and texture vary throughout the shield. When taken with the assumption that the parent materials were the same throughout the region, these discrepancies are indicative of variable temperatures, pressures, and levels of chemically active solutions present during the formation of the rock body. The materials that make up the shield exist in a spectrum of gradations from high to low. Generally, an increase in metamorphic level is accompanied by coarsening of mineral grain sizes and banding of certain minerals.

Grades of Foliated Regional Metamorphic Rocks

Low-grade metamorphic rocks are dense and fine grained. They are formed by gentle dynamothermal metamorphism processes at low temperatures. This means that the metamorphosed rocks are quite similar in superficial appearance to the parent rocks from which they formed. Slate is a common low-grade rock; it is composed of recrystallized shale. Slate's rock cleavage property results from fine foliation bred during low-grade metamorphism. Intermediate-grade metamorphic rocks experience temperatures, pressures, and interference from chemical solutions at levels slightly higher than low-grade rocks. Their component grains are relatively coarse; their folia are regularly spaced. For example, shale and sandstone can metamorphose to schist through intermediate metamorphism. Gneiss is a high-grade metamorphic rock. It exhibits bands of alternately dark- and light-colored minerals. Its grains are nearly the same size as those of granite. High-grade metamorphic rocks often display evidence of plastic deformation as the result of high temperatures present during their formation.

Nonfoliated Metamorphic Rocks

The processes that form nonfoliated metamorphic rocks are similar to those that form foliated rocks; however, the mineral components of the parent rocks that form nonfoliated rocks do not foliate when exposed to directed pressure. Marble, for example, can be produced by the metamorphosis of calcite limestone. Since this type of marble's parent material is only one mineral, the metamorphosed product will not exhibit banding or foliation. Migmatites are rocks of mixed high-grade metamorphism/plutonic origin. At a particular depth, ambient temperatures inside the Earth rise to 600–800 degrees Celsius, which is high enough to melt certain minerals. For example, nonferromagnesian minerals in a gneiss specimen (such as feldspars) possess lower melting points than their ferromagnesian counterparts. At a certain temperature, therefore, the former will melt. If the temperature then stabilizes and drops, the finished product would be a rock made up of bands of ferromagnesian metamorphic rocks alternating with granite.

Pluton, Forceful Injection, Intrusive Contact and Apophyses

The term pluton is used to refer to any **plutonic rock body**. Plutons exist in a wide range of shapes and sizes, determined by the conditions surrounding their formation. Plutons are also called intrusive rocks because they are formed when magma travels underground through cracks in ambient country (host) rocks. Underground magma is highly mobile (laterally and vertically) due at least partially to its lower density as compared to surrounding country rocks. **Forceful injection** is the process in which magma pushes its way into preexisting rocks. Magma can also melt surrounding rocks to clear itself a path or pry out solid portions of rock, which it then replaces. The term **intrusive contact** refers to the surface between a country rock and an intruding pluton. Apophyses are offshoots of a magma body that are able to penetrate Earth's surface, creating a volcanic eruption.

Types of Plutons

A **dike** is a plutonic intrusion that is relatively thin in width when compared to its lateral dimensions. Dikes are usually **discordant**, which means that they cut across existing layers or bodies of rock. They usually form in a near-vertical position when magma moves through existing fractures and then cools. **Sills** are plutonic formations similar to dikes, except that they tend to be laterally oriented rather than vertically oriented; they are often offshoots of dikes. This means that they are usually concordant (they run nearly parallel to preexisting layers of rock). A volcanic neck is an intrusive rock formation created when magma solidifies in a channel that once connected an active volcano to a magma chamber. When a volcano is weathered and eroded, the magma beneath crystallizes into igneous rocks. A **laccolith** is a concordant pluton similar to a sill, but rounded. A **batholith** is a pluton that covers more than 100 square kilometers; if it is smaller than that, it is called a **stock**.

Changes to Earth's Surface Over Time

Geomorphology

Geomorphology is a subdiscipline of physical geography. Geomorphologists study the origins and formative processes of landforms. Observation of weathering and erosion processes, the movement of tectonic plates, mass movements, and the effects of human activity on the environment all contribute to an understanding of the formation and evolution of landforms. Aerial photography (from within Earth's atmosphere or from space) can aid geomorphologists in their quests. Photos taken at intervals allow them to study, for example, the creative and destructive events that occur at plate boundaries. Landscape photography also enables geomorphologists to observe long-term processes of stream erosion. Geomorphology can be applied to prediction and prevention of natural hazards such as landslides; it can also be helpful in assessing and rectifying damage to the natural environment by humans.

Topographic Map

A **topographic (topo) map** is a plot of a portion of land that indicates the contours of the land in that area. Elevation is the vertical distance between a point and mean sea level. Height is the vertical distance between two points (for instance, the distance between the top of a plateau and the bottom of a basin). Relief is the difference in the elevations of the highest and lowest points in a certain area. Topographic maps (or contour maps) use contour lines to connect points with equal elevations. When a particular contour line represents an elevation below the mean sea level, it is crossed with hatch marks. This type of map is basically a two-dimensional representation of three-dimensional features (with elevation as the third dimension) on the Earth's surface. When contour lines on a topographic map are drawn closely together, it indicates that the slopes in a particular geographic area are exceptionally steep. Evenly spaced contour lines indicate a uniform sloping angle. Topographic maps are created from aerial photographs and fieldwork.

Topographic Profile

A **topographic profile** is a representation of the skyline of a particular area (a profile line) on a topographic map. In contrast to topographic maps, topological profiles are viewed horizontally. Creating a topographic profile involves plotting the elevations of contour lines that cross a profile line and connecting these points to construct a cohesive profile. Artists often employ vertical exaggeration (a difference in horizontal and vertical scales on a profile) in creation of a topographic profile to highlight certain features. A true profile exists when the vertical and horizontal scales used in its production are equal.

Geologic Map

Unlike a topographic map, which represents landforms on the Earth's surface, a **geologic map** represents rock or mineral ore formations that exist underneath the surface. An outcrop is a portion of a formation that is exposed at the surface, usually due to weathering and erosion. Often, outcrops are blanketed by sediment, soil, and/or vegetation. A contact is a plane that separates two rock formations. On a geologic map, common rock types (such as limestone, shale, and granite) are represented by graphic patterns or colors. Lines are used to delineate contact planes. Cartographers (those who draw maps) use certain symbols to indicate the presence of horizontal beds, vertical beds, axes in folded rocks, and so on. These maps are extremely useful in the location and recovery of mineral resources and fossil fuels. These formations are identified through analysis of field research data and aerial photography.

Geological Cross Section

A **geological cross section** is created through the addition of geologic information to a topographic profile. Geologists often construct maps that display both topographic and geologic information. Working from one of these maps, it is fairly easy to create a geological cross section. After a topological profile has been plotted, one may add information about subsurface rock structures and compositions underneath the profile line. This process is complicated when rock beds are folded, tilted, or faulted from their horizontal orientation. Vertical exaggeration, which can be useful in the construction of topographic profiles, should not be used in geological cross sections—employment of such a technique would distort the angles and shapes of the represented rock beds.

Mass Movement

A **mass movement** (also called mass wasting) is the downward movement of large amounts of rock and debris due to gravitational forces. The speed at which the material will move and the amount of dislodged material are affected by several factors: the amount of water in the affected material, the climate, the type and extent of weathering, the steepness of the incline, the presence or absence of rooted vegetation, the type of bedrock present and its condition, and the presence or absence of seismic activity. Mass movements cause changes in the landscape of an area. They can also place humans and animals in the affected area in danger.

Rockfall

A **rockfall** is a mass movement wherein various amounts of rock material fall very rapidly (at speeds of 99 miles per hour or more) from a cliff face. This movement may involve a single rock or boulder or may spur an avalanche of tons of rock. The pile of rocks that results from a rockfall is termed a **talus**. When it occurs at a mountain base, a talus may prevent weathering of the mountain. A rockfall may be triggered by an earthquake, excessive rain, ice wedging (common on mountains), or human activity. Such a mass movement may, in turn, spawn an **avalanche**, a rockfall that contributes to a debris flow. The materials in motion in a rockfall often leave "scars" on the slope from which they fall.

Landslide

The term **landslide** may be used to designate several different downslope movements. Normally, a landslide involves the movement of soil and rock as a more or less coherent mass down a slope, although either the bedrock itself or the soil which overlays it may move independently. There are two main categories of landslides. **Glides**, or translational slides, which entails a large portion of rock detached from its bedrock which "glides" outward and downward along a slope. A **slump** (or rotational slide) involves the motion of a relatively cohesive mass along a concave plane—the upper part of the sliding mass ends up below ground level, and the bottom part of the mass ends up above it.

Prediction and Prevention:

The study of soils in an area is useful in estimating the **frequency of geological hazards**, and therefore the likelihood of the occurrence of a mass movement in the near future. For instance, poorly developed soil in an area is indicative of a mass movement in the recent past; well-developed soil indicates that an area has been free of such geological events for a period of time. Also, observation of erosive processes, groundwater drainage, and slope steepness can aid in the prediction of geological hazard occurrence. Civil engineers may attempt to stabilize potential areas of mass movement by several methods. For example, slides may be regraded to lesser inclines. Also, engineers may try to reduce the amount of water in materials on a slope through the implementation of drainage systems or by covering the slope surface with a material, such as plastic, to keep water out. Another method of slope stabilization is the consolidation of loose soil and rock fragments.

Flow

Flow is a type of mass movement that entails viscous motion of surface materials. Flows are characterized by motion of the internal grains of the moving mass (unlike slides). Also, they do not include a clear barrier between the flow material and a stable surface underneath. The velocity of a flow is widely various, dependent on the slope upon which it travels and the presence or absence of water. Flows generally involve one of three types of material: earth, mud, or debris. An **earth flow** is often initiated at the end of a slump slide, when the block of sliding material breaks apart. A **mud flow** involves the motions of soil and relatively high proportions of water. Increased water content increases the velocity of the moving mass from that of an earth flow. Mud flows are common in deserts. A **debris flow** is similar to a mud flow; often, the only distinction between the two is the size of the particles in motion. The motions of both debris flows and mud flows tend to follow pre-existing channels.

Creep

Creep is another landscape-altering mass movement. It involves a shallow mass of soil material moving slowly downward. This type of movement usually occurs so slowly that no one notices it. Creep can be caused by freeze-thaw or wet-dry cycles, depending on the characteristics of the bedrock materials. As with other types of mass movements, the introduction of high amounts of water into creep material will cause it to move more quickly. Though creep does not pose an immediate threat to human or animal life, it can be dangerous through long-term effects on tree roots and the foundations of buildings or other structures.

Solifluction

Solifluction is an intensified form of creep. The existence of permafrost (a layer of earth that remains in a long-term state of freeze that occurs in very cold climates) prevents absorption of surface water. The excess water then enters the topmost "active" layer of soil. That layer is thus more vulnerable to the process of creep than a comparable layer of soil in a warmer climate because of its increased fluidity and the frozen surface over which it slides. Solifluction tends to result in a "wrinkled" landscape with smooth terrain.

Water Movement

The movement of water in streams and rivers plays a key role in landscape evolution. The long-term effect of rivers and streams is to erode the land around them down to sea level, the base level of erosion. There are several theories as to how this occurs:

- **Backwasting** entails the wearing down of river valley slopes parallel to themselves. When the surface between valley slopes is worn down to the base level of erosion, the slopes retreat in parallel layers until all of the land above the widening platform is eroded to the same level.
- **Downwasting** is another theoretical process that explains landscape evolution. This process involves the diminishing of valley slopes through mass movements of soil and rock decomposition.
- A **peneplain** is the result of the erosive process of the land around streams. It is a wide, nearly flat plain of bedrock that exists just above the base level of erosion.
- A **monadnock** is an anomalous portion of especially tenacious rock that rises above a peneplain.

Stream Deposition

Stream deposition is the last phase in the weathering and erosion process performed by water, specifically streams. **Stream erosion** occurs when the movement of water in a stream detaches material from the sides and bottom of the channel through which it flows. This can carve out valleys and wide, meandering streams. Streams then carry the weathered material, as well as material deposited in the stream by other erosive processes, out to sea. Streams transport sediment in three ways:

- The **solid load** consists of the suspended load (sediment grains of various sizes floating in the water) and the bed load (the materials dragged along the bed of a channel by the moving water).
- The **bed load** performs much of the erosion of the sides and bottoms of the channel. A stream's dissolved load is composed of ions produced in the chemical weathering process.
- **Stream deposition** occurs when the stream drops its load of sediment. This can occur due to flooding or intersection of the stream with a larger body of water.

Soil

Soil is a result of the processes of **weathering** and **erosion**. Erosion transports rock particles and ions produced by weathering and deposits those materials, along with organic matter, in unconsolidated layers. Soil, fundamental to life on Earth, varies with regional temperatures, vegetation, rock types, and rock strength; it is made up of various types and ratios of **minerals**, **rocks**, and **organic materials** as well as water and air. The term **soil profile** refers to the composition of a soil's three horizons. Most soils possess an **A horizon** (a dark-colored layer called humus made up largely of decomposed organic matter), a **B horizon** (consisting mainly of the products of weathering, such as clay and rust-colored iron oxides), and a **C horizon** (made up of materials similar to the parent materials underneath). Parent materials are those thought to be present before the formation of the soil above.

Weathering

The rocks at Earth's surface experience physical, biological, and chemical processes that are much different from the processes ambient during their formations. The operation of these processes on Earth materials is called weathering.

Mechanical Weathering

Mechanical weathering causes disintegration of rocks and minerals. In this process, the affected rocks break apart into small fragments but retain their chemical compositions. This type of weathering occurs due to the presence of joints, or cracks, in rocks that allow the penetration of water and vegetative roots. Mechanical weathering occurs most often in cooler climates. The subtypes of mechanical weathering are pressure release, exfoliation, freeze-thaw, and salt-crystal growth:

- **Pressure release**, or surface unloading, occurs when erosion removes materials overlying rock. Decreased pressure causes the underlying rocks to expand and fracture.
- **Exfoliation** often occurs in regions with some moisture that experience substantial diurnal temperature changes. Rocks are subjected to heat during the day, which causes them to expand. At night, the much cooler temperatures cause the rocks to compact. The repeated expansion and contraction creates stress in the outer layers of the rocks, which eventually begin to "peel" off in thin layers. Exfoliation can also be caused by pressure release.

- **Freeze-thaw** operates when water, which has penetrated the joints of a rock, freezes and expands. The resultant pressure widens the joints and can even shatter the rock. If the rock does not fracture, the thawing of ice in the joints admits water further into the rock. Continuous, long-term freeze-thaw activity weakens rocks.
- In **salt-crystal growth**, the evaporation of saline solutions within rocks leaves salt crystals behind. Pressures accompanying this crystallization can be very high.

Chemical Weathering

Chemical weathering refers to the processes by which rocks experience chemical changes (such as decomposition and decay) due to the influence of organic acids. Chemical weathering occurs most often in high temperature, high humidity climates. The two types of weathering are not mutually exclusive; they often occur side by side. The subtypes of chemical weathering are hydration, hydrolysis, oxidation, and solution:

- **Hydration** occurs when salt minerals, which are part of a rock, expand and change due to the absorption of water. For example, anhydrite changes to gypsum with the addition of water. Hydration can cause rocks to fragment mechanically.
- **Hydrolysis** involves a chemical reaction between acidic water and a rock-forming mineral. The interaction breaks the rock down into new materials. For instance, the chemical reaction between feldspar and acidic water produces quartz and clay.
- **Oxidation**, or rusting, which results in yellow, brown, or red discoloration, occurs in iron-bearing minerals when they are exposed to the atmosphere.
- **Solution** is the weathering process whereby an organic acid interacts with certain minerals in a rock, producing ions that are then washed away by erosion. Solution, therefore, is a gradual dissolving process. It produces underground channels and caverns.

Erosion

Erosion also occurs simultaneously with weathering. This term refers to the transportation of Earth materials by wind, water, gravity, and sometimes living organisms.

An **erosion landform** is a landform created by the processes of weathering and erosion. For example, a cliff is an erosion landform. Cliffs are formed when relatively strong rocks are exposed to centuries of wind and water, weathering and erosion. Sandstone, limestone, and basalt are examples of rocks that commonly become cliffs. The canyon provides the classic instance of an erosion landform. Canyons are formed from many years of weathering and erosion processes (often water-based), usually operating on a plateau (a mountain which has been eroded down to a flat but elevated surface). Strata of rocks that resisted the destructive processes remain visible in the canyon walls.

Effects of Human Activity

Human activity can affect the resistance of solid materials such as soil to erosion processes. **Construction** activity has the largest effect on the stability of soil. Clearing trees and other vegetation makes portions of land especially susceptible to runoff. **Agriculture** is another industry that may adversely affect the resistance of Earth materials to erosion. **Animal husbandry** and **urban development** can also lead to increases (smaller than other activities, but still significant) in the levels of eroding materials. With increased erosion, Earth materials are more likely to shift through mass movements, changing natural landscapes and placing humans and other organisms in danger. Increased air pollution can catalyze erosive processes by increasing the speed of rock decay.

Geologic Time and Earth's History

Uniformitarianism

Uniformitarianism is a basic tenet of the science disciplines. It states that the processes which made the world the way it is today are still in effect. This means that careful observation and analysis of the natural processes occurring right now can provide information about the processes which formed the world as it is now known. Simply put, it says that "the present is the key to the past."

An associated (but perhaps less generally accepted) idea is that of **gradualism**, which says that the processes which created the world as it is known operated at the same rate that they do now.

The doctrine of **uniformitarianism** is applicable in all scientific disciplines, from geology to the life sciences to astronomy to physics. In geology, uniformitarianism supplanted the theory of catastrophism, which suggested that earth was formed by isolated, catastrophic events, such as a worldwide flood.

Stratigraphic Correlation

The law of **superposition** states that in bodies of undisturbed sedimentary rocks, the strata at the bottom are older than the strata at the top. **Stratigraphic correlation** is a method used to determine the "correct" or natural stratigraphic position of rock beds which have been separated by disturbances such as metamorphic processes, orogenies, or plutonic formations. This is achieved through the identification of correspondence between two points in a characteristic such as fossil content, lithology (the physical characteristics of a rock), or geologic age. This practice of (theoretically) realigning beds which have been deformed is helpful in identification of the relative ages of rocks in a sedimentary rock sequence.

Important Terms

Geological stratum - a layer of rock which possesses certain attributes which distinguishes it from adjacent layers of rock. Such attributes include, but are not limited to, lithology, chemical composition, and mineralogy.

Stratigraphy - the study of the arrangement, form, distribution, composition, and succession of rock strata. Information gained from such study is then used to form hypotheses about the strata's origins, environments, relations to organic environments, relations to other geologic concepts, and ages.

Chronostratigraphy - an aspect of stratigraphy which focuses on the relative ages of geologic strata. Scientists examine the physical interrelations of strata, the relations of strata to the sequence of organic evolution, and radioactive ages of strata to determine their chronological sequence. When the relative ages of strata have been identified, scientists can examine the constituents and properties of those strata for clues about the sequence of events which made the world what it is today.

Record of the Earth's History

Rocks

One important way in which rocks provide a record of **earth's history** is through the study of **fossils**, which allows scientists to make inferences about the evolution of life on earth. However, the presentation of fossils is certainly not the only record of earth's history contained in rocks. For instance, the **chemical composition** of rock strata may give indications about the atmospheric and/or hydrospheric compositions at certain points in earth's history. Paleomagnetism constitutes another aspect of earth's historical record contained in rocks. Through the study of magnetic orientations of rocks formed at certain times in history, scientists learn more about the form and function of earth's magnetic field then and now.

SEDIMENTS

The study of the **sediments** which make up sedimentary rocks can reveal much about the environment in which they are formed. For example, a study of the **different types** of sediments in a bed, and the **ratios** in which they occur, can indicate the types of rocks exposed at the origination site and the relative abundances of each. Examination of the sorting of a sediment can reveal information about how far the particles traveled from their provenance, as well as the medium which carried the particles. For example, sediments transported by wind tend to be well-sorted, while water moves large particles which are often worn into spheres. The type of weathering experienced by particles in a sedimentary bed can reveal the climate from which they came—mechanical weathering tends to occur in cold and arid climates, while chemical weathering is more common in hot and humid climates. Interpreting the information supplied by sediment can, in turn, reveal information about past conditions on earth.

SOIL

The study of **soil development** can give indications of the **age of certain sedimentary deposits**. For example, the study of soil led to the idea that multiple glaciations have occurred on the North American continent. Examination of the development level of certain areas of soil can also inform earth scientists about natural catastrophic events which have occurred in the past. Study of soil deposits also aided in the determination of how often "ice ages" can be expected to occur. Also, the presence of certain types of soil buried deep beneath the surface can provide indications of past climates.

PREHISTORIC OCEANS

The elements present in the earliest oceans were quite different from those present in the Earth's hydrosphere today. This is largely due to the chemical composition of the atmosphere at that time. The oceans were formed when cooling caused atmospheric clouds to condense and produce rain. **Volcanic gasses** contributed elements such as sulfur and carbon dioxide to the air. Therefore, scientists suspect that the earliest oceans contained high levels of acids (for example, sulfuric acid, hydrochloric acid, and hydrofluoric acid), and low levels of the salts that inhabit the oceans today. The temperature in this early ocean was probably close to 100 degrees Celsius. As **carbon dioxide** began to dissolve in the water, it combined with carbonate ions to form limestone which was deposited on the ocean floor. Consequently, more carbon dioxide was trapped in these rocks. Eventually, **calcium carbonate** began to reduce the acidity of these early oceans. **Weathering** brought different minerals into the ocean, which began to increase its saltiness toward its current levels.

RADIOMETRIC DATING

Radiometric dating is one of the only methods currently available to determine the absolute age of an object such as a fossil or rock body. This process is possible when such an object contains isotopes, the products of radioactive decay. In radioactive decay, the atoms of certain unstable isotopes are transformed through the emissions of either electrons or alpha particles. This process occurs exponentially until it produces a stable final product. The rate of radioactive decay is measured in half-lives: after one half-life has passed, one-half of the atoms of the original element will have decayed. When scientists examine an object which contains isotopes with known half-life periods, they can determine the amount of the isotope that was present at the time of the object's origin. That figure can then be compared with the present level to determine the age of the object.

Gaia Hypothesis

Named for the Greek goddess who organized a living earth from chaos, the **Gaia hypothesis** states that the planet is a **living system**. While this idea is not scientific in the literal sense, it provides a metaphor which is useful in achieving an understanding of the interconnectedness of all of earth's systems. For example, increased levels of carbon dioxide in the atmosphere breed higher levels of plant growth, and these plants help to regulate the amount of carbon dioxide present in the atmosphere. Feedback mechanisms such as this were known before the formulation of the Gaia hypothesis. However, adherence to this idea requires one to study the planet as a whole, rather than focusing on only one of its many aspects in isolation. The fact that earth's atmosphere is quite different from those of the other planets led to the formulation of this idea.

Geologic Time

Geologic time may be measured absolutely using chronometric time, or relatively using chronostratic time. Measurements of chronometric time are achieved through **radiometric dating** and are expressed numerically in number of years. **Chronostratic time**, which places events in sequences, can be estimated through the study of rock bodies. According to the law of original horizontality, the original orientation of sedimentary beds is nearly always horizontal. Therefore, if one observes deformed or slanted strata, the event which disoriented the strata must have occurred after the strata were deposited. Also, a rock body that cuts across another must be newer than the rock body it intersects. Similarly, for a layer of rock to experience erosion and weathering, it must already exist on the surface. These destructive processes can lead to interruptions in the geologic record. Sometimes, sediments are deposited atop a weathered and eroded surface. Such an occurrence is called an unconformity. The most common method used to establish chronostratic time is through stratigraphy, as the name suggests.

Relative geologic time is divided into different units, including two recognized eons: the **Precambrian**, of which little is known due to limited fossil evidence that only reveals ultra-primitive life forms; and the **Phanerozoic**, for which fossil evidence is more abundant and reveals more evolved life forms. **Eons** are the largest units of geologic time.

Scientists also recognize three eras: the Paleozoic, the Mesozoic, and the Cenozoic. Eras contain periods, and periods contain epochs. These units are delineated largely by the conceptions used to divide historical time. They are arranged in a sequence through chronostratigraphy and classified largely on the basis of the fossils found in their associated strata.

Paleontology

Paleontology is the study of ancient plant and animal life. The bulk of information on this subject is provided by the fossil record, which consists of fossilized plants, animals, tracks, and chemical residues preserved in rock strata. There are three general subdivisions within the field of paleontology. The first, **paleozoology**, is the study of ancient animal life, including vertebrate and invertebrate specializations, as well as paleoanthropology, the study of fossil hominids. The second is **paleobotany**, the study of ancient plant life. The third, **micropaleontology**, is the study of microfossils. This field of scientific inquiry is useful in identifying the evolutionary processes that gave rise to present-day life forms. Paleontology also contributes to an understanding of the ways that environmental and geological factors affected evolution.

Evolution

Evolution is the process whereby organisms pass certain acquired traits to successive generations, affecting the attributes of later organisms and even leading to the creation of new species. Charles Darwin is the name often associated with the formulation of natural selection, a vital component of evolution as it is known today. **Natural selection** states that members of a species are not identical—due to their respective genetic make-ups, each individual will possess traits which make it stronger or weaker and more or less able to adapt. The other tenet of natural selection is that members of a species will always have to compete for scarce resources to survive. Therefore, organisms with traits which will help them survive are more likely to do so and produce offspring, passing along the "desirable" traits. Darwin suggested that this process, by creating groups of a species with increasingly different characteristics, would eventually lead to the formation of **a new species**.

Significant Events Leading to Evolution of Man

The **origination of life** is the most fundamental development in the history of life on Earth. Prokaryotic microfossils, the earliest fossils identified by paleontologists, are dated to near 3.5 billion years ago. However, the presence of large amounts of certain carbon and oxygen isotopes in sedimentary rocks dated at about 3.8 billion years ago may indicate the presence of organic material. The next significant event suggested by a drastic change in the fossil record is the huge diversification of species which occurred approximately 543 million years ago, near the end of the Precambrian eon and the beginning of the Phanerozoic. This theoretical evolutionary stage included higher-level tissue organization in multicellular organisms, the development of predator-prey relationships, and, most importantly, the development of skeletons. The final critical step toward the evolution of man is the emergence of life on land about 418 million years ago. This necessitated the evolution of structures which could breathe air, obtain and retain water on land, and support its own weight out of water.

Fossil Record

Fossils

Fossils are the preserved remains or traces of animals, plants, and other organisms from the remote past. These remains may consist of mineralized parts, or impressions left in sediment, or even of entire carcasses. All known fossils make up the fossil record. Scientists use this record to learn about life on ancient Earth and the evolutionary processes which led to life on Earth as it is today. To glean any valuable information from a fossil, scientists must make an attempt to understand the preservation history of a specimen; they must examine the process by which the specimen became a fossil and the natural forces to which it was subjected after fossilization. While certain elements of an organism such as teeth and bone are fairly durable, soft tissues like eyes and skin decay quickly after death. Therefore, to be preserved, an organism must be buried in sediment soon after its death. Since the majority of sediments are deposited on the sea floor, most fossils are preserved marine animals.

Types

On rare occasions, full carcasses of animals are frozen in permafrost terrain, such as the wooly mammoths discovered in Siberia. This type of fossil provides scientists with a wealth of information about an organism because details such as the organism's soft tissue, blood cells, and hints of digested food remain intact. Similarly, small insects may become trapped in tree resin which later hardens into amber, preserving the entire insect. Small bodies may also be preserved when sedimentary concretions form around them. Durable parts of organisms, such as bones, teeth, and shells, may be fossilized when they are buried by sediment soon after the death of the organism. These fragments experience diagenesis with the sediment around them and are preserved. **Permineralization** is the process whereby minerals (such as calcium phosphate or silica) intrude the pore space of an organism's skeleton. Mold fossils or typolites are created when the dissolution of carcasses leave an impression in rock. Trace fossils are impressions left in rock by the movement of an organism, such as footprints or subsurface dwellings.

Precambrian Eon

There is comparatively little evidence to support much elaboration about the environment during the Precambrian time. However, enough is known to divide the eon into three eras. During the earliest **Hadean** era, which occurred 4.5–3.8 billion years ago, the solar system was formed. The earliest microfossils date to the **Archaean** era about 3.8–2.5 billion years ago and reveal the existence of cyanobacteria, photosynthetic organisms which produced oxygen as a byproduct. During the **Proterozoic** era of 2.5 billion to 543 million years ago, the fossil record indicates an abundance of bacteria as well as the appearance of eukaryotic cells. Fossil soils known as paleosols also reveal high levels of metal oxides, indicating that the oxygen levels in the atmosphere were extremely high, probably due to the presence of many cyanobacteria. Fossil dating also proves the emergence of the first animals, called Vendian animals (also known as Ediacaran biota), from late in this era, roughly 650–543 million years ago.

Paleozoic Era

The **Paleozoic Era**, which occurred 543–248 million years ago, dominates nearly half of the Phanerozoic eon. The era began with a huge increase in the diversity of multicellular organisms. Animals, plants, fungi, and insects all experienced rapid evolution during this time. During the early part of this era, marine animals such as trilobites and brachiopods were abundant. Life on land began to proliferate approximately 440–425 million years ago, beginning with plants and expanding to include invertebrates and vertebrates. The presence of limestone outcrops provides evidence of changing sea levels during this era; massive coal deposits also formed during this time. Also, the supercontinent Pangaea came together towards the end of the Paleozoic Era. Earth's climate became warmer and drier during this time, which coincided with a decrease in glacial activity. This era concluded with the most massive extinction event in history. The event's cause is uncertain, but it is known to have eliminated 90% of the planet's living marine species.

Mesozoic Era

The **Mesozoic Era**, which occurred 248–65 million years ago, was the age of the dinosaurs. They evolved at the beginning of the era and all but birds were extinct by its end. The famous K-T extinction event eliminated 85% of all species. This period of time exhibited flora and fauna which were very different from those of the Paleozoic Era. Pangaea began to break apart during the Triassic period, and mammals evolved from a line of "mammal-like reptiles." The Jurassic period saw the emergence of the first birds, as well as a proliferation of crocodiles, sharks, and rays. The first flowering plants evolved during the Cretaceous period. By the time this period began, Pangea had broken into several smaller continents. At the end of this period around 65 million years ago, a massive asteroid hit what is now Mexico's Yucatan Peninsula. Whether the asteroid caused the K-T extinction event, however, is debatable.

Cenozoic Era

The **Cenozoic Era**, which began 65 million years ago and reaches to the present, is subdivided into six epochs delineated by the percentage of fossilized species living at the time of classification in several strata of rocks. Though this naming process occurred in a single area, it has been correlated worldwide. Therefore, unlike the relatively arbitrary subdivisions of other eras, the subdivisions of this era are based on practical experience. The oldest known fossils of modern species date to this period; these species evolved into the forms which are recognized today. The exposure of the Panamanian land bridge spread species across the continents. Homo sapiens evolved and became dominant during this modern period, which also saw the most recent ice age. Fossils from the Cenozoic Era are abundant and of high-quality. As a result, more is known about the flora, fauna, and environmental conditions during this era than any other. Some people also recognize a seventh epoch, the Holocene, which covers the last 11,000 years.

Theories of Earth's Formation

Origination of Earth

Many different theories have been advanced regarding the birth of the planet. The currently most accepted theory, the **nebular hypothesis**, involves the formation of a cloud of dust and gas around the sun, probably due to one or more supernovae. The sun formed from such a cloud of gas and dust, collapsing in on itself through gravitational compaction. Once formed, nuclear fusion of hydrogen began in its core, producing heat and light. Next, other particles derived from the huge supernova began to coalesce, also due to gravitational forces. These accretions of material are called planetesimals. These bodies continued to compact, forming the planets of the solar system. The extreme heat which must have been present during these events indicates that Earth, like the other planets, must have been completely molten at its birth. When it finally began to cool, its constituent elements solidified into rocks.

Living Entities and Nonliving Matter

The elemental components most commonly found in living organisms (hydrogen, oxygen, carbon, nitrogen, sulfur, and phosphorus) are **common** throughout the universe. However, the chemistry of carbon displayed in living beings is **unique**. Also, the **organic compounds** (proteins, certain sugars, and nucleic acids necessary in protein synthesis and the storage and transmission of genetic information) found in live organisms are not found in inorganic matter. Presently on earth, there are no observable instances of the spontaneous generation of these compounds in nonliving matter. Another important factor which distinguishes live organisms from those which are not alive is the ability of life to reproduce itself. Also, organic beings possess the unique ability to react to external stimuli.

Biogenesis and Abiogenesis

Biogenesis is the process of life emerging from life. Modern science has never observed any instance in which life can arise from nonliving materials; rather, all modern organisms are produced by other living organisms like themselves. In a narrower sense, biogenesis is the basis of creation biology, which holds that since life must be created from life, a god figure must have created the earliest life forms on Earth.

Abiogenesis is an oppositional process: the creation of life from nonliving matter. The ancient, now discredited version of abiogenesis involved the generation of complex, fully-formed organisms from nonliving matter (e.g., the creation of mice from putrefying wood). The modern definition of the term is generally applied to the evolution of modern life from simple organisms created by the interactions of nonliving chemicals in the early atmosphere and hydrosphere, although the processes by which this occurred are largely unknown.

Life's Last Common Ancestor

Louis Pasteur disproved the hypothesis of the spontaneous generation of life through his work with bacteria; he proved that even microorganisms are bred from "parents" with similar attributes.

The work of Charles Darwin demonstrated that complex organisms evolve from simpler ones by the process of natural selection. Taken together, these scientific discoveries suggest that all of the life currently on Earth could have evolved from a single, simple, original organism: "life's last common ancestor." This organism must have possessed the capabilities to store information regarding function and reproduction in nucleic acids and to replicate that information with random variations which would have led to the development of different traits. This ancestor must have been constituted of carbon-rich elements and must have contained proteins formed of one set of 20 amino acids, including enzymes to spawn vital processes.

Biochemical Record and Imperfect Design

Biochemical record refers to the genetic coding of organisms. This information may be examined in one organism and compared to that of another. The theory of evolution suggests that modern-day organisms should share certain aspects of their genetic codes due to the fact that certain organisms, like humans and apes, share **common ancestors**. Therefore, investigation of this biochemical record reveals that the closer organisms are on the evolutionary tree, the more similar their DNA will be. Organisms do not need to be perfect to survive, only better at survival than their competitors. Thus, the attributes of each member of an evolved species builds on those of the organisms before it. This means that certain traits which may have been optimal in the past get cemented into the genetic make-up of a species, even if "better" ones are currently available. This is called imperfect design, a phenomenon that lends support to the theory of evolution while contradicting the deterministic the belief that each organism exists for a specific purpose.

Organism Species Classification

The study of the evolutionary relationships between organism species is called **phylogenetics**. In this field of study, scientists make use of cladistic taxonomy to classify species. **Cladistic taxonomy** places species in groups based on "shared derived properties" called synapomorphies, which are physical similarities assumed to be shared by different species because they evolved from a common ancestor. In this method, organism species are placed in successively smaller cladistic groups, originally delineated by Carolus Linnaeus. The divisions of this five-kingdom system are, from broadest to narrowest: Kingdom, Phylum, Class, Order, Family, Genus, and Species. Phylogenetic classification can be expressed graphically through a phylogenetic, or evolutionary, tree. Some modern scientists adhere to the recently developed three-domain system, which features a top-level grouping of domain consisting of Archaea, Eukaryota, and Eubacteria.

Miller-Urey Experiment

The **Miller-Urey experiment**, performed at the University of Chicago in 1953 by Harold Urey and Stanley Miller, demonstrated partial success in producing amino acids through prebiotic chemistry, showing how an environment could have produced amino acids, the basic molecules of life. Chemicals thought to have been present in the atmosphere of early Earth (methane, hydrogen, water, and ammonia) were introduced into a glass bulb to replicate the atmosphere. Another bulb was filled with water to simulate the ocean; this bulb was heated to replicate the effect of the sun. The two bulbs were connected with tubing, which allowed evaporated material in the "atmosphere" to return to the "ocean." Electrodes in the tubing exposed this primordial soup to "lightning." After a few weeks had passed, the two men analyzed the liquid in the contraption, and discovered that the chemical reactions which had taken place produced several amino acids, indicating some feasibility of the creation of molecules basic to life by prebiotic chemistry. These molecules are theorized to have accumulated and led to the chemical evolution of increasingly complex life forms. Some doubt is applied to the success of these experiments, however, as repeated experiments have largely been unsuccessful.

ALTERNATE THEORIES FOR FORMATION OF MOLECULES OF LIFE

Some scientists have theorized that the basic molecules of life may have arrived on Earth from an **extraterrestrial** source. A **carbonaceous meteorite**, which hit Australia several years after the Miller-Urey experiment, was found to contain the same amino acids produced by the experiment in roughly the same proportions. The purine bases of nucleic acids (adenine and guanine) have been shown to exist in meteorites as well. Also, complex molecules vital to life on Earth have been detected in a nebula. Clay theory suggests that organic molecules arose progressively from the "replication platform" of silicate crystals in solution.

RNA WORLD HYPOTHESIS

The **RNA world hypothesis** attempts to explain the development of protocells from simple organic molecules. This hypothesis is a "gene first" hypothesis, meaning that it represents the view that nucleic acids formed before the biochemical reactions and pathways required for self-replication existed. The RNA world hypothesis suggests that nucleotides, the units from which RNA strands are formed, floated in the primordial soup along with other chemicals. Eventually, some of these nucleotides were synthesized into chains, which are said to be the first forms of life. These primitive life forms would have then engaged in competition for free nucleotides; this competition operated as a process of natural selection. The RNA chains then developed the ability to link amino acids into proteins and continued to evolve into the first prokaryotic cells. The discovery that RNA could behave as an enzyme (a ribozyme) lent credence to the idea that RNA could catalyze protein synthesis. Some discredit this hypothesis because there is little evidence that nucleotides could have been formed in the primordial soup.

IRON-SULFUR WORLD THEORY

The **iron-sulfur world theory** is a "metabolism first" model of the evolution of organic molecules into primitive cells. It suggests that the formation of primitive metabolism (a cycle of energy-producing chemical reactions) created an environment in which RNA could later form. The energy produced by these reactions could in turn fuel the development of increasingly complex cells. This hypothesis states that organic molecules were created on the surfaces of iron-bearing minerals near hydrothermal vents on the ocean floor, rather than in the "soup" of the ocean itself. Redox reactions of metal sulfides may have provided the energy necessary for development of self-replicating organisms. This model is attractive because it provides for a succession of developmental steps within a single structure. Critics, however, have pointed out that the spontaneous development of a closed metabolic cycle such as that included in the iron-sulfur theory is unlikely.

EARTH'S ATMOSPHERE

Earth's atmosphere is a mixture of molecules and particles that envelop the planet. Today, this gaseous conglomeration is approximately 78% **nitrogen** and 21% **oxygen**, with trace gases such as the greenhouse gas **carbon dioxide** and the noble gas **argon** making up the remaining 1%. The majority of these elements are concentrated in the lowest ten kilometers of the atmosphere. The atmosphere's lower boundary is the Earth's surface, while its hazy upper boundary is 10,000 kilometers above that. The atmosphere shields the planet's surface from harmful cosmic rays and absorbs much of the ultraviolet radiation beamed towards the planet from the sun. The motion of air within the atmosphere helps to regulate the Earth's temperature through convection and by allowing certain amounts of thermal energy in from, and out to, space.

Formation

According to the best available scientific knowledge, the Earth's atmosphere has evolved through two stages and is currently in its third. This third stage is the only one capable of sustaining life in organisms that need oxygen. The **first atmosphere** is believed to have been composed of helium, hydrogen, methane, and ammonia; these gases probably collected around the planetesimal of the newly-formed Earth over 4 billion years ago. However, the planet was still very hot. This heat, along with the currents of stellar winds, dissipated this primordial atmosphere.

The **second atmosphere** was created about 3.5 billion years ago, just after the crust had solidified. Volcanic activity on the new planet released water vapor, carbon dioxide, sulfur oxide, and nitrogen from the mantle into the atmosphere in a process called outgassing. This atmosphere was called reducing or reductive because it contained little or no oxygen and high amounts of hydrogen. During this time, the greenhouse effect probably prevented the Earth from freezing. Earth's second atmosphere was composed largely of carbon dioxide and water vapor with some nitrogen and minute levels of oxygen. About 3.3 billion years ago, photosynthesizing cyanobacteria evolved, and their respiration processes released large levels of oxygen into the atmosphere. Also, as the Earth cooled, the atmosphere cooled, causing water molecules to condense and produce rain clouds. Over the next few billion years, massive amounts of water then filled the crevices left on Earth's crust after it cooled and condensed, forming oceans and other water bodies. The gases which made up the second atmosphere then began to dissolve in the oceans. Some of these gases, such as carbon dioxide and sulfur oxide, produce acids when they are dissolved in water; this process also contributed to the rising levels of oxygen in the atmosphere. During this period, oxygen levels were actually too high to support life on Earth. It was only after organisms evolved oxidative respiration that the levels of oxygen in the air became balanced. The **third atmosphere**, maintained through gravity, was the result.

Lower Levels

Variations in temperature and air pressure throughout the atmosphere delineate the lower level of the atmosphere into several layers. The lowest three layers are the troposphere, the stratosphere, and the mesosphere. The **troposphere** covers the area from surface level to about 16 kilometers and is the densest level of the atmosphere, containing three-quarters of the body's total mass. Generally, temperatures in this region decrease with increased elevation. Most of the weather experienced on Earth occurs in the troposphere, when the convection of air due to the temperature variations and the presence of moisture cause clouds to form. The **tropopause**, a region of stable temperatures, is the boundary between the troposphere and the stratosphere. The **stratosphere** is located at roughly 16–50 kilometers above the surface. In this region, temperatures increase with altitude due to the ozone layer at this level absorbing ultraviolet radiation from the sun. Unlike the troposphere, this layer is calm and virtually weather-free, which makes it ideal for airplane flight. The stratosphere is separated from the mesosphere by the **stratopause**.

Upper Levels

The **mesosphere** is the layer of the atmosphere approximately 50–80 kilometers above the Earth's surface. Temperatures in the mesosphere drop with increases in altitude; this layer can be as cold as –100 degrees Celsius, making it the coldest layer in the atmosphere. This causes the formation of clouds of ice called noctilucent clouds. The mesosphere is the layer in which most of the meteors that enter the atmosphere burn up and break apart. The **mesopause** separates this layer from the **thermosphere**, the uppermost layer of Earth's atmosphere, about 80–600 kilometers above the surface. Its name, which literally means "sphere of heat," testifies to the fact that it is the warmest layer of the atmosphere; temperatures at this level may reach up to 2,000 °C. This is because the thermosphere absorbs high levels of energy from the sun. Interestingly, this level would not feel very hot, even though the temperature is very high, because the air is so thin.

The thermosphere also contains the **ionosphere**, which is located approximately 80–300 kilometers above the surface of Earth. It is made up of ionized nitrogen and oxygen atoms as well as free electrons. These composite materials justify its classification as a sub-layer. The ionization process occurs in the ionosphere due to the high levels of ultraviolet radiation and x-rays that enter the region. Due to its composition, this level produces the phenomena of aurorae and is a good conductor of electromagnetic radio waves.

Separated from the thermosphere by the **thermopause**, the **exosphere** is the outermost division of Earth's atmosphere at about 600–10,000 kilometers above the surface. The upper boundary of this layer is uncertain and variable because it merges with space. The low-density exosphere is composed mostly of hydrogen and helium.

Earth's Hydrosphere

The collective mass of water found on and beneath the Earth's surface known as the **hydrosphere** was formed from the same processes which formed the Earth's atmosphere. Basically, outgassing from the Earth's mantle through volcanic eruptions thrust steam into the atmosphere. Water molecules then condensed high above the Earth as clouds, which then rained liquid water back to the surface. While the planet was too hot in its earliest stages to sustain liquid water on its surface, the water molecules simply returned to a gaseous form, evaporated back into the atmosphere, and began the cycle anew. Eventually, around 3.3 billion years ago, the planet cooled enough to allow water to remain on the surface in the crustal depressions created during the compaction and cooling processes. Large volumes of rain eventually formed oceans. Later, water weathering and erosion created multitudinous channels, both on the surface and below it, through which the water could flow.

Distribution

Water covers about 70% of the Earth's surface; it exists under the surface in aquifers; on the surface in oceans, seas, rivers, lakes, and within organisms; and above the surface as clouds, water vapor, and precipitation. Large water bodies such as oceans hold about 97.5% of the Earth's water supply. Approximately 2.4% of that supply is contained within the lithosphere, and less than 0.001% of the Earth's water is in the atmosphere at any given time. The total amount of water in the Earth system remains constant, despite the fact that water levels in any particular location fluctuate constantly. Conservation of this water supply is performed through the functions of the water, or hydrologic, cycle.

Seafloor Spreading

Radiometric dating of fossils found in basins on the ocean floor have revealed that the ocean floor crust can be several million years younger than the **continental crust**. This can be explained by the phenomenon of seafloor spreading. As undersea subduction zones are created at convergent boundaries, aspects of the oceanic lithosphere are destroyed when they are forced down into the mantle. The destruction of this crust requires the formation of new crustal material elsewhere, since the diameter of the Earth is not changing. At divergent boundaries, seafloor spreading occurs. When portions of the crust move apart, mantle materials flood up and harden to form new crust. Therefore, the apparent discrepancies in between the age of the ocean floor as revealed by radiometric dating and the age of the oceans as suggested by paleoclimatology can be explained by the fact that new crust is continually being created on the ocean floor at zones of seafloor spreading.

Chapter Quiz

Ready to see how well you retained what you just read? Scan the QR code to go directly to the chapter quiz interface for this study guide. If you're using a computer, simply visit the online resources page at **mometrix.com/resources719/osatearsci108** and click the Chapter Quizzes link.

Atmospheric and Hydrological Systems

Properties of Water and Its Effect on Earth Systems

Water Molecule

The **water molecule** consists of two hydrogen atoms and one oxygen atom (H_2O). The atoms in this molecule are joined through covalent bonding. The two hydrogen-oxygen bonds are at a 105-degree angle from each other, rather than on opposite sides of the oxygen atom. The water molecule has a positive charge on the hydrogen side and a negative charge on the oxygen side. The electrons in the hydrogen atoms are so strongly attracted to the oxygen atom that they are actually closer to the oxygen atom's nucleus than to the nuclei of the hydrogen atoms. This asymmetrical arrangement of atoms in the water molecule characterizes it as a **polar molecule**. This polar quality is the force that causes water molecules to bond so readily with other water molecules; water is a good solvent because of its polar structure.

Specific Heat in Water

The **heat capacity** of a substance is defined as the amount of heat required to raise the temperature of a given amount of the substance one degree; it thus describes the ability of a substance to store heat. The specific heat of a substance is its heat capacity per unit of mass. Specific heat is often expressed as calorie per gram degree Celsius. The specific heat of water is $1\ \text{cal/(g °C)}$. This specific heat is much higher than that of most other substances. Water exhibits this unique property due to its atomic structure. Hydrogen bonding, like that in a water molecule, releases heat, and heat absorption is required to break hydrogen bonds. Thus, one additional calorie of heat causes a small change in the temperature of water because the heat energy is put toward dissolving the hydrogen bonds. Conversely, a slight decrease in the temperature of water is accompanied by the formation of several hydrogen bonds and the release of relatively large amounts of heat energy.

High Specific Heat

The high **specific heat** of the water molecule means that its temperature change when it absorbs or loses an amount of heat will be minimal, especially as compared to other substances. For instance, an ocean or other large body of water can store large amounts of heat from the Sun without becoming terribly hot. Also, the cooling of water bodies after the Sun goes down is accompanied by a release of heat that warms the ambient air. The role that water plays in temperature regulation (both in water and on land) is vital to the maintenance of life on Earth.

Density Changes in Water

Water is one of few substances that is **denser in its liquid form** than it is in its solid form. Fresh (uncontaminated) water is densest at four degrees Celsius. At temperatures above this point, water expands as it warms and contracts as it cools, like other liquid substances. At temperatures below four degrees Celsius, however, water expands as it cools. As it cools from this temperature, water molecules slow to the point at which hydrogen bonds can form. At zero degrees Celsius, the molecules are oriented into a crystalline structure, in which hydrogen bonding keeps them equally spaced at distances far enough apart to make ice less dense than water. Again, this unusual property of water is vital to life on Earth. If, like most substances, the solid form of water was denser than the liquid form, entire oceans would freeze when ice sank; only the top few feet of water would thaw during hot weather. This is not the case, however; ice floats, insulating the water below and thus preventing it from freezing.

Cohesion-Tension Theory

The **cohesion-tension theory** was advanced to explain the method of transport of water from the roots of a plant, where it receives its water supply, to its uppermost leaves, even in the tallest trees. Hydrogen bonds in water molecules form strong bonds with the oxygen atoms in all nearby water molecules. Water moves from plant cells into leaf pores one molecule at a time. As one molecule exits a cell, another water molecule from lower in the plant enters the same cell. This movement, caused by the cohesive properties of the water molecule, creates a tension among all of the (connected) water molecules in the plant and even those in the soil about to enter the plant's roots. This tension provides the force needed to move water upward through a plant from its roots.

Surface Tension of Water

Cohesive forces are attractive forces that act between the molecules of a liquid. In most areas of a liquid, the molecules experience these forces equally from all directions. On the surface of a liquid, however, the molecules are drawn inward toward the center of the liquid's mass but experience no equal force from the outside. This causes the surface to contract and behave like a stretched elastic membrane. This property of a liquid is referred to as its surface tension. Water has a relatively high surface tension; this means that it forms stable, spherical droplets when placed on a nonporous surface. The high surface tension of water is what allows denser objects to float and insects (such as the water strider) to walk atop water bodies.

Role of Water in Maintenance of Life

Living entities need water to live. This is because of the important role of water, often called the **universal solvent**, in facilitating vital chemical reactions within organisms. Living things are made up of molecules suspended in aqueous solutions (substances dissolved in water), and cells are 70–90% water. Thus, the ability of organic molecules to interact with water affects their functions. The reactions between compounds enabled by the presence of water molecules fuel metabolic and digestive processes, as well as processes of cell replication. In addition, organic compounds within a body can be transported in water due to its high surface tension.

Water Cycle and Energy Transfers Involved

Hydrologic Cycle

The **hydrologic (water) cycle** refers to the circulation of water in the Earth's hydrosphere (below the surface, on the surface, and above the surface of the Earth). This continuous process involves five physical actions. Evaporation entails the change of water molecules from a liquid to gaseous state. Liquid water on the Earth's surface (often contained in a large body of water) becomes water vapor and enters the atmosphere when its component molecules gain enough kinetic (heat) energy to escape the liquid form. As the vapor rises, it cools and therefore loses its ability to maintain the gaseous form. It begins to the process of condensation (the return to a liquid or solid state) and forms clouds. When the clouds become sufficiently dense, the water falls back to Earth as precipitation. Water is then either trapped in vegetation (interception) or absorbed into the surface (infiltration). Runoff, caused by gravity, physically moves water downward into oceans or other water bodies.

Evaporation

Evaporation is the change of state in a substance from a liquid to a gaseous form at a temperature below its boiling point (the temperature at which all of the molecules in a liquid are changed to gas through vaporization). Some of the molecules at the surface of a liquid always maintain enough heat energy to escape the cohesive forces exerted on them by neighboring molecules. At higher temperatures, the molecules in a substance move more rapidly, increasing their number with enough energy to break out of the liquid form. The rate of evaporation is higher when more of the surface area of a liquid is exposed (as in a large water body, such as an ocean). The amount of moisture already in the air also affects the rate of evaporation—if there is a significant amount of water vapor in the air around a liquid, some evaporated molecules will return to the liquid. The speed of the evaporation process is also decreased by increased atmospheric pressure.

CONDENSATION

Condensation is the phase change in a substance from a gaseous to liquid form; it is the opposite of evaporation or vaporization. When temperatures decrease in a gas, such as water vapor, the material's component molecules move more slowly. The decreased motion of the molecules enables intermolecular cohesive forces to pull the molecules closer together and, in water, establish hydrogen bonds. Condensation can also be caused by an increase in the pressure exerted on a gas, which results in a decrease in the substance's volume (it reduces the distance between particles). In the hydrologic cycle, this process is initiated when warm air containing water vapor rises and then cools. This occurs due to convection in the air, meteorological fronts, or lifting over high land formations.

PRECIPITATION

Precipitation is water that falls back to Earth's surface from the atmosphere. This water may be in the form of rain, which is water in the liquid form. Raindrops are formed in clouds due to the process of condensation. When the drops become too heavy to remain in the cloud (due to a decrease in their kinetic energy), gravity causes them to fall down toward Earth's surface. Extremely small raindrops are called drizzle. If the temperature of a layer of air through which rain passes on its way down is below the freezing point, the rain may take the form of sleet (partially frozen water). Precipitation may also fall in the form of snow, or water molecules sublimated into ice crystals. When clumps of snowflakes melt and refreeze, hail is formed. Hail may also be formed when liquid water accumulates on the surface of a snowflake and subsequently freezes.

TRANSPORTATION OF WATER IN THE WATER CYCLE

In the **hydrologic cycle**, the principal movement of water in the atmosphere is its transport from the area above an ocean to an area over land. If this transport did not occur, the hydrologic cycle would be less a cycle than the vertical motion of water from the oceans to the atmosphere and back again. Some evaporated water is transported in the form of clouds consisting of condensed water droplets and small ice crystals. The clouds are moved by the jet stream (strong winds in the upper levels of the atmosphere that are related to surface temperatures) or by surface winds (land or sea breezes). Most of the water that moves through the atmosphere is water vapor (water in the gaseous form).

Review Video: Hydrologic Cycle
Visit mometrix.com/academy and enter code: 426578

Structure of the Atmosphere

LAYERS OF THE ATMOSPHERE

The **atmosphere** consists of 78% nitrogen, 21% oxygen, and 1% argon. It also includes traces of water vapor, carbon dioxide and other gases, dust particles, and chemicals from Earth. The atmosphere becomes thinner the farther it is from the Earth's surface. It becomes difficult to breathe at about 3 km above sea level. The atmosphere gradually fades into space.

The main layers of the Earth's atmosphere (from lowest to highest) are:

- **Troposphere** (lowest layer): where life exists and most weather occurs; elevation 0–15 km
- **Stratosphere**: has the ozone layer, which absorbs UV radiation; elevation 15–50 km
- **Mesosphere**: coldest layer; where meteors will burn up; elevation 50–80 km
- **Thermosphere**: where the international space station and most satellites orbit; hottest layer; elevation 80–600 km
- **Exosphere** (outermost layer): consists mainly of hydrogen and helium; extends to ~10,000 km

Review Video: Earth's Atmosphere
Visit mometrix.com/academy and enter code: 417614

Tropospheric Circulation

Most weather takes place in the **troposphere**. Air circulates in the atmosphere by convection and in various types of "cells." Air near the equator is warmed by the Sun and rises. Cool air rushes under it, and the higher, warmer air flows toward Earth's poles. At the poles, it cools and descends to the surface. It is now under the hot air, and flows back to the equator. Air currents coupled with ocean currents move heat around the planet, creating winds, weather, and climate. Winds can change direction with the seasons. For example, in Southeast Asia and India, summer monsoons are caused by air being heated by the Sun. This air rises, draws moisture from the ocean, and causes daily rains. In winter, the air cools, sinks, pushes the moist air away, and creates dry weather.

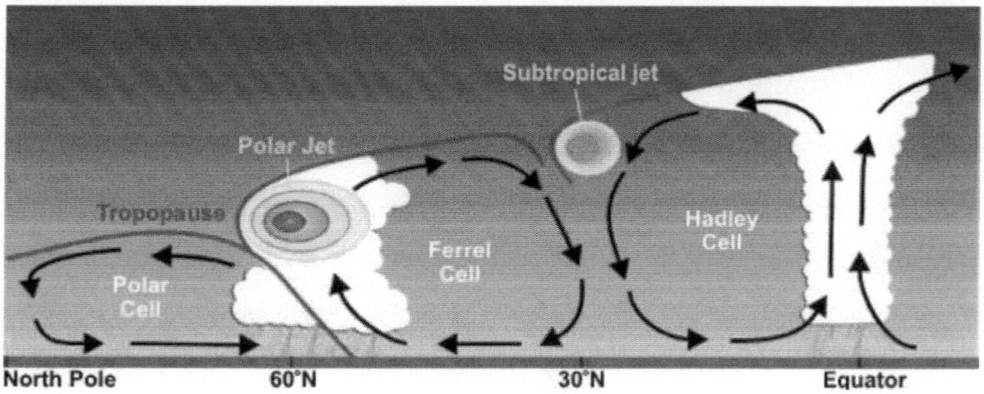

Weather Systems

Weather

Weather is the result of transfers of kinetic (heat) energy due to differences in temperature between objects as well as transfers of moisture in Earth's atmosphere. **Meteorology**, the study of weather, covers the same natural events as climatology, but observes them on a shorter time scale (usually no more than a few days). Rain, fog, snow, and wind are all examples of weather phenomena. The processes that occur at different stages in the hydrologic cycle form the basis of meteorological events. Most of the activity that produces the weather we experience on Earth takes place in the **troposphere**, the lowest level of the atmosphere. Atmospheric pressure, temperature, humidity, elevation, wind speed, and cloud cover are all factors in the study of weather.

Ozone Layer

The **Earth's ozone layer** is the region of the stratosphere with a high concentration of ozone (a form of oxygen) particles. These molecules are formed through the process of **photolysis**, which occurs when ultraviolet light from the sun collides with oxygen molecules (O_2) in the atmosphere. The ultraviolet radiation splits the oxygen atoms apart; when a free oxygen atom strikes an oxygen molecule, it combines with the molecule to create an **ozone particle** (O_3). Ozone molecules may be broken down by interaction with nitrogen-, chlorine-, and hydrogen-containing compounds, or by thermal energy from the sun. Under normal conditions, these creative and destructive processes balance the levels of ozone in the stratosphere. The concentration of ozone molecules in the atmosphere absorbs ultraviolet radiation, thus preventing this harmful energy from reaching the Earth's surface. Ozone particles form in the region of the atmosphere over the equator, which receives the most direct sunlight. Atmospheric winds then disperse the particles throughout the rest of the stratosphere.

Air Mass

An **air mass** is a body of air that exhibits consistent temperatures and levels of moisture throughout. These (usually large) pockets of air tend to come together under relatively still conditions, where air can remain in one place long enough to adopt the temperature and moisture characteristics of the land below it; this often occurs above wide areas of flat land. The region in which an air mass originates and the course of its motion are used to name it. For example, a maritime tropical air mass (denoted mT) is formed over the Gulf of Mexico (a tropical climate) and moves across the Atlantic Ocean (a maritime area). The conditions of an air mass will remain constant as long as the body is still, but when it moves across surfaces with different conditions, it may adopt those qualities. For example, polar air that moves over tropical land areas will be heated by the conditions below. Generally, maritime air masses contain high levels of moisture, and continental air masses are drier.

Meteorological Depression

A **meteorological depression** refers to a **low-pressure zone** (created by rising air) situated between 30- and 60-degrees latitude. These zones vary from approximately 321–3,218 kilometers in diameter. The rising air associated with a depression usually condenses at higher levels in the atmosphere and causes precipitation. Depressions are formed when warm air masses and cold air masses converge. At first, a single front (boundary between converging masses of air with different temperatures) separates the air masses.

A distortion similar to the crest of a water wave develops, creating a small center of low pressure. Then, differentiated warm and cold fronts develop from that center. A mass of warm air forms and rises over the body of cold air. The cold front and the cold air eventually catch up with the warm air, creating an occluded front and causing pressure to rise, effectually slowing the depression's movement. Depressions usually have life spans of four to seven days.

Prevailing Winds and Wind Belts

Wind (the horizontal movement of air with respect to Earth's surface) forms due to pressure gradients (differences) in the atmosphere. Air tends to move from areas of **high pressure** (such as the poles) to areas of **low pressure** (such as the tropics). Prevailing winds, or trade winds, are the winds (named in meteorology for the direction they come from) that blow most frequently in a particular region. For instance, the prevailing winds most common in the region from 90 to 60 degrees north latitude blow from the northeast, and are generally called the Polar Easterlies. Wind belts are created in areas where prevailing winds converge with other prevailing winds or air masses. The Inter-Tropical Convergence Zone (ITCZ), where air coming from tropical areas north and south of the equator come together, is an example of a wind belt.

Review Video: Source of Wind
Visit mometrix.com/academy and enter code: 451712

Coriolis Force

The **Coriolis force**, which gives rise to the **Coriolis effect**, is not really a force at all. Rather, it appears to be there to us because the Earth is a rotating frame of reference and we are inside it. In the atmosphere, air tends to move from areas of high pressure to areas of lower pressure. This air would move in a straight line but for the Coriolis force, which appears to deflect the air and cause it to **swirl**. Really, however, the Earth moves underneath the wind, which creates the impression of swirling air to someone standing on the Earth's surface. The Coriolis force causes winds to swing to the right as they approach the Northern Hemisphere and to the left as they approach the Southern Hemisphere.

Air Stability in the Atmosphere

Air stability is the tendency for air to rise or fall through the atmosphere under its own power. Heated air rises because it is less dense than the surrounding air. As a pocket of air rises, however, it will expand and become cooler with changes in atmospheric pressure. If the ambient air into which rising air ascends does not cool as quickly with altitude as the rising air does, that air will rapidly become cooler (and heavier) than the surrounding air and descend back to its original position. The air in this situation is said to be stable. However, if the air into which the warm pocket rises becomes colder with increased altitude, the warm air will continue its ascent. In this case, the air is unstable. Unstable air conditions (such as those that exist in depressions) lead to the formation of large clouds of precipitation.

Clouds

The four main **types of clouds** are cirrus, cumulous, nimbus, and stratus. A **cirrus** cloud forms high in a stable atmosphere, generally at altitudes of 6,000 meters or higher. Temperatures at these altitudes (in the troposphere) decrease with increased altitude; therefore, the precipitation in a cirrus cloud adopts the form of ice crystals. These usually thin traces of clouds may indicate an approaching weather depression. A cumulous cloud is a stereotypical white, fluffy ball. **Cumulous** clouds are indicators of a stable atmosphere, and also of the vertical extent of convection in the atmosphere—condensation and cloud formation begin at the flat base of a cumulous cloud. The more humid the air, the lower a cumulous cloud will form. A **nimbus** cloud is, generally speaking, a rain cloud. Nimbus clouds are usually low, dark, and formless, sometimes spanning the entire visible sky. A **stratus** cloud is basically a cloud of fog which forms at a distance above the Earth's surface. This type of cloud forms when weak convective currents bring moisture just high enough to initiate condensation (if the temperature is below the dew point).

The four cloud subtypes are cumulonimbus, cirrostratus, altocumulus, and stratocumulus. A **cumulonimbus** cloud is produced by rapid convection in unstable air. This type of cloud (which is often dark) is formed as a large, tall "tower." Collections of these towers (squall lines) often signal a coming cold front. Thunderstorms often involve cumulonimbus clouds. A **cirrostratus** cloud is an ultra-thin formation with a white tint and a transparent quality. An **altocumulus** cloud forms at an altitude from 1,980 to 6,100 meters. Clouds of this type, which appear to be flattened spheres, often form in clumps, waves, or lines. A **stratocumulus** cloud forms as a globular mass or flake. Stratocumulus clouds usually come together in layers or clumps.

Review Video: Types of Clouds
Visit mometrix.com/academy and enter code: 803166

Lightning

Lightning is a natural electrostatic discharge that produces light and releases electromagnetic radiation. It is believed that the separation of positive and negative charge carriers within a cloud is achieved by the polarization mechanism. The first step of this mechanism occurs when falling precipitation particles become **electrically polarized** after they move through the Earth's magnetic field. The second step of the polarization mechanism involves **electrostatic induction**, the process whereby electrically charged particles create charges in other particles without direct contact. Ice particles are charged though this method, and then energy-storing electric fields are formed between the charged particles. The positively-charged ice crystals tend to rise to the top of the cloud, effectively polarizing the cloud with positive charges on top and negative charges at the middle and bottom. When charged clouds conglomerate, an electric discharge (a lightning bolt) is produced, either between clouds or between a cloud and the Earth's surface.

Thunderstorms

A **thunderstorm** is a weather phenomenon that includes lightning, thunder, and usually large amounts of precipitation and strong winds. Thunder is the noise made by the rapid expansion and contraction of air due to the heat energy produced by lightning bolts. A thunderstorm develops when heating on the Earth's surface causes large amounts of air to rise into an unstable atmosphere. This results in large clouds of rain and ice crystals. The associated condensation releases high levels of heat, which in turn power the growth cycle of the cloud. The clouds created during thunderstorms are immense, sometimes reaching widths of several miles and extending to heights of 10,000 meters or more. The precipitation in such clouds eventually becomes heavy enough to fall against the updraft of unstable air; the consequent downpour is often short but intense. The differential speeds at which light and sound travel through the atmosphere enable one to estimate the distance between oneself and the storm by observing the interval between a lightning bolt and a thunderclap.

Hurricanes

Hurricanes form when several conditions are met: Oceanic water must be at least 26 degrees Celsius, the general circulation pattern of wind must be disrupted (this disruption usually takes the form of an atmospheric wave in the easterly trade winds), and the Coriolis force must be in effect. During hurricane season (June to November), easterly waves appear in the trade winds every few days. When such a wave occurs over a body of particularly warm, deep water, it is strengthened by the evaporation of warm air from below. Surrounding winds converge at the low-pressure zone created by the wave; air brought by these winds rises because it has nowhere else to go. The large body of warm, moist air rises high into the atmosphere and consequently condenses into huge clouds. As more and more humid air is drawn upward, this air begins to rotate around the area of low pressure. The storm continues to gain strength and may move toward land.

Tornado

A tornado is a violent rotating column of air that is in contact with both the ground and a cloud. The column is visible because the very low pressure causes water vapor to condense out as visible water droplets. Where the tornado touches the ground it usually stirs up a cloud of dirt and debris like the one in this photo. Tornadoes are the most violent storms on Earth, and the strongest spin at 300 miles per hour.

Review Video: Tornadoes
Visit mometrix.com/academy and enter code: 540439

El Nino

El Niño refers to the **unusual warming of surface waters** near the equatorial coast of South America. This phenomenon occurs during the winter approximately every two to seven years, lasting from a few weeks to a few months. El Nino can cause torrential rains, violent winds, drought, and dangerously high temperatures in surrounding areas. El Nino is caused by a reversal of the atmospheric pressures on the eastern and western sides of the Pacific (normally, pressure is high on the eastern side near South America and lower on the western side near the Indonesian coast). This reversal causes a wave of warm water to flow eastward and sea levels to fall on the western side. The changes in air pressure and ocean temperature cause moisture levels in the western Pacific to rise drastically while the region east of the Pacific experiences drought. The air pressure changes also weaken the region's trade winds, which normally serve to distribute heat and moisture.

Monsoons and Savannahs

The term **monsoon** refers to a unique pattern of moving air and currents that occurs when winds reverse direction with a change in season. India and Southeast Asia experience the most intense monsoons. This area lies between tropical and subtropical climate zones. During the winter season, northeasterly winds (which are generally dry) move from high-pressure subtropical areas to lower-pressure tropical areas. During the summer season, the continents of India and Asia heat up, creating a low-pressure zone. This causes winds to reverse and blow southwesterly across the Indian Ocean, accumulating high levels of moisture, thereby creating large amounts of precipitation during this season.

Savannahs also exist between wet equatorial and dry subtropical climate zones. These regions are characterized by vegetation consisting mainly of shrubs and grass. Savannahs experience dry weather throughout most of the year. A single, brief rainy season that occurs when the Sun is directly above the region interrupts prolonged dry spells.

Influence of Mountains on Climate

At the level of local climate, the presence of mountains forces air to rise to travel above them; this contributes to increased formation of clouds and consequently, increases in levels of precipitation. Mountain chains can affect regional and even global climates by deflecting airflow. The Coriolis force causes most of Earth's atmospheric airflow to move east and west. Therefore, the presence of north-south–oriented mountain chains can alter general circulation patterns. For example, the Rocky Mountains force air to move northward; the air cools near the North Pole before blowing back down. This causes winter temperatures in Canada and parts of the United States to be very cold.

Humidity and Cloud Cover

Humidity is a measure of the amount of water vapor in the air. **Specific humidity** is the expression of humidity as a ratio of aqueous vapor to dry air; it is expressed as a ratio of mass of water vapor per unit mass of natural (dry) air. **Absolute humidity** measures the mass of water vapor in a given volume of moist air or gas; it is expressed in grams per cubic foot or per cubic meter. The equilibrium (or saturated) vapor pressure of a gas is the vapor pressure (created by the movement of molecules) of water vapor when air is saturated with water vapor. **Relative humidity**, usually expressed as a percentage, is the ratio of the vapor pressure of water in air (or another gas) to the equilibrium vapor pressure. In other words, it is a ratio of the mass of water per volume of gas and the mass per volume of a saturated gas. Cloud cover refers to the amount of sky blocked by clouds at a given location.

Measuring Weather

Weather can be measured by a variety of methods. The simplest include measurement of rainfall, sunshine, pressure, humidity, temperature, and cloudiness with basic instruments such as thermometers, barometers, and rain gauges. However, the use of radar (which involves analysis of microwaves reflecting off of raindrops) and satellite imagery grants meteorologists a look at the big picture of weather across, for example, an entire continent. This helps them understand and make predictions about current and developing weather systems. Infrared (heat-sensing) imaging allows meteorologists to measure the temperature of clouds above ground. Using weather reports gathered from different weather stations spread over an area, meteorologists create synoptic charts. The locations and weather reports of several stations are plotted on a chart; analysis of the pressures reported from each location, as well as rainfall, cloud cover, and so on, can reveal basic weather patterns.

Global Warming

The **natural greenhouse effect** of the atmosphere is beneficial to life on Earth; it keeps temperatures on the planet 33 degrees higher than they would be without this phenomenon. Originally, this helped sustain life. However, it has been discovered in the last 20 years that this effect is being intensified by the actions of humans. In the twentieth century, certain activities of mankind, including the burning of fossils fuels like coal and oil, have resulted in an **increase in the levels of greenhouse gases** (such as methane and carbon dioxide) being released into the atmosphere. Also, increasing deforestation has affected the number of photosynthesis-practicing plants. The combined effect of these trends is a higher-than-normal concentration of greenhouse gases in the atmosphere. This, in turn, produces the effect of global warming. The average temperature at the Earth's surface has gone up 0.6 degrees Celsius in the last 100 years. Continuation of this trend is likely to have a detrimental effect on many of the planet's ecosystems, including that of human beings.

Climates and Climate Zones

Climate

Climate is usually defined as the "**average weather**" in a particular area on Earth. The timespan over which climate is measured is variable, but it is generally accepted that the climate of an area does not vary during a human life span (though climate is extremely various in geologic time). This may change, however, due to the increasing greenhouse effect. Meteorologists measure climate by averaging certain quantifiable elements such as rainfall or temperature. Climate may be studied on several different scales:

- **Local climate** refers to the climate of small geographic areas (generally up to tens of miles wide). The local climate of an area is affected by things such as its location relative to an ocean and the presence of mountains near the location.
- A **regional climate** is the climate of a larger geographic area, such as a country. A regional climate may also be delineated due to climate features that are distinctive from the surrounding climate.
- **Global climate** refers to the average weather experienced across the Earth.

Climate Zones

Climate zones are areas of regional climate. These zones are created by the general circulation of the air in Earth's atmosphere. Generally, the warmest air moves from the equator (where the greatest amount of solar energy is received) toward the higher latitudes at the poles. The latitudinal temperature gradient produces atmospheric pressure. At the equator, solar energy heats air near the surface, causing it to rise and decreasing air pressure. The risen air is transported by winds to cooler areas at higher latitudes, where the air then descends (because cool air is heavier than warmer air), creating an area of high pressure. The descended air is then moved by surface winds, either back to the equator or up to higher latitudes, where it encounters colder air. The air then rises again in an area of low pressure. The air in polar regions is very cold, which causes it to sink, creating high pressure. Winds are thus generated to move air from warmer regions to colder ones.

Review Video: Rotation of Low Pressure Systems
Visit mometrix.com/academy and enter code: 258356

Milankovitch Cycles

The phenomenon of **Milankovitch cycles** has been advanced as an explanation of the periodic ice ages experienced on Earth. Variations in the Earth's orbit (including precession, the wobble of the rotational axis, and eccentricities, or variations, in the shape of the orbit path) due to the gravitational attraction between our planet and other celestial bodies affect the amount of solar energy received at different locations on Earth's surface. In the long term, these variations lead to climate changes that, in turn, can cause Earth to enter an ice age. For example, if the Northern Hemisphere receives decreasing amounts of direct sunlight, temperatures will drop. This can cause increased levels of snow buildup, which reflects solar energy, increasing the possibility of glaciation. Milankovitch believed that if all of Earth's orbital variations happened to line up and reinforce one another, the climate change could be severe enough to cause an ice age.

TROPICAL, SUBTROPICAL, AND POLAR CLIMATE ZONES

- The **tropical** (low-latitude) climate zone covers the area around the equator. This area receives a large portion of the sun's solar energy, making average temperatures in this zone fairly high. The consistent levels of hot air in the region indicate that air is often moving upward. This convective process, in turn, produces large levels of precipitation in the area, resulting in a humid climate. Seasons in the tropical zone are delineated by the amount of rainfall, instead of by changes in temperatures.
- **Subtropical** (mid-latitude) climate zones are found about thirty degrees north and south of the equator. These zones generally consist of dry descending air, clear skies, and high atmospheric pressure. Desert climates (extreme heat during the day, cold temperatures at night, and lack of precipitation) are common in these zones.
- **Polar (high-latitude) climate zones are found at the north and south poles.** They are characterized by high air pressure (due to descending air), low temperatures (rarely above freezing), and lack of precipitation (because air cannot evaporate from frozen water).

MARITIME, CONTINENTAL, AND TEMPERATE CLIMATES

- **Maritime climates** are greatly affected by airflow from nearby oceans. This influence prevents extreme temperatures in such regions, which normally experience cool summers and mild winters. Also, maritime climates are usually quite humid, with large amounts of precipitation.
- **Continental climates**, unlike maritime climates, experience variations in temperature with changes in seasons (i.e., cold winters and hot summers). This is because rock and soil have lower heat capacities than water, which serves to moderate ambient temperatures. Continental climates are usually relatively dry.
- A **temperate climate** is one with low variation in average temperature. Temperate climates may be maritime or continental.

INTERACTIONS BETWEEN ATMOSPHERE AND HYDROSPHERE

The **hydrosphere** (all the water on Earth), specifically the oceans, stores much higher quantities of heat energy than the atmosphere is able to hold. Energy in the oceans, like energy in the atmosphere, is transferred around the globe, redistributing heat from areas of low latitudes to areas of high latitudes. Water on the surface of the ocean is driven by atmospheric wind patterns. Energy transfers between the oceans and the atmosphere affect temperatures and precipitation in regions across the globe. For example, the Gulf Stream is an ocean current that exerts an important influence on the climates of the United Kingdom and northwest Europe. This surface current originates in the Gulf of Mexico and carries warm water (about 25 degrees Celsius) northeast across the Atlantic at speeds of three miles per hour. When the ocean cools down at night, it releases warm air, regulating the temperatures of the regions mentioned above. Without the activity of the Gulf Stream, those regions would be as cold as Canada (which is at roughly the same latitude).

> **Review Video: Climates**
> Visit mometrix.com/academy and enter code: 991320

BIOME

A **biome** is the broadest general subdivision of terrestrial ecosystems. This term is used to describe a region that exhibits the distinctive plant and animal life best adapted to an area's particular soil type and climate. This concept is associated with the interrelationships between organisms and their environment. Since vegetation is more abundant than any other species in the biosphere, **biomes** are often classified according to **climax vegetation type** (the type of vegetation that exists in mature or old-growth ecosystems). The global distribution of biomes is closely related to climate and soil variations at different latitudes. The subdivision of a biome may be further differentiated into formation classes, based upon the structural and dimensional characteristics of regional vegetation.

Forest Biomes

The **forest biome** is typified by an abundance of soil and moisture as well as warm temperatures for at least a portion of the year. Trees are the dominant vegetation type in this biome.

Savanna Biome

The **savanna biome** exists between forest and grassland on the spectrum of biomes. It is often situated near the boundary of an equatorial rainforest. This type of biome is commonly found in regions that experience a wet-dry tropical climate. The lack of moisture in the soil during the dry season causes trees in the savanna biome to grow in spacious patterns. This enables the growth of a dense lower layer of grasses and other plants. The trees of the **savanna biome** are similar in height and shape to those found in the monsoon forest. Though fire is a fairly common occurrence in savannas during the dry season, the vegetation in these regions tends to be quite fire resistant. In fact, many geographers believe that such fires prevent rainforest vegetation from overrunning the savanna biome.

Grassland Biome

The **grassland biome** is commonly subdivided into two types: tall-grass prairie and steppe. The **tall-grass prairie subdivision** is characterized by an absence of trees and a high occurrence of tall grasses and broad-leaved herbs called forbs. This kind of biome usually forms in regions with distinct summer and winter seasons in subtropical or midlatitude climates. The **steppe subdivision,** or **short-grass prairie,** is typified by sparse clumps of short grasses, existing alongside the occasional shrub or small tree. Many grass species and forbs populate this kind of region. Steppes are usually found in midlatitude areas with dry continental climates; vegetation grows in wet spring months and becomes dormant during dry summer months.

Desert Biome

The **desert biome** may be subdivided into two types: semidesert and dry desert. The **semidesert subdivision** is found at a wide range of latitudes. It is characterized by thinly-spaced xerophytic shrubs (those adapted to survival in arid climates). **Steppe regions** may be converted to semidesert through; for example, high levels of cattle moving through the area, treading upon and consuming regional vegetation can cause this conversion. The thorn-tree semidesert is found in the tropical zone, which experiences a long, dry hot season and a short, severe rainy season. Thorny vegetation (such as cacti), called thorn-bush or thorn-woods, populate the thorn-tree semidesert.

The **dry desert subdivision** is even barer than the semidesert. Only tough xerophytes, such as cacti and hard grasses, can survive under desert conditions. Many dry desert areas display no plant life at all, due to the unfertile sand that covers the ground.

Tundra Biome

The **tundra biome** may be subdivided into two types: arctic or alpine. The **arctic tundra** exists at very high latitudes near the poles. During the brief summer season in these areas, low vegetation such as herbs, mosses, and grasses are able to grow because above-freezing air temperatures enable melting of the surface layer. The type and occurrence of plant species depends upon the moisture levels in the (usually frozen) ground during the warm season. In the cold season, frost action snaps roots in the ground. Freezing wind and snow kill plants above the ground. **Alpine**

tundra is located at high elevations, above the tree line and below bare mountain tops. Physically, the alpine tundra is quite similar to the arctic tundra.

Various Forests and Formation Classes

- The **low-latitude rainforest formation class** exists in equatorial and tropical climate zones. This class is characterized by many different species of tall, densely-spaced trees, normally with broad leaves. The canopy created by this vegetation casts shade on the ground below, inhibiting the growth of flora on the bottom layer.
- **Monsoon forests** may also be found in tropical latitude zones; however, this formation class exists in regions that experience a wet season and a dry season during which the many tree species lose their leaves. This enables the growth of vegetation on the lower layer of the forest.
- The **subtropical evergreen forest** may be broadleaf or needleleaf (found only in the southeastern United States). This formation class consists of fewer, shorter tree species than the low-latitude rainforest. It also includes a lush lower layer of vegetation.
- The **midlatitude deciduous forest formation class** is common in regions of the northern hemisphere with distinct seasons. During the warm summer season, the tall broadleaf trees in this type of forest form a nearly closed canopy. In the winter season, these trees lose their leaves. The lower level vegetation also varies with the season, growing in the spring and dying out with the summertime formation of a dense upper canopy.
- A **needleleaf forest** is made up largely of conifers (cone-shaped trees with short branches, straight trunks, and small, thin leaves reminiscent of needles). Many trees in this type of forest are evergreen, meaning that they shed their leaves once every several years. The spacing of the trees in this formation class may be dense, preventing the growth of vegetation on the ground. This type of forest is usually located at higher latitudes or regions where orogenies and/or plateaus are found.
- The **sclerophyll forest** contains widely-spaced trees that are able to survive dry, hot seasons (short, with low branches, tough, thick bark, and short, thick leaves).

Surface and Ground Water

Runoff, Watershed, Groundwater and Infiltration

Runoff is precipitation that does not experience evaporation, transpiration by plants, or infiltration (the process in which water transitions from surface water to groundwater). It is an important part of the hydrologic cycle. Runoff, or surface water, moves from the location where it falls as precipitation across the surface of the Earth to an ocean. Rivers and streams are the mechanisms of transportation for surface water. Moving runoff often picks up soil and other materials as it travels. A **watershed** is the area in which runoff moves toward a body of water; such a region is usually bounded by hills and/or mountains. **Groundwater** is precipitation that seeps through the upper layers of the Earth's surface. This process of **infiltration** is also referred to as groundwater recharge. Water moves underground back to the oceans where it originated from at the beginning of the hydrologic cycle. When the water reaches its destination, it is deposited through groundwater discharge.

Water Table and Saturated Zone

The **water table** is the upper boundary of the region in which groundwater moves. It is the level at which water stands in wells. The water table is not level. Rather, it resembles the surface of the Earth, with depressions and elevated portions. This shelf intersects the Earth's surface at streams, springs, and lakes. Low-elevation streams that receive additional water from the water table are called **effluent streams**. This type of stream is common in humid areas. **Influent streams** are those that contribute water to the underground supply; they usually exist in arid regions at high elevations. The saturated zone is the area below the water table; it is so named because the pore space of the rocks in this zone is filled to capacity with water.

Movement of Surface Water to Oceans

Precipitation that does not evaporate or seep into the Earth's surface may fall into a watershed, or it may be **transported** to one by gravity (if, for example, it falls on a hillside). Water that enters a watershed will eventually enter the area's associated body of water. This surface water may move directly to an ocean, or it may move into a transportation medium such as a river or stream (a smaller river); it may also move into a lake, where it will be temporarily stored. A river is a body of water with a detectable current (fluid motion). The velocity of moving water in a river depends largely on the gradient (downward slope); it is also influenced by the shape of the channel through which it moves, the texture of the inside surfaces of the channel, and the amount of sediment in the water.

Coasts

Emergent coasts are those that are rising. Plate tectonics are one mechanism by which a portion of land can rise. Wave-cut platforms provide evidence of this occurrence. Also, Earth's crust may rebound when it is relieved of the pressure caused by an overlying glacier. A **submerged coast** is sinking. In other words, the sea level is rising relative to a submerged coast. This type of coast is usually found where the shoreline has become embayed (the sea extends inland, with fingers of the coast reaching into the ocean). Prior surface water erosion is usually a factor in the formation of a submerged coast. Consequently, wave erosions focus on the portions of land around the embayments, which become sea cliffs. Eventually, the fingers of land jutting into the sea will disappear completely, resulting in a relatively straight coastline. A **plains coast** is surrounded by barrier islands (narrow strips of sandy land separated by the coast by lagoons).

Aeration Zone

The **aeration**, or vadose, **zone** is the area above the water table. This zone consists of three sublayers: the **zone of soil moisture** (the portion of the surface that becomes damp after precipitation), the **intermediate zone** (a transition zone through which water moves downward), and the **tension-saturated zone**, or **capillary fringe** (an area where water is held in thin branches between soil particles). Water actually moves upward from the water table into the capillary fringe. This is accomplished through capillary action, whereby a liquid is drawn upward into a narrow space. Capillary action occurs when adhesive intermolecular forces are stronger between the molecules of the liquid and the molecules of the solid that comprise the tube than they are between the molecules of the liquid alone.

Porosity and Permeability

Porosity is a characteristic of rocks that has a large effect on the rate of transportation of groundwater. It is expressed as the percentage of a rock that is occupied by empty space (pores). The porosity of a rock is determined by several variables. For example, in sedimentary rocks, the amount of cementing material that infiltrated pore space during lithification is a factor that affects the rock's porosity. In igneous and metamorphic rocks, porosity is influenced by the frequency of joints in the material. The measurement of the ability of a rock to transmit water through it is referred to as its **permeability**. A rock's permeability is closely related to the size of the openings in a rock and the extent to which those openings are connected. One rock may have a higher porosity but a lower permeability than another rock.

Aquifer

An **aquifer** is a layer of rock or other material (such as sand or silt) through which groundwater travels laterally between points of deposition. An aquifer is confined when it is bounded from above by a layer of impermeable material. This type of aquifer can often be found below an unconfined aquifer, one that has the water table as its upward boundary. This kind of aquifer is usually close to surface level. An **aquiclude** is a layer of impermeable material. A layer may become an aquiclude when it becomes too saturated to accommodate any more liquid. Other related layers include aquitard and aquifuge layers. Many aquifers are semi-confined, existing at a state between confined and unconfined.

Glaciers and Polar Ice

Glaciers

A **glacier** is a large mass of ice formed by the physical transformation of snow under certain conditions; this ice mass must also exhibit evidence of movement. These ice sheets form only in climates in which some level of snow remains on the ground year-round; this necessitates high amounts of snowfall in the winter and low temperatures in the summer. If a glacier forms on a hill or mountain slope, the formative process may also be influenced by the orientation of said slope, in that the south side of a slope receives more sunlight than the north, and that one side may experience greater wind or precipitation levels than the other. Glaciers are created when snow (solid water) thaws and subsequently freezes again, becoming a granular type of ice called **neve**, which can eventually become **firn**. Neve accumulates and eventually compacts due to the pressure of snow and ice above it, completing the transition to glacier over a long period of time. Glaciers move due to gravity and the force of their own weight.

Movement

The **center of a glacier** flows more quickly than the sides and bottom of the mass because of the friction between the glacier and the surface upon which it moves at the latter two locations. Usually, glacial movement occurs at velocities of 3–300 meters per year. Sometimes, however, the bottom of a glacier detaches from the rock floor and moves downward very rapidly (sometimes up to 6,000 meters per year). This type of movement, called a **glacial surge**, generally occurs in valley glaciers. **Basal slip** is the glacial movement that actually involves the bottom of a glacier sliding along the surface upon which it rests, usually because of melting at the glacier's base. Basal slip leaves polished and scratched ground surface behind; this can be observed after a glacier melts. A glacier is said to move through **plastic flow** when the pressure created by the weight of (brittle) upper layers causes the ice crystals in the lower part of a glacier to become plastic and flow.

Alpine Glaciers

Alpine glaciers (one of the main categories of glacier) form on valley or mountain slopes with summits above the snow line. Gravity is the main proponent of their movement, which usually follows a predefined pathway. The movements of alpine glaciers erode the land over which they travel in two principal ways. **Glacial abrasion** consists of the wearing down of the ground under the base of the moving glacier. **Glacial quarrying** pries surface rocks out of their location and embeds them in the glacier; the deep crevasses that may be left behind by this type of erosion provide much of the information we know about the process. The erosive processes of alpine glaciers produce several different kinds of landforms: for example, cirques (rounded, steep-walled recesses in valley walls), tarns (lakes that form due to uneven erosion), and fjords (deep valleys that are partially below sea level). Glaciers also deposit the materials they acquire along their paths in landforms called **moraines**. Moraines are named for their location of deposition (terminal, lateral, or medial).

Continental Glaciers

Continental glaciers are one of the two general categories of glacier. This type of glacier consists of a large sheet of ice. This type of glacier was prominent during the ice ages, when such formations covered over twenty million square kilometers of land. Unlike alpine glaciers, continental glaciers move over any object in their way (rather than following the path of least resistance). Consequently, this kind of glacier tends to smooth out the land over which it travels, instead of sharpening irregularities, as the movement of alpine glaciers does. Icebergs are formed when portions of a continental glacier breaks off and drifts out to sea. A **kettle** is a landform produced by continental glacial erosion. It is a depression formed when till (debris deposited by ice) builds up around a stationary glacier, which becomes trapped and then melts. A **drumlin** is a small, round hill believed to be created under a moving glacier; these usually appear in groups. **Eskers** are long, thin depositions of stratified sediment.

Rock Glacier

A **rock glacier** is a large, tongue-shaped mass of rock and ice that behaves much like a glacier formed completely of ice. It forms on a slope in a valley and travels slowly (about one meter per year) downward. These bodies form in geographical locations where an ice glacier could not—where warm temperatures in the summer cause much of the snow that piled up in the winter to melt. Though they have not been extensively studied, scientists believe that some rock glaciers are composed of rock particles cemented by ice and others are formed when rocky debris accumulates and becomes frozen into glacial surfaces. Rock glaciers form at high altitudes near eroding cliffs; the altitude allows for some snow to remain into the summertime, and nearby cliffs supply enough rocks to cover the small amount of snow that remains.

Ice Age

An **ice age** is a period of time in which the Earth's climate is significantly colder, enabling the expansion of glaciers and ice sheets. Based on sedimentary deposits (including fossils) and moraine deposits of till left by glaciers, scientists have identified four major ice ages in Earth's past. The most recent of these began about 40 million years ago and intensified about 2.5 million years ago; there have been several expansions and recessions of ice sheets (glacial periods) since that time. Several different hypotheses have been advanced to explain periods of glaciation. Suggested terrestrial causes include the presence of high mountains and large land areas in polar positions. Suggested atmospheric causes include changes in the composition of Earth's atmosphere including, specifically, variations in carbon dioxide levels (related to the greenhouse effect). Suggested astronomical causes include changes in the tilt of Earth's rotational axis, variations in Earth's orbit around the Sun, and changes in Earth's inclination to the plane of its orbit.

Changes in Climate

From about 1900 to the 1940s, most of the glaciers in the Northern Hemisphere were retreating. The global climate during that period of time included a general increase in atmospheric temperatures and changes in annual temperatures and precipitation on Earth. These climatic shifts caused corresponding shifts in ocean currents (and thus populations of marine organisms) and migrations among groups of land animals. Sometime in the 1940s, the climate shifted and began growing generally cooler and wetter than during the preceding years. Consequently, many glaciers expanded or at least halted their recession during this time. This trend once again reversed in the 1970s, when the global climate shifted to warming once again. There is significant debate over what conclusions ought to be drawn, with accusations being made about money on both sides influencing scientific opinion. Currently, a majority of scientists attribute the overall increase of global temperatures to manmade causes.

Oceans

Chemical Composition of Oceans

Salinity is the proportion of salts (inorganic minerals) dissolved in the ocean. These minerals are present as ions within seawater. The proportions of the minerals most commonly found in seawater are as follows: chloride (55%); sodium (31%); sulfate (8%); magnesium (4%); calcium and potassium (1% each); bromide, boric acid, bicarbonate, fluoride, and strontium (less than 1% each). While seawater's salinity may vary, the proportion of salt minerals remains constant. Carbon dioxide, nitrogen, and oxygen are present as dissolved gases in the oceans. The nutrients dissolved in seawater include nitrogen, phosphorus, and silica. The salinity of the oceans is affected by weathering and erosive processes of rocks on land by precipitation (which eventually returns to the seas as runoff), volcanic emissions, and the activity at hydrothermal vents on the deep seafloor. Deep sea vents are created at locations near underwater ridges when mantle material causes the eruption of water containing minerals (such as magnesium) through the lithosphere. The salinity of the ocean affects its electrical conductivity and density.

Island Arc, Oceanic Trench and Continental Shelf

An **island arc** is one potential result of the convergence of two oceanic plates; it is a type of **archipelago** (chain of islands). When one plate subducts the other, the mantle of the subducting plate is partially melted by the increase in temperature of the subducted plate, which also drives water up into the overriding plate's mantle. As the temperature of the mantle increases and absorbs water, it becomes magma riddled with dissolving gases. This low-density material enters and exits the overriding plate. This process creates **volcanic chains**, such as the Pacific's Ring of Fire, which go through alternate periods of high and low activity. An oceanic trench is a long, deep, narrow depression in the oceanic lithosphere. The **Mariana Trench**, located in the Pacific Ocean, boasts the deepest measured location: 10,911 meters below sea level. A **continental shelf** is the submerged edge of a continent. These shelves are often eliminated when an oceanic plate slips under a continental plate at a converging plate boundary.

Each **continental shelf** is a portion of the ocean floor that exists as a platform shallowly submerged off of a beach. This platform has a slight downward grade; its surface is uneven, with a relief (due to glacial activity) up to 100 meters. **Sediment** and **sedimentary rock** make up most continental shelves. The surface of a continental shelf is affected by natural dams, such as tectonic dams (rocks forced upward by tectonic motion) and diapirs (domes of salt that form under sedimentary rocks and push up through the rocks). The presence of these dams creates a depression in which sediment is deposited. A continental shelf experiences an abrupt increase in slope (at an average depth of 133 meters) at the shelf break, the outer boundary of the shelf. The irregular slope that extends downward from the shelf break is called the continental slope; this transition zone connects sea level to the ocean floor (about 3,660 meters below sea level).

Submarine Canyon

A **submarine canyon** is a steep-walled valley in a continental slope. Some believe that these canyons are formed by mass movements of rock along the slope or by turbidity currents (currents initiated by the motion of debris-filled water at the tops of the canyons). It has also been suggested that these canyons were created at a point in time when at least a portion of the relevant area was above sea level; such a point might be the lowering of sea level during the Pleistocene glaciations. These formations occur more often on steeper slopes than on slopes with gentle gradients.

Submarine fans (sediment deposits that travel through the canyon and then spill out onto the seafloor), which are similar to land-bound alluvial fans, form the boundary (called the continental rise) between the continental slope and the ocean floor.

Deep Seafloor

The deepest level of the seafloor, which spans from one continental margin to another, is called the **abyss floor**. The flat, relatively featureless aspects of this floor (which is often covered with either basaltic floods or sediment) are called abyssal plains. **Abyssal hills** are fairly gentle rises along the floor of the abyss. The **ocean ridge system**, which is tall enough in some places to break the ocean surface, stands in sharp contrast to the abyssal plains. The ridge system, including the Mid-Atlantic Ridge, includes the median rift, a long, continuous depression that follows the crest. The floor of the deep ocean also exhibits trenches (the deepest part of the ocean) and chains of volcanic islands called island arcs. Basaltic seafloor volcanoes called **seamounts** are reminiscent of intermediate land volcanoes. Seamounts are not tall enough to reach the ocean's surface. Guyots are enormous undersea volcanoes whose apexes appear to have been shorn off, creating a nearly level underwater shelf. Oceanographers have been unable to establish a consensus explanation of this phenomenon.

Coral Reefs

A **coral reef** is an underwater formation composed mainly of coral (small marine creatures similar to anemones) and algae. These often-beautiful undersea features usually form in warm, clear water. They develop their own ecosystems, composed of a wide variety of plant and animal species. Before he became famous for his theory of genetic evolution, Charles Darwin spent time during an ocean voyage studying reefs, among other things. He identified three major varieties of reef and postulated a successive relationship between them. First, a **fringing reef** (which extends out from and grows along a shoreline) begins to grow around a sinking volcanic island. The fringing reef becomes a **barrier reef** surrounding the still-sinking island when the portion of the reef closest to the shore cannot keep up with the biotic (live) growth of the outer potion; the inner portion becomes a lagoon. This process continues, and the reef continues to spread around the island in a circuit. When the island sinks completely, the coral formation has become an **atoll**.

Sediments on the Ocean Floor

Much of the abyss floor is covered with sediment. The amount of sediment in any location on the ocean floor is related to the age of that portion of the oceanic lithosphere. **Ooze** is a type of sediment that accumulates over time from fragments of deceased surface organisms. The type of ooze deposited varies with depth and chemical conditions. **Calcareous ooze** is ooze made up mostly of the carbonate remains of organisms such as shells. This type of material dissolves at depths below four kilometers. **Siliceous ooze** is that composed of the remains of silica-cell–producing organisms. This type of ooze also dissolves under certain conditions; however, it is more resistant to dissolution than carbonate material. Sediment at the deepest levels of the ocean consists largely of (inorganic) clay, with the occasional appearance of fossils like sharks' teeth. Oceanic sediments provide large amounts of information about the Earth's prehistory, due to their sheer volume and the fact that fossils survive better undersea (without oxygen) than fossils on land.

Sea Breezes

The daily influxes in the strength and direction of wind at ocean coasts are collectively referred to as sea breezes. These phenomena contribute to the climate-mediating function of oceanic bodies. When solar energy hits the coastal surface during a sunny day, the ground warms quickly. Air above this heated land rises through convection, creating a low-pressure zone. Cooler air then flows into the region vacated by the risen air, creating a cool onshore breeze by the middle of the day.

Conversely, when the shore cools after the Sun goes down, the air above it cools and sinks. The direction of wind flow is then reversed, creating an offshore breeze in the evening. Unlike meteorologists, oceanographers name winds for the direction they are headed.

Seawater Motion and Atmospheric Wind Patterns

We can envision the ocean as a series of **layers of water**, loosely connected to one another by friction. Winds over the ocean move the surface layer of water, which exerts a force on the layer below it, which affects the layer below it, and so on. However, the energy generated by the wind decreases with ocean depth, so that after a certain point (usually a depth of 100–200 meters), the wind has little if any effect on the water. Due to the influence of the Coriolis force, surface currents do not move in the same direction as the winds above them; ocean waves seem to move to the right of the wind in the area. This can be explained in terms of **Ekman transport**. This theory states that as each layer of oceanic water is touched by wind, it also experiences the effects of the Coriolis force, which causes it to move 90 degrees to the right (or left, in the Southern Hemisphere) and spiral downward (an Ekman spiral).

Seawater Circulation

At the surface, **atmospheric winds** and the **Coriolis force** are the most influential factors in seawater circulation. Surface waters move in opposite directions on either side of the equator: Northern Hemisphere waters move eastward, and waters in the Southern Hemisphere tend to move westward. In a manner similar to that in which air circulates in the atmosphere, warm surface waters travel from regions near the equator toward the cooler poles, redistributing heat within the oceans. These wide, circular patterns are called gyres. When warm surface water reaches the higher latitudes, it is cooled by interaction with the ambient waters (and ice) and the air in the region. With the resulting increase in density, the water moves downward and cycles back toward the equator. Thus, gravity is the force that most affects deep-water circulation. Some of the water in this "oceanic conveyor belt" then rises back to the surface where it is warmed again and reenters the cycle. Other portions of water remain in the depths of the ocean.

Waves

There are two main processes in operation in the creation of wave motion: disturbing forces (such as wind, changes in atmospheric pressure, the mixing of water of different densities, and earthquakes) and restoring forces (the water's surface tension and gravity). In the creation of a wave, a **disturbing force** drives water into a pile, or crest. The water that makes up this crest comes from an adjacent section of water; therefore, the formation of the crest produces a depression, or trough, on a nearby water surface. Gravity, a **restoring force**, attempts to restore equilibrium by forcing the crest back down to sea level. Due to inertia, however, the gravitational force presses water down below that level, creating another trough. The water displaced by this motion forms another crest, which produces another trough, and the up and down motions continue. When the crest of a wave is higher than its associated trough, the wave moves forward. It is not the water that moves during wave motion, but the wave.

Wave length is defined as the horizontal distance between two equivalent wave phases (that is, the distance separating two sequential crests or troughs). The **velocity** of a wave is the distance it moves during a specified period of time. The **period** of a wave is the length of time required for two equivalent wave phases to pass a certain point. The number of periods that occur in a specified length of time is referred to as the **frequency** of the wave. These measurements vary greatly among waves. One of the largest such occurrences measured a wave length of 792 meters, a velocity of 126 kilometers per hour, and a period of 22.5 seconds.

Wave Erosion

Most **coastal erosion** takes place when waves crash into a shore zone during a storm. It is at this time that the height of a wave (the distance between its upper effective limit and its lower effective limit, or wave base) is the greatest. The upper and lower limits of a wave work on a coastline much like a saw moving horizontally. Like river and stream erosion, most wave erosion is accomplished through abrasion caused by eroded materials (sand and gravel, for instance) carried in the water. Fluctuations in the tide cause coastal erosion indirectly; during low tide, large portions of the shore are exposed and vulnerable to other erosive agents, such as wind and rain. The energy of waves and the strength of the material of which a coastline is composed are the main factors in the rate of wave erosion.

Landforms Created

The **sea cliff** is a landform that is often associated with coastal areas. Particularly large, high-energy waves attack coastlines during storms and abrade portions of a rock face, forming an often steep cliff. The intensity of this effect is related to the durability of the material being eroded and the slope of the land surface. Wave erosion also produces wave-cut platforms, or a truncated sea cliff with a leveled surface. Sometimes these areas remain bare except for the irregularities created by the erosive process; these remnants of cliffs are called stacks. Beaches are created when the portion of the platform closest to the sea is covered with sand or other grainy materials. These formations are constantly being eroded away and reformed. A marine-built terrace (a deposit of material transported by waves) is often formed inland from a beach.

Oceanic Tides

Oceanic tides are the daily oscillations in sea level along coastlines. The number of times sea level changes and the differences in sea level vary with location, but all parts of the ocean experience this phenomenon. Tides occur due to the gravitational force and centripetal acceleration. Both the Sun and the Moon exert gravitational pulls on the Earth; however, the attraction of the Moon is more effective in tide formation, due to the fact that it is closer to our planet (because gravitational attraction varies with distance, among other things). As the Earth rotates, different areas of the oceans are closest to the Moon. Since water is not firmly affixed to the surface, it is disturbed by the Moon's gravitational pull, which creates an exceptionally long wave. Centripetal acceleration is the force that keeps the Earth and Moon in orbit around the Sun; this force is experienced equally at all points on the Earth's surface. The combined influence of these two forces produces the rhythmic pattern of oceanic tides.

Review Video: Spring and Neap Tides
Visit mometrix.com/academy and enter code: 825792

Coastal Upwelling

Coastal upwelling occurs due to the combined effects of wind and Ekman transport. Wind often blows parallel to a coastline; Ekman transport causes warm surface water along the shore to swing outward, away from land. Coastal upwelling happens when cooler water swells up from higher depths to replace the water moving away from the coast. The water that rises during coastal upwelling contains high levels of nutrients. Plants near the surface absorb these nutrients and consequently experience population growth. Fish and other marine organisms then come to the surface to feed on the plentiful vegetation. Thus, areas of coastal upwelling are some of the most fertile in the ocean.

Effects of Ozone Depletion on Marine Life

Ozone depletion affects marine life due to the harm caused by ultraviolet radiation. In the oceans, this electromagnetic energy can penetrate depths to 20 meters. This radiation can cause cell damage in marine species. Small organisms, such as plankton (plant and animal species), are especially susceptible to damage. When these organisms, which exist on the lowest tier of the food chain, are killed or mutated, effects radiate upward on the food chain. This process has the potential to decrease the global food supply. Ultraviolet radiation also affects fish, amphibians, shrimp, and other organisms in their developmental stages, decreasing their future reproductive capabilities. Again, this damage can move up the food chain and impact entire ecosystems.

Effects of Pollution on Oceans

Sewage, oil, garbage, and industrial waste are commonly disposed of in Earth's oceans. Also, the use of pesticides in agriculture can indirectly contribute to pollution as these chemicals are picked up by rainwater moving back to the oceans. **Ocean pollution** has many harmful effects, both within oceanic ecosystems and across the rest of the globe. For example, pesticides deposited in the ocean contaminate the normally clean water in which algae thrive. When the algae die, a number of the fish that depend on algae (or other underwater plant life) for sustenance will die as well. This can affect local economies (not to mention food supplies) that depend on fishing. Also, when toxic waste is dumped into an ocean, it may be consumed by organisms low on the food chain. If it does not kill these organisms, they can be eaten by larger predators. Pollutants can continue to move up the food chain and eventually be consumed by humans. Lead, for instance, is commonly found in seafood eaten by humans.

Chapter Quiz

Ready to see how well you retained what you just read? Scan the QR code to go directly to the chapter quiz interface for this study guide. If you're using a computer, simply visit the online resources page at **mometrix.com/resources719/osatearsci108** and click the Chapter Quizzes link.

Natural Hazards and Human Environmental Interaction

Impact of Earth Science

Forest Management

Since 1950, about half the forests on Earth have been removed to make room for development, livestock pasture, or new cropland or because the trees were used for lumber, fuel, or paper pulp. **Deforestation** reduces natural resources such as wood, other plants, and wildlife. It also reduces ecological health by damaging runoff and erosion control, climate stabilization, carbon dioxide sequestration, and wildlife habitat. The US Forest Service manages 155 national forests in ways that are supposed to allow sustainable yield and multiple uses; logging is allowed to the point that the trees can be replaced in a reasonable time, and recreation, hunting, and fishing are encouraged. Management of forest fires is controversial. Preventing or extinguishing all fires allows dry matter and small trees to accumulate on forest floors, and these increase the likelihood that a surface fire will become a destructive crown fire. Many experts favor the use of prescribed fires, and allowing surface fires to burn, to remove the forest floor buildup.

Rangeland

Rangeland is unfenced land where grasses and small plants grow. These grasses and plants provide food for cattle, sheep, horses, bison, and other grazers and for goats, deer, and other browsers. When too many animals graze or browse in the same range (or any grassland) area for too long, it deteriorates. This is due to **overcropping** of grasses, which destroy the roots, and **overbrowsing** of other plants. But it is also caused by trampling, especially near surface water, which kills the grass roots, causes erosion, and pollutes the water. Significant overgrazing leads to desertification (reduced productivity). In many cases, the desire for rangeland has caused deforestation, as has been common in the South America rainforest.

The US Department of Agriculture manages about a hundred million acres of federal rangeland and influences management of millions more, both public and private, in the United States.

Old Growth Forest and Tree Plantations

Old growth forest are forests made up of trees that are a hundred or more years old. Some are over a thousand years old, like the sequoia redwoods. These forests may have a dominant type of tree but also contain a number of other species, and the trees are of varied ages and sizes. **Old second-growth forest**—the result of growth after destruction of a forest (secondary succession)—is considered old-growth forest, as is virgin forest. Tree plantations, or tree farms, typically contain only one or a few types of trees that are all of the same age. They provide some forest services, such as producing oxygen, absorbing carbon dioxide, and providing ground cover, which reduces erosion, as well as habitat for some animals. However, their lack of tree diversity does not support as much wildlife diversity as old-growth forests. Monoculture tree farms are more susceptible to biological pests, and repeated planting and harvesting can degrade the soil.

American Land Use for Transportation

In the United States, up to 70% of urban land is used for transportation—for parking lots, roads, and highways, as well as for light rail trains and subways and for airports. The national highway system includes about 160,000 miles. The areas devoted to automobile use have high concentrations of pollutants from gasoline and from wear and tear on tires, brake pads, and lubricating oil. Air pollutants from automobiles include hydrocarbons, carbon dioxide, carbon monoxide, nitrogen oxides, ozone, and volatile organic compounds (VOCs). Water is polluted by many of the same chemicals when it runs off the roads.

In some places, large areas are used for canals and channels that provide routes for transportation by water and/or reroute water to allow transportation by land. In Florida, canals cover thousands of miles; New Orleans is famous for its canals. In addition to navigation, canals are important for flood control and agricultural irrigation.

Public and Federal Land

The US Forest Service manages 193 million acres of grasslands and forests. More than 51 million acres are set aside in the National Wilderness Preservation System. Those lands, including 30 million acres managed by the US Forest Service, are managed by four federal agencies. There are 63 national parks, managed by the National Park Service. Some US wetlands are managed by the federal government under the rules of the Clean Water Act, but many are unprotected. There are over 1,100 national parks in the world. Wilderness areas, wildlife refuges, and other nature reserves cover 12% of the land on Earth. Much of this area is uninhabitable—or nearly so—tundra, ice, and desert. Allowing other uses of lands in reserve is controversial. While some think we should use the lumber, oil, minerals, and other resources that are found there, others believe that protected reserves are crucially important for maintaining biodiversity and allowing future evolution.

Ecological Conservation Options

The following are ecological conservation options:

- **Preservation**: Keeping ecosystems from deteriorating in the first place. Preservation attempts include keeping cars and off-road vehicles off sensitive lands such as dunes and tundra.
- **Remediation**, also called rehabilitation: Improving the state of a deteriorated ecosystem. Remediation attempts include filling in old mining sites and improving the slope of the land so that vegetation can grow and runoff will be reduced.
- **Restoration**: Returning an ecosystem to its previous condition. Restoration activities include demolishing dams that block rivers, planting submerged aquatic vegetation in estuaries where it has died off, and replacing invasive plants with specimens of native species.
- **Mitigation**: Reducing the deterioration of an ecosystem. Mitigation includes remediation and restoration, as well as establishment of new areas that will function as the deteriorated ecosystem did. For example, replacing a disturbed wetland with a new wetland established somewhere else by rerouting water would be compensatory mitigation.

Sustainable Strategies for Land and Freshwater Use

Smart growth prevents urban sprawl. Ecocities have high-density housing, plentiful green areas, convenient mass transportation, and stores and workplaces within walking distance to reduce the use of private cars. Less land is used, and less pollution is generated, per person. Sustainable agricultural land choices include no-till planting, organic farming, low-volume irrigation, polyculture planting, and not overgrazing grasslands. In forests, biodiversity is preserved and improved by having larger continuous areas of trees, which prevent edge effects and allow natural migration and movement of wildlife, by not allowing mining, and by allowing only sustainable cutting. Freshwater resources can be used more sustainably by reducing the amount of water used in irrigation, recycling industrial cooling and cleaning water, using graywater for yard and city plant watering, reducing personal water use, and xeriscaping.

Global Reserves of Minerals

Earth's crust contains 3,000 different minerals spread unevenly among nations. **Uncommon minerals** that are beautiful, such as emeralds and rubies, are called gems. **Common minerals** include:

- Silicates, the most common, are used for sand and gravel and to make glass
- Carbonates, such as calcite and dolomite, form chalk and marble
- Oxides, which contain metals, such as hematite, which contains iron, and bauxite, which contains aluminum

Ores contain enough minerals to make them profitable to mine. High-grade ores contain larger percentages of minerals than low-grade ores. While any given mineral will never be used up, high-grade ores can be depleted. Mining of low-grade ores causes more environmental destruction. According to some experts, if developing countries use minerals at the same rate as the United States, the minerals will become scarce. One group working for sustainable mineral use is the UN's Intergovernmental Forum for Mining, Minerals, Metals, and Sustainable Development.

Overfishing

Efficient modern fishing methods (including GPS systems, spotter planes, and factory ships) and government subsidies allow more fish to be taken than in the past. The **larger fish species** (tuna, cod) have been harvested to the point where they are not as profitable. This has shifted the fishing to smaller individuals of the large species and then to smaller species of fish (mackerel). This is called **fishing down the food chain** (or down the food web). Catching these smaller fish for human consumption makes them unavailable for the remaining larger fish, which fail to reestablish their populations. The result of this **overfishing** is that we are left with fewer and fewer food fish. Integrated coastal management programs and marine reserves can improve the numbers (and biodiversity) of fish in the ocean. The United Nations Convention on the Law of the Sea (UNCLOS) sets guidelines for sustainable use of ocean fishes. However, these guidelines are not followed by many fishing nations or by pirate fishers.

US Energy Consumption

Until the Industrial Revolution, wood was the most used energy source, along with animals to provide horsepower. Between 1880 and 1920, America's use of non-animal energy grew by about 400%. **Coal** became the dominant energy source. By 1950, Americans were using mostly oil, gas, diesel fuel, and natural gas. In 2000, about 80% of US energy came from fossil fuels. The remainder came mostly from **nuclear plants**, with some from wood and hydropower and a smaller percentage from geothermal, biofuels, solar energy, and other "alternative" energy sources. Total energy use increased slowly, along with population size, until the Industrial Revolution. It dipped somewhat in the late 1970s and 1980s, when oil prices rose during what was then called "the energy crisis." US energy use is now around 100 quadrillion BTUs per year.

Present Global Energy Use

The world consumes more than 15 terawatts—15 trillion watts—of commercial energy per year. That's actually only 1% of the energy we use on Earth, but the other 99% comes directly from the Sun and is not captured and delivered commercially. At present, most (76%) of the commercial energy comes from fossil fuels, and about 6% comes from nuclear power. Renewable energy sources such as solar energy captured for light or heat, geothermal energy, wind power, hydropower, and energy in biomass provide the other 18%. (In the United States, renewable energy resources provide only 7%.) Per capita use varies widely. In 2003, the lowest per person annual energy use—less than the energy in 500 kilograms of oil—was in Peru, Myanmar/Burma, Bangladesh, Nepal, and Pakistan, and in many parts of Africa. The highest use—more than 20 times that—was in Iceland.

Future Global Energy Needs and Sources

The human population will continue to grow, and developing countries will likely become bigger energy users. It is expected that reserves of conventional oil will continue to be used rather than being conserved, and they will probably be almost depleted before 2100. Energy conservation will help make energy use more sustainable. Examples include less personal car use and more mass transportation, higher-mile-per-gallon (including electric and hydrogen cell) vehicles, more-efficient machines (like Energy Star appliances), and reduced waste. Smaller providers, but more of them, and individual families and businesses are likely to deliver smaller amounts of energy, in contrast to the huge electric power companies of today. Reliance on the types of energy that are most available in an area will help. For example, Iceland has the highest per capita energy use of the world, but all of its energy is renewable geothermal energy and hydropower.

Review Video: Renewable and Nonrenewable Resources
Visit mometrix.com/academy and enter code: 840194

Effects of Burning Fossil Fuels on the Environmental

Burning fossil fuels (naturally-occurring hydrocarbon compounds that may be used by humans for fuel), especially coal, releases harmful elements into the atmosphere. The chemical reaction of coal combustion, for example, produces large amounts of carbon dioxide. When these gases reach the atmosphere, they inhibit the release of infrared photons into space; carbon dioxide molecules absorb the photons and may reflect them inward, back toward the Earth. This phenomenon is called the **greenhouse effect**. While the greenhouse effect is desirable, to a certain degree, to maintain a comfortable climate on the planet, increased levels of carbon dioxide can change the balance of energy in the atmosphere. This is termed **global warming**. Coal burning can also cause acid rain. Sulfur dioxide, a byproduct of burning coal, rises to the atmosphere and combines with water molecules to form sulfuric acid. This acid rain falls back to Earth, where it can cause harm to plants, animals, water bodies, and exposed structures. Burning gasoline can also contribute to the formation of acid rain.

Outdoor and Indoor Air Pollutants

The major outdoor air pollutants are carbon dioxide and carbon monoxide; sulfur dioxide and sulfuric acid; nitrogen oxides, nitric acid, and nitrates (or nitrate salts); particulates, or suspended particulate matter (SPM); ozone (at ground level); and VOCs (volatile organic compounds) such as hydrocarbons (including methane) and various solvents.

Indoor air pollutants include outdoor pollutants plus radioactive radon-222, cigarette smoke, cooking- and heating-fire smoke, formaldehyde, and assorted very small particles.

Concentrations of most pollutants are measured in parts per million by volume (ppm or ppmv), milligrams per cubic meter of air (mg/m^3), or micrograms per cubic meter of air ($\mu g/m^3$). Radon is usually measured in picocuries per liter of air (pCi/L).

Remediation and Reduction Strategies for Air Pollution and Acid Deposition

Acid deposition results from dispersion of primary air pollutants—from power plants, industry, automobiles, and other sources—and their subsequent formation of secondary pollutants: sulfuric acid, sulfates, nitric acid, and nitrates. When these are deposited downwind, they corrode rock and metal, intensify respiratory diseases, acidify drinking water (and other bodies of water), increase mercury in fish to toxic levels, kill fish, and weaken trees. The US Clean Air Act of 1970 required the Environmental Protection Agency (EPA) to set air quality standards for the major air pollutants. Air pollution, as well as acid deposition in some areas, has been reduced by burning less coal, scrubbing pollutants from the exhaust before it leaves the smokestack or car tailpipe, and increased energy efficiency. Remediation of some acidified lakes has been accomplished by application of limestone, which is basic, to neutralize the acid. Since 1970, the EPA has set emission standards for many hazardous air pollutants, including volatile and toxic chemicals.

Noise Pollution

Sources of unwanted sounds at disturbing levels include motorcycles, trucks, other vehicles, industrial processes, alarms, airplanes, construction and destruction equipment (jackhammers), and noisy neighbors. The **effects of noise pollution** include stress; stress-related health effects, such as spikes in blood pressure; many other health effects; loss or disturbance of sleep; interference with communication; lowered productivity; and noise-induced hearing loss. According to the Occupational Safety and Health Administration, 85 decibels of noise for 8 hours can induce hearing loss. Control measures include the personal actions of wearing ear plugs or hearing protection devices. Legal control of most noise pollution is the responsibility of local and state governments. The Environmental Protection Agency and other federal agencies have some control over transport and construction equipment. Though the federal Noise Control Act of 1972 and Quiet Communities Act of 1978 are still in effect, they are not funded.

Water Pollution

Water pollution is a change in water that reduces the ability of water organisms to live in it or makes it unusable by humans. **Point source pollution**, as from the outflow pipe from a factory into a river, is traceable to a specific point, or polluter. **Nonpoint source pollution**, such as runoff from city streets, is spread out and cannot be traced to someone or somewhere specific. The top three sources of water pollution are agriculture, industry, and mining:

- Agriculture pollutes with water and sediments contaminated with such things as nitrates, phosphates, pesticides, oxygen-demanding wastes from plants and animals, and microbial pathogens such as viruses, bacteria, and protozoa.
- Industry pollutes with inorganic chemicals such as arsenic and mercury, organic chemicals such as petroleum products, and heat.
- Mining pollutes with sediments, sulfuric acid, and toxic chemicals, such as mercury and arsenic.

Some of the effects of **water pollution** include eutrophication, death of aquatic organisms, buildup of toxins in fish, and early death for 3.2 million people per year. Because many water sources are not suitable for human use, many countries purify their piped water as a government service. The first step is often holding the water in reservoirs to increase dissolved oxygen and decrease sediment. Commonly, the second step is disinfection with chlorine, ozone, or sunlight. Improving and maintaining water quality is a more sustainable way to provide potable water:

- In agriculture, organic farming would reduce nitrates, phosphates, and pesticides; oxygen-demanding plant and animal wastes would be composted for later application to the soil; this would keep many pathogens out of streams, and streamside areas could be kept planted to reduce erosion.
- In industry, arsenic, mercury, and other chemicals could be removed from industrial processes or reduced or at least removed from effluent (outgoing wastewater).

Cultural Eutrophication

Eutrophication is the process or end result of addition of plant nutrients to aquatic ecosystems. Eutrophication happens normally because of **erosion of sediments** from the surrounding land that contain organic matter and that run off into surface water systems (streams, ponds, rivers, and estuaries). Cultural eutrophication is the same process or end result but speeded up by human activities. Because nitrogen and phosphorus are common waste products of agriculture lands, sewage treatment plants, urban areas, and other areas used by humans, the nearby surface waters receive more than the natural background amounts of plant nutrients. The result is often an algal bloom near the surface, which blocks sunlight from plants growing beneath them and kills them. The alga depletes its resources and dies, and then the bacteria that decompose plant and algal materials deplete the water of oxygen. The end results include loss of biodiversity and anoxia (low oxygen).

Septic Systems and Sewage Treatment Systems

Septic systems are used when waste and wastewater from a building (usually a home) flow into a septic tank that contains bacteria that digest some of the waste. The semi-decomposed slurry and fluid exits the tank and flows through perforated lines and/or drainage tiles set in the ground. From these, it enters the soil, where additional natural decomposers remove most of the remaining pollutants.

Sewage treatment occurs when waste and wastewater from buildings and gutters enter sewer pipes, which carry them to a wastewater (sewage) treatment plant. There, large objects are removed by screens and by gravity in a settlement tank. The remaining material enters a second tank, where most of the organic solids settle to the bottom. That much of the process is called primary treatment. In secondary treatment, most of the remaining organic material is digested by bacteria. Usually the remainder is then chlorinated to kill the bacteria and bleach the water before it is returned to the environment.

Solid Waste

Municipal solid waste combines household and workplace trash. It contains many **recyclable items** (paper products, metals, glass, plastic), many **compostable materials** (food wastes, yard trimmings), and other items (disposable diapers, e-waste, old furniture). Industrial solid waste is the non-toxic trash from manufacturers, mines, and farms. **Hazardous** (or toxic) waste contains dangerous (pathogenic, corrosive, explosive, carcinogenic, chemically reactive, volatile, flammable) organic compounds and heavy metals. In developed countries, half of municipal solid waste goes to landfills and about 15% to incinerators. Only a third is composted or recycled. In many developing countries, municipal solid waste goes to open dumps. Integrated waste management combines disposal, recycling, and composting with reduction. Some experts think we could cut out 90% of our municipal solid waste through the four Rs:

- Refuse what you don't need.
- Reduce what you use, and press manufacturers to reduce packaging and use of resources.
- Reuse as much as possible.
- Recycle most of what is left.

Biodiversity

Biodiversity decreases when species become extinct, endangered, or threatened. These conditions can result from **overuse of a species** as a resource (food fishes), **overuse of resources** a species needs (water), or **resource competition** from alien species introduced purposely (marine toads, kudzu) or by mistake (zebra mussels). Biodiversity also decreases when niches and natural processes are lost because of **habitat loss**. Habitat is degraded when people pollute or divide large natural areas into small ones. Habitat is destroyed by deforestation and urban sprawl. One way to maintain our remaining biodiversity is to conserve habitat in acceptable nature reserves. For example, Costa Rica's reserves include areas for sustainable use by local people (hunting, gathering wood, farming) and for ecotourism and also separate areas where plants and animals are not disturbed.

The Convention on International Trade in Endangered Species of Wild Flora and Fauna (CITES), signed by 171 nations, outlaws distribution of organisms (or their parts) of species that are considered endangered or threatened.

Greenhouse Effect

The **greenhouse effect** is the warming of the Earth due to greenhouse gases (carbon dioxide, water vapor, methane, and nitrous oxide) in the troposphere. Without this effect, it would be too cold for life on Earth. However, humans' release of unnatural amounts of greenhouse gases into the air has increased the greenhouse effect and warmed the Earth's surface and troposphere by 0.74 degrees Celsius since 1906. This has caused melting of ancient ice, a rise in sea level (4–8 inches in the last century), and climate change (in distribution of rain and snow, in ambient temperatures and humidity, and in storm patterns). The Kyoto Protocol, signed by 189 nations by 2005, called for a decrease in and allowed trading of greenhouse gas emissions. In 1990, the Intergovernmental Panel on Climate Change began releasing its climate change assessment reports; these prompted many more to take climate change more seriously and engage in the Copenhagen Climate Change Conference of 2009.

Important Terms

- **Acute effect**: Immediate and short-term response (from slight discomfort to death)
- **Aquaculture**: Growing fish for consumption in contained bodies of water (ponds, rice paddies) or underwater cages. A third of the world's sea fish comes from aquaculture.
- **Biomagnification**: The increase in the amount of a toxin as it is passed up the food chain. For example, when three toxin-containing animals are eaten by an animal higher on the food chain, the predator stores the toxins from all three prey.
- **Bioremediation:** Conversion of hazardous wastes to other substances by the action of certain enzymes and bacteria
- **Carcinogen:** A chemical, radiation, or virus that causes cancer
- **Chronic effect**: Long-lasting response (like intellectual disabilities or cancer)

- **Cost-benefit analysis**: A weighing of the pros (better public health, higher-quality environment) and cons (traditional costs, external costs, missed opportunities) of an action as compared to taking no action. The ideal result of environmental cost-benefit analysis is that no one will be harmed and many will benefit.
- **Dose-response relationship**: The cause-and-effect connection between the amount (dose) of a substance that an organism takes into its body and the effect (response) in the organism. Both frequency and amount of exposure are important, as are individual characteristics.
- **Drift-net (also gillnet) fishing**: Fishing with long nets attached to buoys. Bycatch, or incidental capture, includes whales and turtles.
- **Environmental risk analysis**: The process of predicting the statistical probability of damage from a hazard to the environment or human health
- **Externalities**: External costs and benefits. They are parts of an economic exchange that are not usually considered and therefore not reflected in the stated price. The health effects of air pollution, for example, are external costs; they are not usually included in the price of kilowatt hours of electricity.
- **Hazardous chemical**: A chemical that can harm humans or animals by burning, exploding, interfering with respiration, irritating the skin, or causing an allergic reaction
- **Heat island**: An area with a higher temperature than its surroundings. Urban heat islands are caused by their construction from heat-retaining materials and the concentration of machines giving off exhaust heat.
- **Long line fishing**: Fishing with long lines fitted with many hooks set with bait. Bycatch includes sea mammals, seabirds, and turtles.
- **Marginal cost**: The cost of one more action or making one more product (change in cost over change in quantity)
- **Mutagen:** A chemical or radiation that causes changes in DNA molecules
- **Phytoremediation**: Filtering hazardous wastes out of the environment by the action of some plants
- **Planned development**: Development that results from considered and decided plans. A number of planned areas are green cities, in which car traffic is reduced, public transportation is very available, and there are common green spaces between areas of high-density housing and stores.
- **Primary air pollutant**: Harmful chemical that enters the air as a result of combustion or another process
- **Purse-seine fishing**: Fishing with circular nets held down at the bottom with weights and up at the top with floats. Tuna are typically caught by this method. Bycatch has included dolphins and turtles.
- **Secondary air pollutant**: Harmful chemical that forms when a primary air pollutant reacts with the air or another primary air pollutant
- **Smog:** Named for a combination of smoke and fog, smog is a combination of chemicals in the air. Photochemical smog, which includes ozone, forms from hydrocarbons and nitrogen oxides in sunlight.
- **Suburban sprawl, or urban sprawl**: More and more people moving from cities to suburbs. About half of Americans live in suburbs. Sprawl causes loss of agricultural lands, forests, grasslands, and wetlands. As suburbs grow, two or more may meet each other between cities, making a very large urban area called a megalopolis, like the one that goes from Boston to Washington, D.C.

- **Sustainability**: Ability to sustain life in our environment. Sustainability allows some kinds of economic growth but requires full-cost pricing. That is, external costs and marginal costs must be reflected in prices of goods and services.
- **Temperature inversion**: The reversal of the normal temperature change of air with elevation. In a temperature inversion, there is a layer of warmer air above cooler air near the Earth's surface. This situation can trap air pollutants near the ground.
- **Teratogen:** A chemical that causes birth defects in a fetus or embryo within someone taking in the chemical
- **Toxic chemical**: A chemical that can harm or kill humans or animals, for example, a poison, carcinogen, mutagen, or teratogen
- **Trawler fishing**: Fishing by pulling nets through the water. This method catches large marketable fish but also small fish and other creatures considered unusable, or bycatch. Nets dragged along the ocean bottom destroy habitat. Supertrawlers are huge ships with huge nets that can catch fish a mile beneath the surface.
- **Urbanization**: More and more people moving from rural to urban and suburban areas. For example, about 80% of people in the continental United States live on less than 2% of the land. About 200 years ago, only 5% lived in cities.

History and Impact of Science

Greenhouse Effect

The **greenhouse effect** refers to a naturally occurring and necessary process. **Greenhouse gases**, which are ozone, carbon dioxide, water vapor, and methane, trap infrared radiation that is reflected toward the atmosphere. Without the greenhouse effect, it is estimated that the temperature on Earth would be 30 degrees less on average. The problem occurs because human activity generates more greenhouse gases than necessary. Practices that increase the amount of greenhouse gases include the burning of natural gas and oil, farming practices that result in the release of methane and nitrous oxide, factory operations that produce gases, and deforestation practices that decrease the amount of oxygen available to offset greenhouse gases. Population growth also increases the volume of gases released. Excess greenhouse gases cause more infrared radiation to become trapped, which increases the temperature at the Earth's surface.

Ozone Depletion

Ultraviolet light breaks O_2 into two very reactive oxygen atoms with unpaired electrons, which are known as **free radicals**. A free radical of oxygen pairs with another oxygen molecule to form **ozone** (O_3). Ultraviolet light also breaks ozone (O_3) into O_2 and a free radical of oxygen. This process usually acts as an ultraviolet light filter for the planet. Other free radical catalysts are produced by natural phenomena such as volcanic eruptions and by human activities. When these enter the atmosphere, they disrupt the normal cycle by breaking down ozone so it cannot absorb more ultraviolet radiation. One such catalyst is the chlorine in chlorofluorocarbons (CFCs). CFCs were used as aerosols and refrigerants. When a CFC like CF_2Cl_2 is broken down in the atmosphere, chlorine free radicals are produced. These act as catalysts to break down ozone. Whether a chlorine free radical reacts with an ozone or oxygen molecule, it is able to react again.

Human Impacts on Ecosystems

Human impacts on **ecosystems** take many forms and have many causes. They include widespread disruptions and specific niche disturbances. Humans practice many forms of **environmental manipulation** that affect plants and animals in many biomes and ecosystems. Many human practices involve the consumption of natural resources for food and energy production, the changing of the environment to produce food and energy, and the intrusion on ecosystems to provide shelter. These general behaviors include a multitude of specific behaviors, including the use and overuse of pesticides, the encroachment upon habitat, over hunting and over fishing, the introduction of plant and animal species into non-native ecosystems, and the introduction of hazardous wastes and chemical byproducts into the environment. These behaviors have led to a number of consequences, such as acid rain, ozone depletion, deforestation, urbanization, accelerated species loss, genetic abnormalities, endocrine disruption in populations, and harm to individual animals.

Global Warming

Global warming may cause the permanent loss of glaciers and permafrost. There might also be increases in air pollution and acid rain. Rising temperatures may lead to an increase in sea levels as polar ice melts, lower amounts of available fresh water as coastal areas flood, species extinction because of changes in habitat, increases in certain diseases, and a decreased standard of living for humans. Less fresh water and losses of habitat for humans and other species can also lead to decreased agricultural production and food supply shortages. Increased desertification leads to habitat loss for humans and other species. There may be more moisture in the atmosphere due to evaporation.

Acid Rain and Eutrophication

Acid rain is made up water droplets for which the pH has been lowered due atmospheric pollution. The common sources of this pollution are **sulfur** and **nitrogen** that have been released through the burning of fossil fuels. This can lead to a lowering of the pH of lakes and ponds, thereby destroying aquatic life, or damaging the leaves and bark of trees. It can also destroy buildings, monuments, and statues made of rock.

Eutrophication is the depletion of oxygen in a body of water. It may be caused by an increase in the amount of nutrients, particularly **phosphates**, which leads to an increase in plant and algae life that use up the oxygen. The result is a decrease in water quality and death of aquatic life. Sources of excess phosphates may be detergents, industrial run-off, or fertilizers that are washed into lakes or streams.

Waste Disposal Methods

- Landfills – **Methane** (CH_4) is a greenhouse gas emitted from landfills. Some is used to generate electricity and some gets into the atmosphere. CO_2 is also emitted, and landfill gas can contain nitrogen, oxygen, water vapor, sulfur, mercury, and radioactive contaminants such as tritium. **Landfill leachate** contains acids from car batteries, solvents, heavy metals, pesticides, motor oil, paint, household cleaning supplies, plastics, and many other potentially harmful substances. Some of these are dangerous when they get into the ecosystem.
- Incinerators – These contribute to air pollution in that they can release nitric and sulfuric oxides, which cause **acid rain**.
- Sewage – When dumped in raw form into oceans, sewage can introduce **fecal contaminants** and **pathogenic organisms**, which can harm ocean life and cause disease in humans.

Effects of Consumerism

Economic growth and quality of living are associated with a wasteful cycle of production. Goods are produced as cheaply as possible with little or no regard for the **ecological effects**. The ultimate goal is profitability. The production process is wasteful, and often introduces **hazardous byproducts** into the environment. Furthermore, byproducts may be dumped into a landfill instead of recycled. When consumer products get dumped in landfills, they can leach **contamination** into groundwater. Landfills can also leach gases. These are or have been dumping grounds for illegal substances, business and government waste, construction industry waste, and medical waste. These items also get dumped at illegal dump sites in urban and remote areas.

Ethical and Moral Concerns

Ethical and moral concerns related to genetic engineering arise in the scientific community and in smaller communities within society. Religious and moral beliefs can conflict with the economic interests of businesses, and with research methods used by the scientific community. For example, the United States government allows genes to be patented. A company has patented the gene for breast and ovarian cancer and will only make it available to researchers for a fee. This leads to a decrease in research, a decrease in medical solutions, and possibly an increase in the occurrence of breast and ovarian cancers. The possibility of lateral or incidental discoveries as a result of research is also limited. For example, a researcher working on a genetic solution to treat breast cancer might accidentally discover a cure for prostate cancer. This, however, would not occur if the researcher could not use the patented gene in the first place.

Energy Production

- **Coal-fired power plants**: These generate electricity fairly cheaply, but are the largest source of **greenhouse gases**.
- **Gasoline**: Gasoline is cheap, generates less CO_2 than coal, and requires less water than coal. But it nevertheless releases a substantial amount of CO_2 in the aggregate and is a limited resource. The burning of gas and other fossil fuels releases carbon dioxide (a greenhouse gas) into the atmosphere.
- **Nuclear power plants**: A small nuclear power plant can cheaply produce a large amount of electricity. But the waste is potentially harmful and a substantial amount of **water** is required to generate electricity. The cost of storing and transporting the **radioactive waste** is also very large.
- **Hydropower**: Hydropower is sustainable and environmentally benign once established. A disadvantage is that the building of a dam and the re-routing of a river can be very **environmentally disruptive**.
- **Wind power**: Wind power is sustainable, non-polluting, and requires little to no cooling water. But it will not produce power in the absence of **wind** and requires a large area over which the turbines can be laid out.
- **Solar power**: Solar power is sustainable, can be used for a single house or building, and generates peak energy during times of peak usage. But production is limited to when the sun is shining, the panels themselves are expensive to make, and making the panels generates harmful **toxins**.
- **Geothermal power:** Geothermal power is sustainable, relatively cheap, and non-polluting. Disadvantages are that it can only be utilized in areas with specific **volcanic activity**.

Remote Sensing

Remote sensing refers to the gathering of data about an object or phenomenon without physical or intimate contact with the object being studied. The data can be viewed or recorded and stored in many forms (visually with a camera, audibly, or in the form of data). Gathering weather data from a ship, satellite, or buoy might be thought of as remote sensing. The monitoring of a fetus through the use of ultrasound technology provides a remote image. Listening to the heartbeat of a fetus is another example of remote sensing. Methods for remote sensing can be grouped as radiometric, geodetic, or acoustic. Examples of **radiometric remote sensing** include radar, laser altimeters, light detection and ranging (LIDAR) used to determine the concentration of chemicals in the air, and radiometers used to detect various frequencies of radiation. **Geodetic remote sensing** involves measuring the small fluctuations in Earth's gravitational field. Examples of **acoustic remote sensing** include underwater sonar and seismographs.

CELL PHONES AND GPS

A **cell phone** uses **radio waves** to communicate information. When speaking into a cell phone, the user's voice is converted into an electrical signal which is transmitted via radio waves to a cell tower, then to a satellite, then to a cell tower near the recipient, and then to the recipient's cell phone. The recipient's cell phone converts the digital signal back into an electrical signal.

A similar process occurs when data is transmitted over the **Internet** via a wireless network. The cell phone will convert any outgoing communication into a radio wave that will be sent to a wireless router. The router is "wireless" in the sense that the router is not wired to the phone. But the router is connected to the Internet via a cable. The router converts the radio signal into digital form and sends the communication through the Internet. The same basic process also occurs when a cell phone receives information from the Internet.

Wireless networks use radio frequencies of 2.4 GHz or 5 GHz.

Global Positioning System (GPS) is a system of **satellites** that orbit the Earth and communicate with mobile devices to pinpoint the mobile device's **position**. This is accomplished by determining the distance between the mobile device and at least three satellites. A mobile device might calculate a distance of 400 miles between it and the first satellite. The possible locations that are 400 miles from the first satellite and the mobile device will fall along a circle. The possible locations on Earth relative to the other two satellites will fall somewhere along different circles. The point on Earth at which these three circles intersect is the location of the mobile device. The process of determining position based on distance measurements from three satellites is called **trilateration**.

Effects of Natural Processes on Climate Change

NATURAL PROCESSES THAT IMPACT THE CLIMATE

Many natural processes have extreme effects on Earth systems.

- **Volcanic eruptions** have largely short-term effects on global temperature due to the emissions of ash and CO_2, which affect how sunlight is absorbed and reflected in the atmosphere.
- **Asteroids** usually burn up in the atmosphere, but impacts of significant sizes can cause similar effects to that of volcanos, such as introducing chemicals into the atmosphere or severely damaging ecosystems.
- **Ocean currents** and **subsurface processes** within the earth also can change how temperature variation is distributed across the Earth.
- **Magmatic cycles** of temperature change cause surface level heating and cooling, referred to as **El Nino** (heating) and **La Nina** (cooling).
- **Solar variations** usually come in cycles which also have powerful effects on the temperature of the planet. These temperature changes affect the temperature of the climate directly, but also influence systems such as weather, oceanic currents, and ecological systems.

Chapter Quiz

Ready to see how well you retained what you just read? Scan the QR code to go directly to the chapter quiz interface for this study guide. If you're using a computer, simply visit the online resources page at **mometrix.com/resources719/osatearsci108** and click the Chapter Quizzes link.

Pedagogical Content Knowledge

Developing Scientific Understanding

Scientific understanding involves not merely the knowledge of scientific theories and equations, but a comprehension of how science is done, how we come to know these theories (and how confident we are in them), and how the different domains of science fit together. Students are unlikely to develop a good scientific understanding merely by being presented with isolated facts. Rather, research suggests that a scientific understanding is best fostered by **inquiry** and by **problem-based learning** approaches, which help students develop their own critical thinking and reasoning skills. In these methods, students are not just provided with facts and theories to memorize but are led to "discover" principles on their own, through experimentation and analogy. The instructor must still provide guidance in the process; if students are completely left to their own devices they may be confused or arrive at incorrect conclusions that may do more harm than good. Furthermore, assessments used in the classroom should promote **higher-order learning**, focusing not just on repetition of facts but on reasoning and evaluation of claims. It is critical that students understand that science is a process and a way of knowing, not a collection of facts.

Prior Knowledge

Students vary in their prior knowledge and capabilities, and science instruction is not a one-size-fits-all process. Sometimes prior knowledge helps student, in that they already have some knowledge about the subject in question, but sometimes prior knowledge may seem to conflict with the new information being taught—a dilemma sometimes called the "**paradox of continuity**." Learning therefore can require a **conceptual change**, in a way that allows the students to reformulate their understanding to fit new information.

Students' experience and developmental characteristics can also affect their science learning. Some students learn more effectively through different **learning styles**, or modalities: some learn best from what they see (**visual learners**), others from what they hear (**auditory learners**), still others from handling objects (**tactile learners**), and others from active participation (**kinesthetic learners**). **Abstract thinking** develops during adolescence and may develop more rapidly in some students than others; students who have not fully developed this capability may benefit from more structured teaching methods. Adolescents tend to be at a stage in their social development in which they learn well in cooperative group activities.

Planning Activities

Instructors should be aware of and sensitive to students' different preferred styles of learning and prepare lessons that engage all these styles. The instructor should also try to tie lessons to students' individual interests in order to promote active engagement. A **positive learning environment** is one that adapts to students' individual needs and that often involves students working cooperatively.

In science in particular it's important for instructors not to exclude women and minorities, since they have been excluded so much in the past that it's easy to do so unconsciously. The instructor should make an effort to mention scientists of different ethnicities and genders and make it clear that women and minorities can be and are capable scientists.

Students currently learning English have their own needs that must be addressed. The instructor can help English learners, for instance, by speaking slowly and clearly, by writing down and providing definitions of key terms, by using visual aids and graphic organizers (which also may help visual learners who are not English language learners), and by giving access to translating devices if necessary. English learners can also benefit from working in groups with capable English speakers who can help explain instructions and procedures they don't understand.

Motivation and Engagement

Regardless of how clearly and accurately an instructor explains the topic, the students may not learn if they're unengaged and not paying attention. Therefore, it's important for the teacher to engage the students' interest and keep their attention. One of the advantages of inquiry-based learning is that it actively involves the students and keeps them more engaged by relating the topic to their interests and goals and finding ways to tie the topics in to the students' own experiences, prior knowledge, and daily lives. This requires the teacher to get to know the students and their interests, but this has other benefits as well: the students are also more engaged when there is a good relationship between the teachers and students.

Students also tend to be more engaged by collaborative group activities than by working on their own. Adolescents are at a stage in their social development in which they are increasingly driven to form social attachments with their peers. They are comfortable working in groups and benefit from collaborative learning environments.

Texts Used in the Classroom

Science instruction often involves the students acquiring information from textbooks and handouts, but not all students may be able to effectively use these texts without guidance. Most textbooks have various features designed to make it easier to locate information: an **index**, a **table of contents**, and often a **glossary** and/or a list of important variables and formulas. An instructor can explain how to use these features at the beginning of the year and perhaps even assign an activity that involves making use of them.

It may also be helpful to teach **active reading** techniques. One such technique is **pre-reading**—skimming and reading the headings before reading the text in depth, making predictions and building background knowledge. The instructor can also encourage active reading techniques through providing graphic organizers or techniques like **SQ3R**—a method that involves the student first Surveying the chapter, then formulating Questions about each section, then Reading the section, Reciting the main ideas (putting them in their own words), and Reviewing the material.

In the modern classroom, textbooks aren't the only kind of text that students can take advantage of. An effective teacher can also show students how to find information online, through web searches and reference sites.

Total School Program

While the science teachers plan the curriculum for their classes, they must also be aware of the **total school program**—the overall objectives for the students' learning in all subjects. The science teacher must be aware of school-wide objectives, and make sure that they are being adequately met in his or her class. The science instructor may also have a role in *setting* those objectives, in conjunction with other teachers and administrators; the science instructor in this case should work cooperatively with the rest of the team and ensure that any issues unique or important to the science classroom are properly addressed and incorporated into the objectives.

The science teacher must also be mindful of the statewide objectives. State standards lay out the curriculum requirements for the course and specify topics that must be covered. Students must master these topics to be ready not only for standardized exams, but to ensure that no gaps in understanding exist prior to advancing to the next grade-level.

Supportive Learning Environment

Creating a learning environment that supports student inquiries involves both setting certain procedures and expectations in the class and providing resources that lend themselves to inquiry-based learning. To encourage inquiry-based learning, the instructor should encourage students to ask questions, but try to guide them toward finding answers for themselves rather than giving direct answers to their questions. The instructor should pose questions that require higher-order thinking rather than rote recall or yes or no answers and include a time for reflection in each lesson. Lessons in inquiry-based classrooms are centered around projects and experiments rather than lectures—in fact, one increasingly popular technique is to "**flip the classroom**," having the students read the lesson or watch video lectures you provide as their homework and freeing up class time for discussion and analysis.

An inquiry-centered classroom environment should put a priority on student collaboration. The instructor should give the students assignments that involve their working together as much as practical. It is helpful to have some online resources that facilitate collaboration and sharing of information, such as a class website, and perhaps a class blog and wiki. Many online resources allow students to share documents and work on them together.

Participation in Scientific Investigation

Scientific investigations are an important part of science teaching, and it is vital that all students are given the opportunity to participate. Ideally, there will be enough space and equipment for the students to work in small groups on an experiment, but in practice this may not be possible. In this case, one solution is to have rotating stations in the classroom, where for one day or for part of the period one group works on one experiment, while another group works on a different activity that uses different equipment; as they rotate through the different stations, all the students will have the opportunity to do every activity, just not in the same order.

Another important part of making it possible for all students to participate in scientific investigations is to ensure that they all have the means to understand and carry out the instructions. Going over the procedure in a lecture may not be enough; it may be better to have a written handout and/or a screencast that the students can watch and refer back to as needed. Students with special needs must also be accommodated; for instance, English language learners can be given definitions of key terms.

Active Learning, Inquiry, and Reflection

Active learning and inquiry-based learning are two related pedagogical techniques that have been shown by research to be effective in teaching science. **Active learning** refers to teaching by making the student an active participant in the learning process. A class in which the instructor lectures, the students take notes, and the students later demonstrate their learning of the topic by taking a written exam is *not* engaged in active learning, and is not likely to be as effective. Active learning can include experiments that the students perform, interactive online simulations of processes that they can't physically experience in the classroom, and having the students create presentations and projects rather than have exams and worksheets as the main assessments.

Inquiry-based learning is a form of teaching by asking questions, having discussions, and helping students do their own research rather than just presenting them with lists of facts and formulas to be learned. Inquiry-based learning is effective not only because it involves the students directly, but because allowing them to formulate their own questions engages their curiosity and critical thinking. **Reflection** is also an important part of inquiry-based learning, having students think back on what they learned and how they learned it.

Modeling Scientific Thought

Modeling, in a pedagogical context, refers to *showing* the students what they should do, rather than telling them. This doesn't mean just demonstrating an activity at the front of the classroom while the students watch passively; effective modeling also involves the students as active participants. The important thing is that the teacher sets an example of the principles he or she wants to convey.

To model scientific attitudes, therefore, means to demonstrate and embody those attitudes. To instill curiosity and skepticism in students, the teacher should display those attributes. If the teacher doesn't know the answer to a question, the teacher should not be afraid to say "I don't know"—but should follow that by trying to find the answer, by looking it up online or by performing an experiment. When discussing a topic and coming up with questions about it, the instructor should come up with questions as well—ideally questions the instructor honestly doesn't know the answer to. On the other hand, the instructor should not be too quick to accept answers—not, for instance, immediately latching onto the first answer found online, but looking for multiple sources of information and analyzing their credibility.

Inquiry-Based Scientific Investigation

An **inquiry-based scientific investigation** is one that follows the **scientific method**. While the scientific method is often formalized in different ways, there are some essential aspects. The investigator formulates a specific **question** that the investigation will answer. Usually this question is based on an **observation** that the investigation is intended to explain. The investigator then does some background **research**, reviewing previously published information on the subject in question. For a professional scientist, this will usually involve reading articles in scientific journals; in a classroom setting, a web search may suffice. The investigator may formulate a **hypothesis**—a proposed possible answer to the question.

The investigator decides how to **gather evidence** to find an answer to the question and prove or disprove the hypothesis, designing an **experiment** that will test the hypothesis, and selecting the proper tools to carry it out. The investigator makes **predictions** as to what will happen in the experiment if the hypothesis is true or if it is not. The investigator then carries out the experiment, gathers data, and analyzes the results, drawing **conclusions** based on the data.

There remain other important steps: **communication** of the results to others, defending the results, and possibly formulating further questions.

Formulating Scientific Questions

Formulating scientific questions is an important part of an inquiry-based investigation; an investigation starts with a specific question, and then an experiment is designed to answer that question. The question usually is based on an observation: the student observes a phenomenon and then formulates a question about what was observed. The question should be as concrete, objective, quantitative, and measurable as possible. "Why did this object move?" is a vague and abstract question that cannot be easily answered. "Did this object move because of this force?" is more concrete. "What is the relationship between this force and the motion of this object?" is a good quantitative question that can potentially be answered by experiment.

To help the student to formulate a question, the instructor can first guide students through an observation, encouraging the students to think of anything about the observation they're curious about or that they don't understand. The instructor can then help the students come up with questions addressing the subject of their curiosity, and then gradually guide the students into making the questions more specific and measurable.

Hypotheses

The **hypothesis** is an educated guess as to the answer to the central question of a scientific investigation. It is an important part of the investigation because it helps guide the inquiry and suggest specific lines of investigation that can prove or disprove the hypothesis: the experiment at the heart of the investigation should be designed such that it will have different results depending on whether or not the hypothesis is correct.

It is important that the hypothesis is an *educated* guess; the student may not know the answer to the question, but there should be some basis for choosing the hypothesis—by extrapolation from known cases, or by analogy with similar scenarios. If the student has trouble coming up with a hypothesis, the instructor might prompt the student to think of similar situations the student understands better, or to research such situations that have been investigated before, and then to consider what those situations imply about the present question. Even a very loose analogy can be enough to make a hypothesis—for the purposes of the investigation, it doesn't matter that the student chooses a hypothesis that turns out to be *right*, only that it relates to the question.

Scientific Results

There are many methods that can be used to analyze and evaluate scientific results. Often **graphs** help investigators and readers visualize data better. If one variable is plotted against another and the points seem to form a straight line, that is evidence that a linear relationship may exist between these variables; if they form a parabola, they may have a quadratic relationship; and so on. In more advanced classes, **statistical methods** may be useful, from methods as simple as taking the **mean** of multiple measurements and comparing the means of sets of data rather than the individual points, to methods as complex as calculating **standard deviations** and **correlation coefficients**. All of these methods help show the relationships between quantities and can help to evaluate possible explanations of a result.

Error analysis is another important part of evaluating results. Students should have an idea of what possible sources of error exist in the experiment, and whether they are **random** or **systematic**. Random error can be identified by taking repeated measurements and seeing how close they are; identifying systematic error involves a more thoughtful consideration of what could lead results to be off in one direction or the other.

Higher-Level Thinking Skills

Students should be encouraged to engage in not just rote memorization and learning of procedures, but in higher-order thinking as well that involves putting together what they've learned in constructive ways. The most commonly used model of different levels of thinking in education is **Bloom's taxonomy**, which divides cognitive processes into six categories or levels. The lowest level, **Remember**, involves simple recall of data. The next, **Understand**, requires students to be able to explain or discuss concepts in their own words. Then come **Apply**, using the concepts in practice; **Analyze**, drawing connections and comparisons between ideas; **Evaluate**, judging and justifying ideas; and **Create**, synthesizing something new from the concepts.

It's easy to design activities that utilize the lower levels of Bloom's Taxonomy. Engaging the higher orders of thinking is more difficult, but it is important for developing a more thorough understanding of a topic. Some verbs commonly associated with each level of Bloom's Taxonomy give clues as to how to promote them. "Create", for example, is associated with the verbs "construct," "plan," and "design" (among others)—certainly designing an experiment to answer a specific question fits here. "Evaluate" is associated with "appraise," "argue," and "justify"—students could be asked to assess a scientific claim and argue for or against it.

Systematic Observations and Measurements

In a scientific investigation, observations are not haphazard; there are certain systematic principles that must be followed for useful observations. As far as possible, the observations should be **quantitative**; there should be some measured value recorded, and not simply a qualitative observation such as "it is longer". Measurements should be taken by a consistent method and recorded with proper units—and with an estimate of their **uncertainty**. A measurement taken with a meter stick with markings every millimeter, for instance, has an uncertainty of ±0.5 mm.

It is also important when making observations to vary only one quantity at a time. If you want to measure how a plant's growth is affected by temperature and by amount of light, it isn't useful to change both factors for each measurement—that would make it impossible to see how much of the effect was produced by each change. Rather, it is better to do at least one set of measurements in which the temperature is held constant and the amount of light is changed, and another where the reverse is true, so that the effects of each factor can be isolated. In many cases, an **experimental control** is also desirable.

Students' Prior Knowledge

Prior knowledge refers to the knowledge the student has about the subject matter before it's covered in class. This may come from previous classes, from books and television, from peers or parents, from experience, or from other sources. It's useful to know what prior knowledge students possess before the lesson begins, and there are a number of ways of finding out. One way is through **formative assessments**, assessments that are designed not to test what the student has learned but to test what the students already know in order to guide lesson planning. Another popular way of testing prior knowledge is a **K-W-L chart**, in which students write down what they *know* about the topic, what they *want* to know, and, after the lesson, what they *learned*.

The instructor can use the students' prior knowledge as a starting point for the lesson; having the students share what they already know can help introduce the topic. Prior knowledge may also guide the instructor's approach to the topic, since it may carry some assumptions or preconceptions that will affect the way the student might react to different presentations. In some cases, prior knowledge may even lead to misconceptions that must be overcome.

Performance in Inquiry-Based Investigations

The stereotypical classroom assessment may be a multiple-choice quiz, but this is not generally the most effective way of assessing student learning in an inquiry-based classroom. There may be a place for written exams as summative assessments, but more effective assessment methods will engage students' higher-order thinking processes and may involve collaboration and active participation.

For example, in a science class, a lab report can be a useful assessment; after performing an experiment, students may be asked to turn in a written account of the procedure and results. Along similar lines, a laboratory journal that students keep during an experiment can also be used for assessment, or a field journal for longer-term projects. The instructor may require students to compile all their work in a portfolio, to be turned in at the end of the semester or at shorter intervals; this can serve as a summative assessment in lieu of or in addition to a traditional exam. To assess the student's participation in a classroom activity as objectively as possible, rather than make a subjective judgment call the instructor can use checklists or a detailed rubric prepared ahead of time.

Assessment and Instruction

An **assessment** is an activity designed to measure students' knowledge, learning, or abilities, such as an exam. Assessments are not limited to testing how much the student has learned after a lesson; there are also formative assessments used before or during a lesson to test the student's prior knowledge and how well they are learning the topic.

There are important relationships between assessment and instruction, and the two must be designed together. Formative assessments guide instruction, since the instructor should take into account students' prior knowledge in planning a lesson, and if a formative assessment shows that students are not learning what the instructor expects, the instructor should use that information to try a different pedagogical approach. As for summative assessments, they should be designed to match the learning objectives; the instructor should make sure that the summative assessment is designed to test that the students have met the specific instructional goals of the lessons.

Ongoing Assessment

Ongoing assessment is vital in science instruction for several reasons. For one thing, formative assessments are important so that the instructor can be informed of the students' prior knowledge and plan the lesson accordingly. If the instructor learns from a formative assessment that the students lack some prior knowledge necessary to the lesson, then the instructor will have to be sure to cover that first; if the instructor learns that the students have a significant misconception about the topic, then the instructor may have to plan for a conceptual change. During the lesson, further formative assessments can monitor students' learning and inform the instructor whether the students are absorbing the information and methodologies that the instructor intends them to absorb, or whether the pace of the lesson should be changed or different pedagogical methods adopted.

Ongoing assessments can also benefit the students by reinforcing the subject matter. The assessments give the students another opportunity to put what they have learned to use, and may help them better retain it. They also give the students an idea of how well they are learning, and what topics they might need to review or about which they should ask more questions.

Types of Assessments

Assessments are divided into two main categories: **summative assessments** that measure how well students have learned the subject matter at the end of a unit, and **formative assessments** that are used before or during a lesson to test the student's prior knowledge and how well they are learning the topic. Both these types of assessment are important, and both can be carried out in a number of ways. Assessments can also be **formal**—data-driven, standardized assessments the results of which can be compared against preset benchmarks—or **informal**—less structured assessments based around performance and content. An effective science classroom utilizes a variety of different assessment methods.

For example, a **performance assessment** is an assessment that requires the student to demonstrate skills by completing a task, rather than by selecting a pre-set answer or filling in a blank. A **self-assessment** is an activity in which the student assesses his or her own work, perhaps using a rubric provided by the instructor; these are often not graded and serve to inform the student of his or her own learning. A **peer assessment** is an activity in which the student's work is assessed not by the instructor, but by a fellow student.

Review Video: Formative and Summative Assessments
Visit mometrix.com/academy and enter code: 804991

Combatting Misconceptions

One of the reasons it's important to gauge students' prior knowledge of a topic is because some of that prior knowledge may be incorrect or misleading, and the student may have misconceptions about the topic that must be overcome. Simply telling the students that their prior beliefs were incorrect is unlikely to be effective, and it may in fact be counterproductive, leading to their misconceptions being reinforced instead of removed. Rather, a better goal is to bring about a **conceptual change**, a gradual revision and rearrangement of prior knowledge to accommodate new ideas, in which the student is an active participant.

There are several research-based methods of bringing about conceptual change. One method is to promote **cognitive conflict**: presenting data or demonstrations that contradict the students' prior conceptions, and guiding the students into finding a resolution to the conflict. Another is the use of **refutational texts** that discuss and refute various views on the topic. Other methods include **collaborative argumentation**, in which students are encouraged to discuss, defend, and evaluate their positions; and **persuasive pedagogy**, applying methods of persuasion such as response shaping and reinforcing.

Reliability and Validity

Two measurements of the soundness of an assessment are reliability and validity. An assessment is **reliable** if it yields consistent results; students' scores on the assessment should not depend on external circumstances and should be similar for different questions that test the same skill. An assessment is **valid** if it measures what it is meant to measure. These two qualities can vary independently; it is possible for an exam to have a high reliability but a low validity, or vice versa.

The reliability of an assessment can be affected by many factors. Longer tests tend to be more reliable; tests with a short time limit so that many students cannot complete all the questions, or must rush to do so, tend to be less reliable. Reliability is also affected by difficulty; a test is most reliable when the questions are not so easy that almost every student answers the questions correctly, but not so hard that almost none do. It requires finding a suitable middle ground of difficulty. An assessment will tend to be more valid if it is designed to cover all the material that it is supposed to cover, but only that material. It will be less valid if it has hidden biases against certain categories of student.

Assessment as a Learning Experience

Though an obvious purpose of assessments is to allow the instructor to assign students a grade in the class, the assessments themselves can provide learning experiences. For one thing, as the students see what questions on the assessment they are unable to answer, or do not answer correctly, this helps them see what topics they have not fully learned and may need to further review. On the other hand, the questions that the students got right will help build their confidence and perhaps help them better remember in the future what they learned about those topics. Assessments also give students further practice with the methods and concepts they are testing, which may further work to reinforce them. They may also help students to learn new problem-solving strategies; as students go over the assessment after the fact and discuss how they were supposed to solve a particular problem, the answer might give them information about a strategy they were previously unaware of or underutilizing.

Equitable Use of Assessments

One important consideration that must be kept in mind in designing assessments is that they must be **equitable**—they must not be biased toward or against any part of the student population. Every student must have an adequate opportunity to demonstrate his or her skills and knowledge. There are many biases that may carelessly enter into assessments: cultural biases, language biases, biases against students with special needs.

There are a number of steps that instructors can take to ensure that assessments are equitable. Questions should not rely on "common knowledge" that may not be common to students of different cultures. Students with special needs must be provided with adequate accommodations. English language learners should be given definitions or paraphrases of difficult words and sentences. Other steps that can be taken toward making assessments more equitable include clearly laying out learning outcomes and grading rubrics, using many different methods of assessment that allow students to show their accomplishments in different ways, and ensuring that the subject matter covered in assessments is closely matched to what the instructor teaches in class.

Sharing Criteria and Results

It's important to share the evaluation criteria of assessments with students so that the students will know what to expect from the assessments and prepare accordingly, and so that during the assessment they will know where to best focus their time and attention. If the students have no idea how an assessment will be graded, then the assessment is not fair or equitable; students will not know what aspects of the assessment they should focus on the most and doing well on the assessment may be largely a matter of luck. Sharing the rubric for the assessment ahead of time makes the instructor's expectations clear and ensures that the students know what specifically they will be tested on and can prepare accordingly.

It is also important to share the results of assessments with the students. If the students know the results of their assessments, they can gauge their own progress and learning, and decide where they need to focus in the future and what topics they may need to revisit. Knowing their assessment results may also help students evaluate their study strategies and judge whether or not they are working and how or if they might need to be revised.

Scientific Inquiry Skills for Elementary Students

The six abilities that **grades K-4 students** should acquire are as follows:

- They should be able to ask questions about objects, organisms, and events in the environment.
- They should be able to devise a simple investigation to answer a question.
- They should be able to use tools such as magnifying glasses, rulers, and balances to gather data and make observations.
- They should be able to use the gathered data and observations to provide an explanation.
- They should be able to talk about, draw pictures, or use another method to communicate the results of an investigation and what they learned.
- With respect to the nature of scientific inquiry and scientists, students should understand that investigations involve formulating questions and answers, using different methods of discovering and disclosing answers, using basic tools, observing, sharing answers, and looking at and understanding others' work.

SCIENTIFIC INQUIRY SKILLS FOR MIDDLE GRADE STUDENTS

The five abilities that **grades 5–8 students** should acquire are as follows:

- They should be able to reformulate and clarify questions until they can be answered through scientific investigation.
- They should be able to create and carry out a scientific investigation, interpret the data to provide explanations, and use further data to revise explanations.
- They should be able to identify the tools necessary to gather and analyze data. They should be able to use computer hardware and software to store, organize, and gather data.
- They should be able to provide descriptions and explanations, create models, and make predictions based on the body of knowledge they possess.
- They should be able to explain cause and effect relationships using explanations and data from experiments.

SCIENTIFIC INQUIRY SKILLS FOR OLDER STUDENTS

The six abilities that **grades 9–12 students** should acquire are as follows:

- They should be able to identify questions and concepts that guide scientific investigation. In other words, they should be able to create a hypothesis and an appropriate experiment to test that hypothesis.
- They should be able to design and conduct a scientific investigation from start to finish. This includes being able to guide the inquiry by choosing the proper technologies and methods, determining variables, selecting an appropriate method for presenting data, and conducting peer review.
- They should be able to use technology and mathematics in investigations.
- They should be able to formulate and revise scientific explanations and models.
- They should be able to recognize and analyze alternative explanations. In other words, they should be able to devise other possibilities based on the current body of knowledge.
- They should be able to communicate and defend a scientific argument in both written and oral form.

Chapter Quiz

Ready to see how well you retained what you just read? Scan the QR code to go directly to the chapter quiz interface for this study guide. If you're using a computer, simply visit the online resources page at **mometrix.com/resources719/osatearsci108** and click the Chapter Quizzes link.

OSAT Practice Test

Want to take this practice test in an online interactive format?
Check out the online resources page, which includes interactive practice questions and much more: **mometrix.com/resources719/osatearsci108**

1. Which of the following statements correctly compares rocks and minerals?

a. Minerals may contain traces of organic compounds, while rocks do not.
b. Rocks are classified by their formation and the minerals they contain, while minerals are classified by their chemical composition and physical properties.
c. Both rocks and minerals can be polymorphs.
d. Both rocks and minerals may contain mineraloids.

2. Which of the following is the best description of mineraloids?

a. Mineraloids are organic compounds found in rocks.
b. Mineraloids are inorganic solids with the same chemical composition but with different crystalline structures.
c. Mineraloids are inorganic solids containing one or more minerals with the same crystalline structure.
d. Mineraloids are similar to minerals, but they lack a crystalline structure.

3. All of the following are branches of petrology EXCEPT:

a. Metamorphic petrology
b. Igneous petrology
c. Mineralogical petrology
d. Sedimentary petrology

4. Which of the following is NOT one of the five major physical properties of minerals?

a. Chemical composition
b. Hardness
c. Luster
d. Streak

5. Which of these minerals would have the lowest score on the Mohs scale?

a. Gypsum
b. Fluorite
c. Talc
d. Diamond

6. A mineral's true color is observed by:

a. Conducting a streak test on white paper
b. Conducting a streak test on unglazed porcelain tile
c. Inspecting the mineral's outer surface
d. Shining a light on the mineral to inspect its luster

7. Galena, pyrite, and magnetite are examples of minerals with which of the following types of luster?

a. Pearly
b. Greasy
c. Adamantine
d. Metallic

8. According to the Dana classification system, gold, silver, and copper belong to which class?

a. Organic
b. Elemental
c. Oxide
d. Sulfide

9. According to the Dana classification system, minerals that contain the anion SO_4^{2-} are part of which chemical class?

a. Sulfate
b. Sulfite
c. Halide
d. Phosphate

10. Minerals that form on the sea floor from discarded shells are most likely part of which chemical class?

a. Sulfate
b. Organic
c. Carbonate
d. Silicate

11. The lithification process results in the formation of which of the following types of rocks?

a. Sedimentary
b. Intrusive igneous
c. Extrusive igneous
d. Metamorphic

12. Which of the following types of rock solidifies deepest beneath the Earth's surface?

a. Hypabyssal
b. Plutonic
c. Volcanic
d. Detrital

13. Which of the following factors directly contributes to soil erosion?

a. Air pollution from cars and factories
b. Use of pesticides
c. Deforestation and overgrazing
d. Water pollution caused by excess sedimentation

14. Physical weathering of rocks can be caused by all of the following EXCEPT:

a. The freezing and thawing of water on the surface of rocks
b. Changes in temperature
c. Oxidation
d. Changes in pressure due to the removal of overlying rocks

15. Which of the following is NOT an example of chemical weathering of rocks?

a. Highly acidic rainwater causes dissolution of rocks.
b. Anhydrous minerals in rocks absorb water, causing them to enlarge and create fractures within the rocks.
c. Salt water penetrates fractures in rocks and leaves behind salt crystals that cause fractures.
d. Iron atoms in rocks react with atmospheric oxygen, which causes oxidation.

16. Which of the following lists several phases of the sedimentary cycle in the correct order?

a. Erosion, weathering, transportation, deposition
b. Weathering, erosion, deposition, transportation
c. Weathering, deposition, erosion, transportation
d. Weathering, erosion, transportation, deposition

17. Which of the following is required for the process of diagenesis (also called lithification)?

a. Magma
b. Water
c. Wind
d. Sulfur

18. Nondetrital sedimentary rock is produced by:

a. Chemical precipitation.
b. Cooling of magma just below the Earth's surface.
c. Physical weathering processes.
d. Weathering of igneous rock.

19. Leaching in the "A" soil horizon results from:

a. The accumulation of cations in the "B" horizon.
b. The accumulation of cations in the "O" horizon.
c. Contact with acid solutions generated in the "O" horizon.
d. Contact with acid solutions generated in the "B" horizon.

20. Which of the following statements is true of minerals (such as olivine) that are found at the top of Bowen's reaction series?

a. They are classified as metamorphic.
b. They weather more quickly than rocks found lower in the series.
c. They crystallize at lower temperatures than rocks found at the bottom of the series.
d. They can only be made artificially.

21. Metamorphic rock is produced when which of the following undergoes profound changes as a result of exposure to intense pressure and heat?

a. A batholith
b. A protolith
c. An igneous rock
d. A sedimentary rock

22. All of the following are examples of metamorphic rocks EXCEPT:

a. Granite
b. Quartzite
c. Slate
d. Marble

23. When metamorphic rock is stressed unevenly during recrystallization, it can result in:

a. Foliation
b. Contact metamorphism
c. Regional metamorphism
d. Extrusion

24. Which of the following statements correctly describes a distinction between regional and contact metamorphism?

a. Regional metamorphism results from intense heat, while contact metamorphism is caused by extreme pressure.
b. Regional metamorphism results from extreme pressure, while contact metamorphism is caused by intense heat.
c. Regional metamorphism occurs when magma is injected into surrounding rock, while contact metamorphism occurs when a large area of rock is subjected to intense heat and pressure.
d. Regional metamorphism occurs when a large area of rock is subjected to intense heat and pressure, while contact metamorphism occurs when magma is injected into surrounding rock.

25. When two tectonic plates are moving laterally in opposing directions, this is called a(n):

a. Transform boundary
b. Compressional boundary
c. Oppositional boundary
d. Lateral boundary

26. Which of the following statements correctly describes a difference between the lithosphere and the asthenosphere?

a. The asthenosphere is composed of atmospheric gas, while the lithosphere is composed of liquids and solids.
b. The asthenosphere is hotter and more fluid than the lithosphere.
c. The lithosphere is hotter and has a different chemical composition than the asthenosphere.
d. Heat is transferred through conduction in the asthenosphere, while it is transferred through convection in the lithosphere.

27. The most recently formed parts of the Earth's crust can be found at:

a. Subduction zones
b. Compressional boundaries
c. Extensional boundaries
d. Mid-ocean ridges

Refer to the following for question 28:

After a laboratory experiment that involved using various chemical solutions, you and your lab partner are asked to clean up your workspace. The teacher states that any chemicals that have been poured into a new container should be disposed of, but the chemicals still in their original bottles can be placed into storage.

28. Which of the following is NOT a recommended storage practice for laboratory chemicals?

a. Chemicals should be stored at the appropriate temperature and humidity.
b. Chemicals should be dated when received and when opened.
c. Chemicals may be routinely stored on bench tops.
d. Chemicals should be stored on shelves with raised outer edges.

29. Which of the following events directly results in a volcanic eruption?

a. A batholith forms beneath the Earth's surface.
b. Magma fills vertical and horizontal fractures in the Earth's crust, creating sills and dikes.
c. An oceanic plate is subducted by a continental plate.
d. A dike reaches the Earth's surface, and a plume passes through it.

30. Cinder cone volcanoes are created by:

a. A series of explosive eruptions
b. Gradual eruptions over time
c. A combination of both explosive and gradual eruptions over time
d. None of the above

31. Island chains like the Hawaiian or Midway Islands are created when:

a. Tectonic plates move apart and magma rises to the surface.
b. The subduction process creates magma, which rises above the ocean's surface to form islands.
c. Underwater earthquakes produce mountains that protrude above the water's surface.
d. A tectonic plate gradually moves over a fixed plume of magma that rises from the mantle.

32. Which of the following is true of a volcano that is thought to be dormant?

a. It will probably never erupt again, and it is quite safe for people to live near its base.
b. It is expected to erupt some time again in the future, but danger is not imminent.
c. It is expected to erupt soon, and evacuation should be commenced.
d. It is a shield volcano that is erupting, but people living near the volcano should not expect their lives to be significantly disrupted.

33. The mountain below has the oldest rock in its core and the youngest rock in its outer layers. Which of the following terms best describes the mountain?

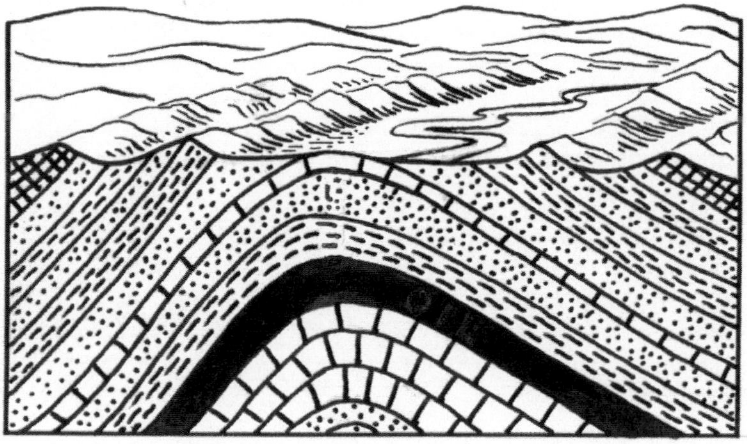

a. Syncline
b. Anticline
c. Fault-block
d. Graben

34. When fault-block mountains like those in the Western United States are formed, sections that are lifted by tensional forces are called:

a. Antiforms
b. Faces
c. Horsts
d. Rifts

35. Which of the following is thought to be a direct result of the Dynamo Effect?

a. The motion of tectonic plates over the mantle
b. The heating of the Earth's atmosphere
c. The production of the Earth's magnetic field
d. None of the above

36. The Earth's magnetic field protects it from:

a. Excess heat from the Sun
b. Radio waves from black holes
c. Solar wind
d. Impacts from space debris

37. In 1912, Alfred Wegener proposed a theory often referred to as "the Pangaea Theory." This theory was based on which of the following ideas?

a. The Earth's magnetic poles have reversed several times throughout history.
b. Tectonic plates move because of convection currents in the mantle.
c. Mountains are formed by tectonic plates pushing against one another.
d. The continents once formed a single land mass, but they have since drifted apart.

38. The Richter scale determines the magnitude of an earthquake by:

a. Comparing its destructiveness to that of other earthquakes
b. Measuring the amount of seismic energy it releases
c. Ascertaining the farthest distance from the epicenter at which the earthquake can be felt
d. Measuring the depth of the earthquake

39. An earthquake with a Richter magnitude of 1.5 can be expected to have which of the following effects on an urban area with high standards for building construction?

a. The earthquake will probably not be felt, and will not cause damage.
b. There may be slight damage to well-constructed buildings over a small area.
c. There will be serious damage to well-constructed buildings over a large area.
d. There will be catastrophic damage and many people will be injured.

40. The process that causes lithospheric plates to move over the surface of the mantle is called:

a. Conduction
b. Convection
c. Tension
d. Subduction

41. Which of the following statements correctly describes the relationship between temperature and density in water?

a. As the temperature of liquid water decreases, density decreases monotonically.
b. As the temperature of frozen water (ice) increases, density increases monotonically.
c. Water in the solid state generally has a higher density than water in the liquid state.
d. Water in the liquid state generally has a higher density than water in the solid state.

42. Ammonia has a specific heat capacity greater than that of water. This means that:

a. Water vaporizes at a higher temperature than ammonia.
b. It takes more energy to increase the temperature of ammonia than it does to increase the temperature of water.
c. Water is always denser than ammonia.
d. Water is only denser than ammonia at higher temperatures.

43. Water that evaporates from oceans can precipitate over land due to the process of:

a. Transpiration
b. Advection
c. Sublimation
d. Interception

44. Water is likely to have the shortest residence time in which of the following types of reservoirs?

a. A glacier
b. A lake
c. A river
d. The atmosphere

45. What is the point of a phase diagram where a substance can exist as a solid, a liquid, and a gas?

a. Isothermal point
b. Isobaric point
c. Triple point
d. Critical point

Refer to the following for question 46:

> The planet's oceans are experiencing climate changes, pollution, and overfishing. In some areas, zones that would normally host abundant aquatic life are now considered "dead zones."

46. The main human-caused reason for these "dead zones" is:

a. Evaporation
b. Invasive species
c. Use of chemical fertilizers
d. Global warming

47. The majority of the solar energy that reaches Earth is absorbed by:

a. Glaciers
b. Landmasses
c. Oceans
d. The Earth's atmosphere

48. The majority of weather phenomena occur in which part of the Earth's atmosphere?

a. Troposphere
b. Stratosphere
c. Hydrosphere
d. Ionosphere

49. According to the Köppen Climate Classification System, regions with continental climates are most commonly found:

a. In the interior regions of large landmasses
b. Near the equator
c. Near the Earth's poles
d. In places with high temperatures year-round

50. Tropical climate zones are characterized by:

a. Extreme temperature variations between night and day
b. Extreme temperature variations between seasons
c. Frequent rainfall
d. All of the above

51. Which of the following is a true statement about the Earth's oceans?

a. Oceans comprise about 50% of the Earth's surface.
b. The deepest point in the ocean is about 6,000 meters below sea level.
c. The ocean is divided geographically into four areas: the Atlantic, Pacific, Mediterranean, and Indian.
d. The ocean's salinity is usually between 34 and 35 parts per thousand, or 35,000 parts per million.

52. A guyot is defined as:

a. Any undersea mountain more than 1,000 meters high
b. A seamount with a flattened top
c. An undersea mountain chain
d. A trough in the ocean floor

53. Approximately 96.5% of seawater is composed of:

a. Hydrogen and sodium
b. Hydrogen and oxygen
c. Oxygen and sodium
d. Chlorine and sodium

54. Which of the following statements correctly describes a difference between surface and subsurface ocean currents?

a. Subsurface currents are caused only by temperature variations, while surface currents are caused by changes in air pressure.
b. Subsurface currents are caused by temperature and density variations, while surface currents are caused by changes in air pressure.
c. Subsurface currents are caused by temperature and density variations, while surface currents are caused by wind.
d. Surface currents are caused by changes in air temperature, while subsurface currents are caused by changes in water temperature.

55. The Coriolis effect in the Earth's oceans is caused by:

a. The Earth's rotation
b. The Earth's magnetic field
c. Variations in the density of seawater
d. The Gulf Stream

56. Which of the following statements correctly describes an effect of the Gulf Stream?

a. It increases humidity along North America's west coast.
b. It makes the climate of South America colder.
c. It makes the climate of Northern Europe warmer.
d. It makes the climate of the Caribbean milder and less humid.

57. Thermohaline circulation is caused by:

a. Temperature differences between seawater only
b. Salinity differences between seawater only
c. Variations in seawater density caused by both temperature and salinity differences
d. Variations in seawater density caused by extreme wind and storm events

58. When cold, nutrient-rich water is allowed to rise to the surface because winds parallel to a landmass's coast blow the surface water towards the open sea, this is called:

a. Ekman transport
b. The Coriolis effect
c. Upwelling
d. Downwelling

59. The frequency of ocean waves is measured by:

a. The vertical distance between a wave's crest and trough
b. The horizontal distance between the crests of two subsequent waves
c. The time between two subsequent wave crests
d. The number of wave crests that pass a given point each second

60. When the accumulation of snow and ice exceeds ablation, which of the following occurs as a direct result?

a. An iceberg breaks free from a glacier.
b. A glacier gradually forms.
c. A glacier slowly erodes.
d. A lake forms within a glacier.

61. The Cretaceous-Tertiary event, during which non-avian dinosaurs became extinct, occurred approximately how long ago?

a. 10,000 years ago
b. 15.5 million years ago
c. 38 million years ago
d. 65.5 million years ago

62. Which of the following techniques is NOT a radiometric dating process?

a. Potassium-argon dating
b. Stratigraphic dating
c. Uranium-lead dating
d. Chlorine-36 dating

63. In the field of geology, the term "uniformitarianism" refers to the belief that:

a. Catastrophic events like mass extinctions are the main forces that have shaped the Earth.
b. The Earth's crust has not undergone any dramatic changes since its formation.
c. The natural forces that shape the Earth have remained relatively constant over geologic time.
d. The Earth's stratigraphy is more or less uniform at any given geographic location.

64. In the field of stratigraphy, the relative ages of rocks may be determined by examining which of the following types of evidence?

a. The dates the rocks were formed and the ages of fossils deposited within the rocks
b. Evidence of changes in detrital remanent magnetism when the rock was deposited
c. The vertical layering pattern of the rock
d. All of the above

65. Which of the following is an example of an absolute age?

a. A fossil is 37 million years old.
b. A rock is less than 100,000 years old.
c. An organic artifact is between 5,000 and 10,000 years old.
d. All of the above

66. In geochronology, which of the following is the longest time period?

a. An epoch
b. An era
c. An eon
d. An age

67. Which of the following correctly lists the periods that make up the Mesozoic era, from earliest to most recent?

a. Jurassic, Triassic, Cretaceous
b. Permian, Triassic, Jurassic
c. Triassic, Jurassic, Cretaceous
d. Triassic, Jurassic, Permian

68. In his work, *The Origin of Life*, Alexander Oparin argued that:

a. Life arose spontaneously from other decaying organic matter.
b. Life originated in deep-sea vents.
c. Life arose on Earth through a "primordial soup" that is no longer possible because of atmospheric oxygen.
d. Life emerged as part of an autocatalytic network.

69. According to current theories, the Earth was formed approximately how long ago?

a. 50 million years ago
b. 1.25 billion years ago
c. 4.5 billion years ago
d. 15 billion years ago

70. The most severe mass extinction event in Earth's history was the:

a. Cretaceous-Tertiary Event
b. Permian-Triassic Event
c. Ordovician-Silurian Event
d. Late Devonian Event

71. According to the theory of evolution, which of the following life forms is thought to have appeared first on Earth?

a. Eukaryotes
b. Arthropods
c. Prokaryotes
d. Amphibians

72. The Cambrian Explosion is best described as:

a. A great migration of flora and fauna between North and South America that vastly increased biodiversity on both continents.
b. The emergence of multicellular life about one billion years ago.
c. The increase in the pace of evolution ushered in by the emergence of sexual reproduction about 1.2 billion years ago.
d. The dramatic increase in biodiversity that began about 530 million years ago and resulted in the emergence of complex animals over a period of millions of years.

73. Which of the following is considered observational evidence in support of the Big Bang Theory?

a. Expansion in the redshifts of galaxies
b. Measurements of cosmic microwave background radiation
c. Measurements of the distribution of quasars and galaxies
d. All of the above

74. The Cosmological Principle is best described as:

a. An assumption that cannot be tested empirically because it has no observable implications
b. A scientific hypothesis that has been repeatedly validated in empirical tests
c. A working assumption that has testable structural consequences
d. A law of physics that defies empirical testing

75. Redshift is observed when:

a. A light-emitting object moves away from an observer.
b. A star begins to decrease the amount of light it emits.
c. A light-emitting object moves toward an observer.
d. A magnetic field bends observed light.

76. Which of the following statements best describes the physical structure of the universe?

a. Galaxies are the largest structures in the universe, and they are distributed evenly throughout space.
b. Superclusters are the largest structures in the universe, and they are distributed evenly throughout space.
c. Superclusters are the largest structures in the universe, and they are unevenly distributed so that large voids exist in space.
d. Filaments are the largest structures in the universe, and they surround large, bubble-like voids.

77. Which of the following statements about galaxies is true?

a. Galaxies are the only structures in the universe that do not contain dark matter.
b. Galaxies are gravitationally bound, meaning structures within the galaxy orbit around its center.
c. Galaxies typically contain over one trillion stars.
d. Galaxies are composed of clusters and superclusters.

78. The structure of the Milky Way galaxy is best described as:

a. Spiral
b. Starburst
c. Elliptical
d. Irregular

79. The Hertzsprung-Russell (H-R) Diagram is used primarily to:

a. Determine a star's age by comparing its temperature and luminosity.
b. Measure a star's size by estimating its luminosity.
c. Determine a galaxy's luminosity when its size is known.
d. Group galaxies by their morphological types.

80. The distance from the earth to the sun is equal to which of the following?

a. One astronomical unit
b. One light-year
c. One parsec
d. One arcsecond

81. The energy radiated by stars is produced by:

a. Neutronicity
b. Nuclear fusion
c. Nuclear fission
d. Gravitational confinement

82. The stream of charged particles that escape the Sun's gravitational pull is best described by which of the following terms?

a. Solar wind
b. Solar flare
c. Solar radiation
d. Sunspots

83. Which of the following planets in our solar system is NOT a gas giant?

a. Saturn
b. Neptune
c. Venus
d. Jupiter

84. The asteroid belt in our solar system is located between:

a. Earth and Mars
b. Neptune and Pluto
c. Uranus and Saturn
d. Mars and Jupiter

85. Which of the following is a proposed explanation for the formation of black holes?

a. High-energy collisions
b. Gravitational collapse
c. Accretion of matter
d. A and B

86. A total solar eclipse can be observed only by viewers located:

a. Within the penumbra but outside of the umbra
b. Within the umbra
c. Within either the umbra or the penumbra
d. Outside of the Moon's penumbra

87. The atomic number of an element is defined by:

a. The total number of protons and electrons it contains
b. The total number of electrons it contains
c. The total number of protons it contains
d. The total number of neutrons it contains

88. Which of the following statements best describes the main distinction between the isotopes carbon-12 and carbon-13?

a. They have different atomic numbers.
b. They have different mass numbers.
c. They have experienced different degrees of radioactive decay.
d. Both A and B are true.

89. Which of the following statements is NOT true of electrons?

a. They comprise only a tiny fraction of an atom's mass.
b. They are arranged in levels and usually occupy the lowest energy level possible.
c. They are negatively charged.
d. They have a substructure that includes a nucleus.

90. Chemical compounds are formed when:

a. Valence electrons from atoms of two different elements are shared or transferred.
b. Valence electrons from multiple atoms of a single element are shared or transferred.
c. The nuclei of two atoms are joined together.
d. The nucleus of an atom is split.

91. The state of matter in which atoms have the strongest bond is:

a. Plasma
b. Liquid
c. Solid
d. Gas

92. Which of the following statements is true of a closed thermodynamic system?

a. It cannot exchange heat, work, or matter with its surrounding environment.
b. It can exchange heat and work, but not matter, with its surrounding environment.
c. It can exchange heat, but not work or matter, with its surrounding environment.
d. It can exchange matter, but not heat or work, with its surrounding environment.

93. The formula for calculating kinetic energy is:

a. $\frac{1}{2}mv^2$
b. $\frac{1}{2}mv$
c. mgh
d. mgv

94. Which law of classical thermodynamics states that energy can neither be created nor destroyed?

a. Zeroth
b. First
c. Second
d. Third

95. James Hutton is best known for:

a. Establishing the first observable evidence for the Big Bang Theory
b. Suggesting the Third Law of Thermodynamics
c. Proposing the theory of uniformitarianism
d. Introducing the Law of Superposition

96. Which of the following is the correct formula for converting Fahrenheit to Celsius?

a. $^{o}C = \frac{5}{9}(^{o}F - 32)$
b. $^{o}C = \frac{9}{5}(^{o}F - 32)$
c. $^{o}C = \frac{5}{9}(^{o}F + 32)$
d. None of the above

97. A calorimeter is used to measure changes in:

a. Heat
b. Mass
c. Weight
d. Volume

98. Commercial nuclear reactors generate electricity through the process of:

a. Nuclear fission
b. Nuclear fusion
c. Nuclear depletion
d. Radioactive decay

99. Which of the following can be inferred based on the results of the regression analysis shown in the following figure?

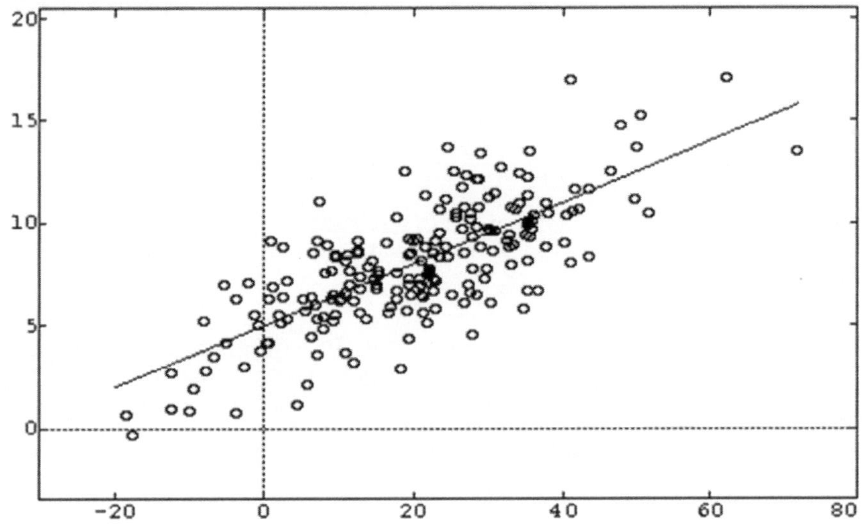

a. A change in the independent variable causes a change in the dependent variable.
b. A change in the dependent variable causes a change in the independent variable.
c. There is a weak positive correlation between the two variables.
d. There is a weak negative correlation between the two variables.

100. Random error could be caused by which of the following problems?

a. Imperfectly calibrated equipment
b. Extraneous disturbances that cannot be controlled
c. Consistent human error in the use of lab equipment
d. Failure to account for a specific variable

Answer Key and Explanations

1. B: It is true that rocks are classified by their formation and the minerals they contain, while minerals are classified by their chemical composition and physical properties. Choice A is incorrect because rocks may contain traces of organic compounds. Choices C and D are incorrect because only minerals can be polymorphs and only rocks contain mineraloids.

2. D: Mineraloids can be defined as substances that resemble minerals but lack a crystalline structure. They are typically found in rocks. Minerals with the same chemical composition but with different crystalline structures are known as polymorphs.

3. C: Mineralogical petrology is not a branch of petrology. Petrologists study the various categories of rocks, including metamorphic, igneous, and sedimentary. Some petrologists, called experimental petrologists, also study changes in the geochemistry of materials that are exposed to extreme temperatures and pressures. Minerals are studied by mineralogists, not petrologists.

4. A: Chemical composition is not one of the physical properties used to classify minerals. The five major physical properties used to classify minerals are luster, hardness, cleavage, streak, and form. There is a separate classification system based on the chemical composition of minerals.

5. C: On the Mohs scale of mineral hardness, talc has the lowest possible score (a one). Diamond is a ten, which is the highest possible score, and gypsum and fluorite have a score of two and four, respectively. Minerals can always scratch minerals that have a Mohs score lower than their own.

6. B: A mineral's true color is observed by conducting a streak test on unglazed porcelain tile. Paper is not appropriate for a streak test because it does not have the correct physical properties. External observation (inspecting the mineral's outer surface) is not sufficient to establish true color since streak tests sometimes reveal a color that is different from the substance's external hue. Finally, the luster test is not used to determine color.

7. D: Galena, pyrite, and magnetite are examples of minerals with a metallic luster. Opal is an example of a mineral with a greasy luster, and diamonds have an adamantine luster. Muscovite and stilbite are examples of minerals with a pearly luster. Other types of luster include dull, silky, waxy, and sub-metallic.

8. B: According to the Dana classification system, gold, silver, and copper belong to the elemental class. Members of the oxide class include chromite and magnetite, and hydrocarbons and acetates are members of the organic class. Sulfide minerals include pyrite and galena.

9. A: According to the Dana system, minerals that contain the anion SO_4^{2-} are part of the sulfate class. Sulfate minerals are typically formed in environments where high salinity water evaporates. Gypsum is an example of a mineral that belongs to the sulfate class.

10. C: Minerals that form on the sea floor from discarded shells are most likely part of the carbonate class. Minerals that form in karst regions and evaporitic settings may also be carbonates. Examples of minerals in the carbonate class include aragonite, dolomite, calcite, and siderite.

11. A: The lithification process results in the formation of sedimentary rocks. During lithification, existing rock is compacted and liquid is squeezed from its pores. Eventually, the rock is cemented together, resulting in sedimentary rock.

12. B: Plutonic, or intrusive, rock forms deep beneath the Earth's surface and cools slowly. Volcanic, or extrusive, rock solidifies at or near the surface. Hypabyssal rock forms below the Earth's surface but not at a depth as great as plutonic rock. Detrital rock is a type of sedimentary rock.

13. C: Overgrazing and deforestation directly contribute to soil erosion by destroying the natural ground cover that normally prevents soil from being washed and blown away. These activities can ultimately result in desertification, which renders land unsuitable for agriculture.

14. C: Physical weathering of rocks can be caused by changes in temperature and pressure, as well as the freezing and thawing of water on the surfaces of rocks. Oxidation is a chemical process, not a physical one. Therefore, it is considered an example of chemical rather than physical weathering.

15. C: When salt water penetrates fractures in rocks and leaves behind salt crystals that cause the rock to fracture, it is considered physical rather than chemical weathering. Chemical weathering involves changes in the molecules that make up the rocks, while physical weathering occurs when external factors act on the rock without changing its chemical composition in any way.

16. D: Weathering causes erosion, which often leads to transportation and the deposition of eroded material. After the eroded material is deposited in a new location, lithification proceeds and the sedimentary cycle begins anew.

17. B: Water is a key element in the lithification of sedimentary rock. After it is squeezed from the compressed material, it forms a chemical cement that holds the sedimentary rock in place. This cementation process is followed by recrystallization of the rock when equilibrium is reached.

18. A: Non-detrital sedimentary rock is produced by chemical precipitation. In contrast, detrital sedimentary rocks are comprised of pre-existing rocks, such as quartz, or weathered products of pre-existing rocks, such as clay.

19. C: Leaching in the "A" soil horizon results from contact with acid solutions generated in the "O" horizon, which is the uppermost organic layer of soil. Cations that are leached in the "A" soil horizon accumulate in the "B" soil horizon below.

20. B: Minerals (such as olivine) that are found at the top of Bowen's reaction series weather more quickly than minerals found lower in the series. This is because minerals high in the series crystallize at higher temperatures than those found lower in the series. This means they are less stable and more susceptible to weathering than rocks that crystallize at lower temperatures, such as quartz.

21. B: Metamorphic rock is produced when a protolith undergoes profound changes after being exposed to extreme heat and pressure. A protolith is any rock that is transformed through this process. The original rock may be sedimentary, igneous, or metamorphic. The extreme heat and pressure that serve as the catalyst for this transformation may be produced by the intrusion of magma or tectonic activity, among other factors.

22. A: Quartzite, marble, and slate are all examples of metamorphic rocks, while granite is one of the most common types of igneous rocks.

23. A: When metamorphic rock is stressed unevenly during recrystallization, it can result in foliation. Foliation is characterized by banded rock, and it occurs when certain types of minerals are reoriented during recrystallization due to uneven shortening or compression of the rock.

24. D: Regional metamorphism occurs when a large area of rock is subjected to intense heat and pressure, while contact metamorphism occurs when magma is injected into surrounding rock, also known as country rock. When contact metamorphism occurs, the rocks closest to the hot magma undergo the greatest changes.

25. A: When two tectonic plates are moving laterally in opposing directions, this is called a transform boundary. When there is friction at transform boundaries and pressure builds up, it can result in shallow earthquakes (usually at a depth of less than 25 meters). California's San Andreas Fault is an example of a transform boundary.

26. B: It is true that the asthenosphere is hotter and more fluid than the lithosphere. The asthenosphere is a hot, ductile layer within the upper mantle upon which the lithosphere, or the uppermost mantle and Earth's crust, is situated. Heat is transferred within the asthenosphere through a process called convection, which sometimes causes movement in the tectonic plates that make up the lithosphere.

27. D: The most recently formed parts of the Earth's crust can be found at mid-ocean ridges. New crust forms here when magma erupts from these ridges and pushes preexisting crust horizontally towards the continental plates. Such ridges include the Mid-Atlantic Ridge and the East Pacific Rise.

28. C: Chemicals should not be stored routinely on bench tops. Each chemical should be stored in a location for that specific type of chemical. When in use, chemicals may be temporarily kept on bench tops, but only in the quantities that are required for that particular situation. Chemicals should be returned to an appropriate location after use.

29. D: A volcano occurs when a dike (a vertical fracture in the Earth's crust that fills with magma) reaches the Earth's surface and a plume (a spurt of magma) passes through it. Batholiths are large masses of igneous rock that form beneath the Earth's surface, and a sill is a horizontal fracture in the Earth's crust that fills with magma. When an oceanic plate is subducted by a continental plate, it results in the formation of mountain ranges and volcanic arcs.

30. A: Cinder cone volcanoes are created by a series of explosive eruptions. Gradual eruptions produce shield volcanoes, and composite volcanoes are the result of a combination of gradual and explosive eruptions over time.

31. D: Island chains like the Hawaiian or Midway Islands are created when a tectonic plate gradually moves over a fixed plume of magma that rises from the mantle. When this plume erupts through the Earth's crust, a volcano that rises above the water's surface is formed, which creates an island. The tectonic plate gradually shifts so that the next time the fixed plume erupts, it affects a different point on the plate. This creates another volcanic island near the first one.

32. B: A volcano that is thought to be dormant is expected to erupt some time again in the future, but danger is not imminent. Dormant volcanoes are expected to erupt again in the future because they still show signs of internal volcanic activity. Extinct volcanoes are not expected to erupt again because they show no signs of activity. Active volcanoes are either erupting or about to erupt.

33. B: Since the mountain in the figure has the oldest rock in its core and the youngest rock in its outer layers, it is best described as an anticline. Any mountain that results from a crustal fold and has an upward, convex shape is called an antiform. Mountains in which the rocks are progressively older from the outer layers to the core are anticlines. Synclines have downward, or concave, folds, and fault-block mountains result when faults in continental crust cause certain sections to lift or tilt. Grabens are a formation associated with fault-block mountains.

34. C: When fault-block mountains such as those in the Western United States are formed, sections that are lifted by tensional forces are called horsts. Blocks that are lowered in elevation are called grabens. The term "rift" refers to the entire area that is affected by the separation of a continental plate.

35. C: The Earth's magnetic field is thought to be produced by the Dynamo Effect. According to this theory, the Earth's rotation combined with the convection of metals within the Earth's core produce electric currents. When these currents flow through an existing magnetic field in the core, this produces a secondary magnetic field which reinforces the primary field and creates a self-sustaining dynamo.

36. C: The Earth's magnetic field protects it from solar wind. Solar wind is a stream of highly charged radioactive particles that emanate from the Sun, and these particles are deflected by the magnetic field. The magnetic field is shaped like a bowl that covers the side of the Earth facing the Sun. It deflects most solar particles, but some are trapped in the Van Allen belt. Particularly strong bursts of solar wind allow particles to pass through this belt into the Earth's ionosphere and upper atmosphere, creating geomagnetic storms and auroras.

37. D: In 1912, Alfred Wegener proposed that the continents once formed a single land mass called Pangaea, but they have since drifted apart. Theories about the Earth's magnetic fields and plate tectonics did not emerge until years later. Once they did, they helped produce evidence to support Wegener's theory.

38. B: The Richter scale determines the magnitude of an earthquake by measuring the amount of seismic energy it releases. The formula used to calculate an earthquake's Richter magnitude takes the logarithm of the horizontal amplitude of the earthquake's seismic waves into account, and also makes adjustments for the position of the seismograph relative to the earthquake.

39. A: An earthquake with a Richter magnitude of 1.5 will probably not be felt, and will not cause any damage. Earthquakes with magnitudes of less than 2.0 are usually not felt, and those with magnitudes of less than 5.0 typically do not seriously damage well-constructed buildings. Earthquakes with magnitudes of 6.0 or greater can cause damage to even well-constructed buildings.

40. B: The process that causes lithospheric plates to move over the surface of the mantle is called convection. The mantle rock in the lower portion of the mantle is heated by the Earth's core and slowly rises to the surface, pushing aside cooler rock that is already there. This hotter rock eventually cools and is pushed aside by hotter rock that rises from below. This cycle, called convection, creates constant movement in the mantle that contributes to the motion of the tectonic plates.

41. D: Water in the liquid state generally has a higher density than water in the solid state (ice). Unlike most other substances, which become progressively denser as they grow colder, water's density only increases until it reaches a maximum density around 4 °C, after which it begins to decrease as the temperature drops further.

42. B: The fact that water's specific heat capacity is second only to that of ammonia means that it takes more energy to increase the temperature of ammonia than it does to increase the temperature of water. Specific heat capacity refers to the amount of energy required to increase the temperature of a substance by one degree Celsius. Ammonia has the highest specific heat capacity of all substances, and the specific heat capacity of water is the second highest.

43. B: Water that evaporates from oceans can precipitate over land due to advection. Advection is the horizontal movement of air masses by wind. Moist air over the ocean is transported horizontally over land; as this air rises and cools (often by convection or lifting over terrain or fronts), the water vapor condenses and can precipitate over land masses.

44. D: Water is likely to have the shortest residence time in the atmosphere. Water molecules linger in the atmosphere for an estimated 9 days, while their residence time in glaciers may range from 20 to 100 years. Water molecules reside in lakes for approximately 50 to 100 years, and they stay in rivers for two to six months.

45. C: A triple point on a phase diagram indicates a precise temperature and pressure where a substance can simultaneously exist as a solid, a liquid, and a gas. Isothermal means constant temperature and would refer to a vertical line rather than a point. Isobaric means constant pressure and would refer to a horizontal line rather than a point. The critical point indicates a particular temperature and pressure beyond which the substance is neither a liquid nor a gas, but a supercritical fluid.

46. C: The main human-caused reason for "dead zones" in portions of oceans and lakes that normally host abundant aquatic life is the use of chemical fertilizers. These fertilizers, which are high in nitrogen and phosphorous, enter lakes and rivers in water runoff and become concentrated in certain areas. This concentration, called eutrophication, eventually depletes the water's oxygen levels and renders it incapable of supporting life.

47. C: The majority of the solar energy that reaches Earth is absorbed by the oceans, which make up 71 percent of the Earth's surface. Because of water's high specific heat capacity, oceans can absorb and store large quantities of heat, thus preventing drastic increases in the overall atmospheric temperature.

48. A: The majority of weather phenomena occur in the Earth's troposphere. The troposphere is the lowest layer of the atmosphere, extending from Earth's surface up to roughly 8–15 kilometers in altitude. It contains the majority of the mass of Earth's atmosphere and 99 percent of its water vapor.

49. A: According to the Köppen Climate Classification System, regions with continental climates are most commonly found in the interior regions of large landmasses. Continental climates are characterized by large seasonal temperature variations, with warm or hot summers and cold winters. Precipitation is often moderate and can occur throughout the year.

50. C: Tropical climate zones are characterized by frequent rainfall, especially during the monsoon season, and by moderate temperatures that vary little from season to season or between night and day. Tropical zones do experience frequent rainfall, which leads to abundant vegetation.

51. D: It is true that the ocean's salinity is usually between 34 and 35 parts per thousand, or 35,000 parts per million. Oceans comprise about 70.8% of the Earth's surface, and the ocean's deepest point is over 10,000 meters below sea level. The Mediterranean is considered a sea, not an ocean.

52. B: A guyot is defined as a seamount with a flattened top. The term "seamount" refers to any undersea volcano that is more than 1,000 meters tall. Undersea troughs are called trenches, and undersea mountain chains are called mid-ocean ridges.

53. B: Approximately 96.5% of seawater is composed of hydrogen and oxygen. Although seawater does contain sodium, chlorine, magnesium, sulfur, and other dissolved solids, its primary components are the same substances that make up fresh water.

54. C: It is true that subsurface currents are driven by temperature and density variations, while surface currents are driven by wind. Ocean currents affect vast quantities of seawater and strongly influence the climate of Earth's landmasses.

55. A: The appearance of the Coriolis effect in the Earth's oceans is caused by the Earth's rotation. The Coriolis effect results when free objects such as water move over a rotating surface such as the Earth. As water moves from the poles towards the equator, it curves slightly westward, while water moving in the opposite direction (from the equator towards the poles) moves slightly eastward.

56. C: The Gulf Stream, which is a surface current that originates in the Gulf of Mexico and travels across the Atlantic Ocean, makes the climate of Northern Europe warmer. After traveling up the eastern coast of the US, the Gulf Stream splits into two forks. The North Atlantic Drift travels across the ocean to warm Europe, while the southern fork travels toward West Africa.

57. C: Thermohaline circulation is caused by variations in seawater density caused by both temperature and salinity differences. This process, which affects subsurface ocean currents, contributes to the mixing of seawater and accounts for the relative uniformity of the water's physical and chemical properties.

58. C: When cold, nutrient-rich water is allowed to rise to the surface because winds parallel to a landmass's coast blow the surface water towards the open sea, it is called upwelling. Upwelling brings nutrient-rich deep water that is enriched by the decomposition of dead organisms to the surface, supplying nutrients for phytoplankton growth. These phytoplankton are then consumed by zooplankton, which in turn are eaten by larger organisms.

59. D: The frequency of ocean waves is measured by the number of wave crests that pass a given point each second. The crest of a wave is its highest point, and the trough is its lowest point. The horizontal distance between two subsequent crests is called wavelength, and the height is the vertical distance between a single wave's trough and crest.

60. B: When the accumulation of snow and ice exceeds ablation, a glacier will gradually form. Ablation is the sloughing off of ice and snow through melting, evaporation, sublimation, and wind erosion. When snow and ice accumulate faster than ablation occurs, a glacier will form and continue to gain mass until the rate of ablation overtakes the rate of accumulation.

61. D: The Cretaceous-Tertiary event, during which non-avian dinosaurs became extinct, occurred approximately 65.5 million years ago. It is the most recent of the five major extinction events that have occurred throughout the Earth's history.

62. B: Stratigraphic dating is not a radiometric dating process because it does not consider the radioactive properties of materials to estimate their dates. Instead, it relies on the law of superposition to estimate relative ages by comparing the relative depths of materials.

63. C: In the field of geology, the term "uniformitarianism" refers to the belief that the natural forces, laws, and processes that shape the Earth have remained relatively constant over geologic time. This belief contradicts catastrophism, which maintains that dramatic events have been the primary forces involved in shaping the Earth.

64. D: The field of stratigraphy is divided into several subfields, each of which focuses on a unique aspect of sedimentary material and yields unique insights about the material's age. In the subfield of chronostratigraphy, a material's age is estimated by determining when it was formed or deposited. The study of the vertical layering of rock types is called lithostratigraphy, and the study of fossil ages in rock layers is called biostratigraphy. Magnetostratigraphy examines data about changes in detrital remanent magnetism (DRM) at the time rocks were formed.

65. A: When a fossil is determined to be 37 million years old, this is an example of an absolute age. Absolute dating, which can be accomplished through the use of radiometric techniques, establishes precise ages for materials, while stratigraphic techniques only produce relative dates. Relative dating can establish approximate ages for rocks and fossils based on clues in the surrounding rock, but it cannot be used to determine absolute age.

66. C: In geochronology, an eon is the longest time period, followed by an era, an epoch, and then an age. The lengths of these units vary, but eons are usually hundreds of millions of years to two billion years.

67. C: The Mesozoic era is composed of the Triassic, Jurassic, and Cretaceous periods. It was preceded by the Paleozoic era, of which the Permian is the last period. The Triassic period ended about 200 million years ago, and was followed by the Jurassic period. The Jurassic period gave way to the Cretaceous period just under 150 million years ago.

68. C: In his 1924 work, *The Origin of Life*, Alexander Oparin argued that life arose on Earth through a "primordial soup" that is no longer possible because of atmospheric oxygen.

69. C: According to current theories, the Earth was formed approximately 4.5 billion years ago. This date has been established through the use of radiometric dating performed on meteorite fossils.

70. B: The most severe mass extinction event in Earth's history was the Permian-Triassic Event. It occurred approximately 251.4 million years ago, and resulted in the extinction of 96 percent of all marine species and 70 percent of terrestrial vertebrate species.

71. C: Prokaryotes, or simple cells that lack a nucleus, are thought to have appeared on Earth approximately 3.8 billion years ago, according to the theory of evolution. Eukaryotes, or complex cells, are thought to have emerged 2 billion years ago, and arthropods are thought to have developed about 570 million years ago. Amphibians are thought to have emerged approximately 360 million years ago.

72. D: The Cambrian Explosion is best described as the dramatic increase in biodiversity that began about 530 million years ago and resulted in the emergence of complex animals over a period of millions of years. Evidence for this "explosion" of life comes mainly from fossil records. There are many possible explanations for it, ranging from an increase in oxygen levels to the development of eyes.

73. D: Expansion in the redshifts of galaxies, measurements of cosmic microwave background radiation, and measurements of the distribution of quasars and galaxies are all considered observational evidence in support of the Big Bang Theory. The abundance of certain "primordial elements" is also consistent with the theory.

74. C: The Cosmological Principle is best described as a working assumption that has testable structural consequences. The principle, which underlies existing cosmological theories, assumes that the view of the universe possessed by observers on Earth is not distorted by their observational location. The observable implications of this theory are homogeneity (the same types of observational evidence are available regardless of one's vantage point within the universe) and isotropy (the same observational evidence is available by looking in any given direction from a single vantage point).

75. A: Redshift is observed when a light-emitting object moves away from an observer. The observation of cosmological redshift supports the notion that the universe is expanding and the distance between Earth and distant galaxies is increasing. Redshift is an increase in the wavelength of light that appears visually as a movement toward the "red" end of the spectrum.

76. D: The physical structure of the universe is thought to consist of filaments (walls of superclusters, clusters, and galaxies) that surround large, bubble-like voids. Filaments are the largest structures in the universe, with some forming huge structures like the Great Wall and the Sloan Great Wall.

77. B: It is true that galaxies are gravitationally bound, so that structures within them orbit around the center. Galaxies do contain dark matter, and only the largest "giant" galaxies contain over one trillion stars. The smallest "dwarf" galaxies contain as few as 10 million stars. Clusters and superclusters are composed of many galaxies.

78. A: The structure of the Milky Way galaxy is spiral, meaning it has curved "arms" stretching out from a central point. While spiral galaxies have a flat, disc-like appearance, elliptical galaxies are more three-dimensional and appear to be roughly the same shape regardless of the viewing angle.

79. A: The Hertzsprung-Russell (H-R) Diagram is used primarily to determine a star's age by comparing its temperature and luminosity. These two variables are plotted, and a given star's values can be compared to those of other stars to estimate its age and evolutionary stage. Stars on the Main Sequence of the diagram have roughly proportional luminosity and temperature values, while white dwarf stars have low luminosity relative to their temperature. Some giant stars have low temperatures relative to their luminosity.

80. A: The average distance from the earth to the sun is equal to one astronomical unit (AU). An AU is equal to 93 million miles and is far smaller than a light-year or a parsec. A light-year is defined as the distance light can travel in a vacuum in one year, and is equal to roughly 63,241 AU. A parsec is the parallax of one arcsecond and is equal to 2.0626×10^5 astronomical units.

81. B: The energy radiated by stars is produced by nuclear fusion. This is the process whereby the nuclei of individual atoms bind together to form heavier elements and release energy outward. By the time this energy, which is created in the star's core, reaches the outer walls of the star, it exists in the form of light.

82. A: The stream of charged particles that escape the Sun's gravitational pull is called solar wind. Solar wind is composed primarily of protons and electrons, and these particles are deflected away from the Earth by its magnetic field. When stray particles do manage to enter the atmosphere, they cause the auroras (northern and southern lights) and geomagnetic storms that can affect power grids.

83. C: Venus is not a gas giant. The four gas giants are Jupiter, Saturn, Uranus, and Neptune. While these gas giants are larger than Earth and are composed mostly of gases, Venus is a terrestrial planet that is comparable in size to the Earth.

84. D: The asteroid belt in our solar system is located between Mars and Jupiter. The asteroid belt is populated by asteroids and dwarf planets that are distributed thinly enough that spacecraft can pass through the belt with relative ease.

85. D: Gravitational collapse and high-energy collisions are both proposed explanations for the formation of black holes. Gravitational collapse occurs when the outward pressure exerted by an object is too weak to resist that object's own gravity. Collisions that produce conditions of sufficient density could also, in theory, create black holes. The accretion of matter is considered observational evidence for the existence of black holes.

86. B: A total solar eclipse can be observed only by viewers located within the umbra. The umbra is the darkest part of the shadow, and the light source is not visible from it. The penumbra is the lighter portion of the shadow from which the light source is partially visible. In a solar eclipse, the Moon passes between the Earth and the Sun, and viewers in the umbra experience a total solar eclipse.

87. C: The atomic number of an element is defined by the total number of protons it contains, and elements are arranged on the periodic table by atomic number. The atomic mass of an element is the sum total of its protons and neutrons, averaged over all of its isotopes.

88. B: The main distinction between the isotopes carbon-12 and carbon-13 is that they have different mass numbers. Isotopes of a given element all have the same atomic number, since atomic number (also known as proton number) is the defining characteristic of each element. However, they have different neutron numbers, which causes them to have varying mass numbers as well. Both carbon-12 and carbon-13 are stable isotopes, meaning they do not experience observable radioactive decay.

89. D: Electrons are elementary particles with no known components, so it is not true that they have a nucleus. Electrons are negatively charged, and they are arranged in levels. Electrons gravitate toward the lowest energy level possible, and they have very little mass (roughly $\frac{1}{1,836}$ of the mass of a proton).

90. A: Chemical compounds are formed when valence electrons from atoms of two different elements are shared or transferred. Valence electrons are the electrons located in the outermost shell of the atom, and they occupy the highest energy level. Atoms may form compounds by sharing valence electrons (covalent bonding) or by transferring electrons.

91. C: The state of matter in which atoms have the strongest bond is the solid state. Matter, which is defined as any substance that has mass and occupies space, can exist as a solid, liquid, gas, or plasma. The atoms or molecules that form solids possess the strongest bonds, while those that form plasma possess the weakest bonds.

92. B: A closed thermodynamic system can exchange heat and work, but not matter, with its surrounding environment. In contrast, an isolated system cannot exchange heat, work, or matter with its surrounding environment, so its mass and energy levels always remain constant. Open systems can exchange heat, work, and mass with their surrounding environments.

93. A: The formula for calculating kinetic energy is $\frac{1}{2}mv^2$, where m = mass and v = velocity. Kinetic energy is defined as the energy of an object in motion. Potential energy, or stored energy, is measured using the formula mgh, where m = mass, g = gravity, and h = height.

94. B: The first law of classical thermodynamics states that energy can neither be created nor destroyed. The zeroth law is concerned with thermodynamic equilibrium, and the second and third laws discuss entropy.

95. C: James Hutton is best known for proposing the theory of uniformitarianism. This geological theory, which is essentially the opposite of catastrophism, suggests that the laws and forces acting on the Earth have remained basically the same since the beginning of geologic time.

96. A: The correct formula for converting Fahrenheit measurements to Celsius measurements is $°C = \frac{5}{9}(°F - 32)$, where °F is the temperature in Fahrenheit.

97. A: A calorimeter is used to measure changes in heat. This instrument uses a thermometer to measure the amount of energy necessary to increase the temperature of water.

98. A: Commercial nuclear reactors generate electricity through the process of nuclear fission. The fission process is used to heat water, which in turn generates steam that is used to produce electricity. This process is controlled to ensure safety, but it does produce nuclear waste that requires the use of extensive procedures to dispose of it safely.

99. C: The results of the regression analysis show that there is a weak positive correlation between the two variables, as evidenced by the fact that data points with higher values for the independent variable (x-axis) also have higher corresponding values for the dependent variable (y-axis). However, correlation does not equal causation, and it cannot be established that a change in the independent variable causes a corresponding change in the dependent variable without additional information.

100. B: Random error could be caused by extraneous disturbances that cannot be controlled. Random error is that which does not affect experimental results in a consistent, patterned way. In contrast, systematic error affects all experimental results consistently. For example, if an instrument is calibrated improperly, all experimental results will be skewed in the same direction.

How to Overcome Test Anxiety

Just the thought of taking a test is enough to make most people a little nervous. A test is an important event that can have a long-term impact on your future, so it's important to take it seriously and it's natural to feel anxious about performing well. But just because anxiety is normal, that doesn't mean that it's helpful in test taking, or that you should simply accept it as part of your life. Anxiety can have a variety of effects. These effects can be mild, like making you feel slightly nervous, or severe, like blocking your ability to focus or remember even a simple detail.

If you experience test anxiety—whether severe or mild—it's important to know how to beat it. To discover this, first you need to understand what causes test anxiety.

Causes of Test Anxiety

While we often think of anxiety as an uncontrollable emotional state, it can actually be caused by simple, practical things. One of the most common causes of test anxiety is that a person does not feel adequately prepared for their test. This feeling can be the result of many different issues such as poor study habits or lack of organization, but the most common culprit is time management. Starting to study too late, failing to organize your study time to cover all of the material, or being distracted while you study will mean that you're not well prepared for the test. This may lead to cramming the night before, which will cause you to be physically and mentally exhausted for the test. Poor time management also contributes to feelings of stress, fear, and hopelessness as you realize you are not well prepared but don't know what to do about it.

Other times, test anxiety is not related to your preparation for the test but comes from unresolved fear. This may be a past failure on a test, or poor performance on tests in general. It may come from comparing yourself to others who seem to be performing better or from the stress of living up to expectations. Anxiety may be driven by fears of the future—how failure on this test would affect your educational and career goals. These fears are often completely irrational, but they can still negatively impact your test performance.

Elements of Test Anxiety

As mentioned earlier, test anxiety is considered to be an emotional state, but it has physical and mental components as well. Sometimes you may not even realize that you are suffering from test anxiety until you notice the physical symptoms. These can include trembling hands, rapid heartbeat, sweating, nausea, and tense muscles. Extreme anxiety may lead to fainting or vomiting. Obviously, any of these symptoms can have a negative impact on testing. It is important to recognize them as soon as they begin to occur so that you can address the problem before it damages your performance.

The mental components of test anxiety include trouble focusing and inability to remember learned information. During a test, your mind is on high alert, which can help you recall information and stay focused for an extended period of time. However, anxiety interferes with your mind's natural processes, causing you to blank out, even on the questions you know well. The strain of testing during anxiety makes it difficult to stay focused, especially on a test that may take several hours. Extreme anxiety can take a huge mental toll, making it difficult not only to recall test information but even to understand the test questions or pull your thoughts together.

Effects of Test Anxiety

Test anxiety is like a disease—if left untreated, it will get progressively worse. Anxiety leads to poor performance, and this reinforces the feelings of fear and failure, which in turn lead to poor performances on subsequent tests. It can grow from a mild nervousness to a crippling condition. If allowed to progress, test anxiety can have a big impact on your schooling, and consequently on your future.

Test anxiety can spread to other parts of your life. Anxiety on tests can become anxiety in any stressful situation, and blanking on a test can turn into panicking in a job situation. But fortunately, you don't have to let anxiety rule your testing and determine your grades. There are a number of relatively simple steps you can take to move past anxiety and function normally on a test and in the rest of life.

Physical Steps for Beating Test Anxiety

While test anxiety is a serious problem, the good news is that it can be overcome. It doesn't have to control your ability to think and remember information. While it may take time, you can begin taking steps today to beat anxiety.

Just as your first hint that you may be struggling with anxiety comes from the physical symptoms, the first step to treating it is also physical. Rest is crucial for having a clear, strong mind. If you are tired, it is much easier to give in to anxiety. But if you establish good sleep habits, your body and mind will be ready to perform optimally, without the strain of exhaustion. Additionally, sleeping well helps you to retain information better, so you're more likely to recall the answers when you see the test questions.

Getting good sleep means more than going to bed on time. It's important to allow your brain time to relax. Take study breaks from time to time so it doesn't get overworked, and don't study right before bed. Take time to rest your mind before trying to rest your body, or you may find it difficult to fall asleep.

Along with sleep, other aspects of physical health are important in preparing for a test. Good nutrition is vital for good brain function. Sugary foods and drinks may give a burst of energy but this burst is followed by a crash, both physically and emotionally. Instead, fuel your body with protein and vitamin-rich foods.

Also, drink plenty of water. Dehydration can lead to headaches and exhaustion, especially if your brain is already under stress from the rigors of the test. Particularly if your test is a long one, drink water during the breaks. And if possible, take an energy-boosting snack to eat between sections.

Along with sleep and diet, a third important part of physical health is exercise. Maintaining a steady workout schedule is helpful, but even taking 5-minute study breaks to walk can help get your blood pumping faster and clear your head. Exercise also releases endorphins, which contribute to a positive feeling and can help combat test anxiety.

When you nurture your physical health, you are also contributing to your mental health. If your body is healthy, your mind is much more likely to be healthy as well. So take time to rest, nourish your body with healthy food and water, and get moving as much as possible. Taking these physical steps will make you stronger and more able to take the mental steps necessary to overcome test anxiety.

Mental Steps for Beating Test Anxiety

Working on the mental side of test anxiety can be more challenging, but as with the physical side, there are clear steps you can take to overcome it. As mentioned earlier, test anxiety often stems from lack of preparation, so the obvious solution is to prepare for the test. Effective studying may be the most important weapon you have for beating test anxiety, but you can and should employ several other mental tools to combat fear.

First, boost your confidence by reminding yourself of past success—tests or projects that you aced. If you're putting as much effort into preparing for this test as you did for those, there's no reason you should expect to fail here. Work hard to prepare; then trust your preparation.

Second, surround yourself with encouraging people. It can be helpful to find a study group, but be sure that the people you're around will encourage a positive attitude. If you spend time with others who are anxious or cynical, this will only contribute to your own anxiety. Look for others who are motivated to study hard from a desire to succeed, not from a fear of failure.

Third, reward yourself. A test is physically and mentally tiring, even without anxiety, and it can be helpful to have something to look forward to. Plan an activity following the test, regardless of the outcome, such as going to a movie or getting ice cream.

When you are taking the test, if you find yourself beginning to feel anxious, remind yourself that you know the material. Visualize successfully completing the test. Then take a few deep, relaxing breaths and return to it. Work through the questions carefully but with confidence, knowing that you are capable of succeeding.

Developing a healthy mental approach to test taking will also aid in other areas of life. Test anxiety affects more than just the actual test—it can be damaging to your mental health and even contribute to depression. It's important to beat test anxiety before it becomes a problem for more than testing.

Study Strategy

Being prepared for the test is necessary to combat anxiety, but what does being prepared look like? You may study for hours on end and still not feel prepared. What you need is a strategy for test prep. The next few pages outline our recommended steps to help you plan out and conquer the challenge of preparation.

Step 1: Scope Out the Test

Learn everything you can about the format (multiple choice, essay, etc.) and what will be on the test. Gather any study materials, course outlines, or sample exams that may be available. Not only will this help you to prepare, but knowing what to expect can help to alleviate test anxiety.

Step 2: Map Out the Material

Look through the textbook or study guide and make note of how many chapters or sections it has. Then divide these over the time you have. For example, if a book has 15 chapters and you have five days to study, you need to cover three chapters each day. Even better, if you have the time, leave an extra day at the end for overall review after you have gone through the material in depth.

If time is limited, you may need to prioritize the material. Look through it and make note of which sections you think you already have a good grasp on, and which need review. While you are studying, skim quickly through the familiar sections and take more time on the challenging parts.

Write out your plan so you don't get lost as you go. Having a written plan also helps you feel more in control of the study, so anxiety is less likely to arise from feeling overwhelmed at the amount to cover.

STEP 3: GATHER YOUR TOOLS

Decide what study method works best for you. Do you prefer to highlight in the book as you study and then go back over the highlighted portions? Or do you type out notes of the important information? Or is it helpful to make flashcards that you can carry with you? Assemble the pens, index cards, highlighters, post-it notes, and any other materials you may need so you won't be distracted by getting up to find things while you study.

If you're having a hard time retaining the information or organizing your notes, experiment with different methods. For example, try color-coding by subject with colored pens, highlighters, or post-it notes. If you learn better by hearing, try recording yourself reading your notes so you can listen while in the car, working out, or simply sitting at your desk. Ask a friend to quiz you from your flashcards, or try teaching someone the material to solidify it in your mind.

STEP 4: CREATE YOUR ENVIRONMENT

It's important to avoid distractions while you study. This includes both the obvious distractions like visitors and the subtle distractions like an uncomfortable chair (or a too-comfortable couch that makes you want to fall asleep). Set up the best study environment possible: good lighting and a comfortable work area. If background music helps you focus, you may want to turn it on, but otherwise keep the room quiet. If you are using a computer to take notes, be sure you don't have any other windows open, especially applications like social media, games, or anything else that could distract you. Silence your phone and turn off notifications. Be sure to keep water close by so you stay hydrated while you study (but avoid unhealthy drinks and snacks).

Also, take into account the best time of day to study. Are you freshest first thing in the morning? Try to set aside some time then to work through the material. Is your mind clearer in the afternoon or evening? Schedule your study session then. Another method is to study at the same time of day that you will take the test, so that your brain gets used to working on the material at that time and will be ready to focus at test time.

STEP 5: STUDY!

Once you have done all the study preparation, it's time to settle into the actual studying. Sit down, take a few moments to settle your mind so you can focus, and begin to follow your study plan. Don't give in to distractions or let yourself procrastinate. This is your time to prepare so you'll be ready to fearlessly approach the test. Make the most of the time and stay focused.

Of course, you don't want to burn out. If you study too long you may find that you're not retaining the information very well. Take regular study breaks. For example, taking five minutes out of every hour to walk briskly, breathing deeply and swinging your arms, can help your mind stay fresh.

As you get to the end of each chapter or section, it's a good idea to do a quick review. Remind yourself of what you learned and work on any difficult parts. When you feel that you've mastered the material, move on to the next part. At the end of your study session, briefly skim through your notes again.

But while review is helpful, cramming last minute is NOT. If at all possible, work ahead so that you won't need to fit all your study into the last day. Cramming overloads your brain with more information than it can process and retain, and your tired mind may struggle to recall even previously learned information when it is overwhelmed with last-minute study. Also, the urgent nature of cramming and the stress placed on your brain contribute to anxiety. You'll be more likely to go to the test feeling unprepared and having trouble thinking clearly.

So don't cram, and don't stay up late before the test, even just to review your notes at a leisurely pace. Your brain needs rest more than it needs to go over the information again. In fact, plan to finish your studies by noon or early afternoon the day before the test. Give your brain the rest of the day to relax or focus on other things, and get a good night's sleep. Then you will be fresh for the test and better able to recall what you've studied.

Step 6: Take a Practice Test

Many courses offer sample tests, either online or in the study materials. This is an excellent resource to check whether you have mastered the material, as well as to prepare for the test format and environment.

Check the test format ahead of time: the number of questions, the type (multiple choice, free response, etc.), and the time limit. Then create a plan for working through them. For example, if you have 30 minutes to take a 60-question test, your limit is 30 seconds per question. Spend less time on the questions you know well so that you can take more time on the difficult ones.

If you have time to take several practice tests, take the first one open book, with no time limit. Work through the questions at your own pace and make sure you fully understand them. Gradually work up to taking a test under test conditions: sit at a desk with all study materials put away and set a timer. Pace yourself to make sure you finish the test with time to spare and go back to check your answers if you have time.

After each test, check your answers. On the questions you missed, be sure you understand why you missed them. Did you misread the question (tests can use tricky wording)? Did you forget the information? Or was it something you hadn't learned? Go back and study any shaky areas that the practice tests reveal.

Taking these tests not only helps with your grade, but also aids in combating test anxiety. If you're already used to the test conditions, you're less likely to worry about it, and working through tests until you're scoring well gives you a confidence boost. Go through the practice tests until you feel comfortable, and then you can go into the test knowing that you're ready for it.

Test Tips

On test day, you should be confident, knowing that you've prepared well and are ready to answer the questions. But aside from preparation, there are several test day strategies you can employ to maximize your performance.

First, as stated before, get a good night's sleep the night before the test (and for several nights before that, if possible). Go into the test with a fresh, alert mind rather than staying up late to study.

Try not to change too much about your normal routine on the day of the test. It's important to eat a nutritious breakfast, but if you normally don't eat breakfast at all, consider eating just a protein bar. If you're a coffee drinker, go ahead and have your normal coffee. Just make sure you time it so that the caffeine doesn't wear off right in the middle of your test. Avoid sugary beverages, and drink enough water to stay hydrated but not so much that you need a restroom break 10 minutes into the test. If your test isn't first thing in the morning, consider going for a walk or doing a light workout before the test to get your blood flowing.

Allow yourself enough time to get ready, and leave for the test with plenty of time to spare so you won't have the anxiety of scrambling to arrive in time. Another reason to be early is to select a good seat. It's helpful to sit away from doors and windows, which can be distracting. Find a good seat, get out your supplies, and settle your mind before the test begins.

When the test begins, start by going over the instructions carefully, even if you already know what to expect. Make sure you avoid any careless mistakes by following the directions.

Then begin working through the questions, pacing yourself as you've practiced. If you're not sure on an answer, don't spend too much time on it, and don't let it shake your confidence. Either skip it and come back later, or eliminate as many wrong answers as possible and guess among the remaining ones. Don't dwell on these questions as you continue—put them out of your mind and focus on what lies ahead.

Be sure to read all of the answer choices, even if you're sure the first one is the right answer. Sometimes you'll find a better one if you keep reading. But don't second-guess yourself if you do immediately know the answer. Your gut instinct is usually right. Don't let test anxiety rob you of the information you know.

If you have time at the end of the test (and if the test format allows), go back and review your answers. Be cautious about changing any, since your first instinct tends to be correct, but make sure you didn't misread any of the questions or accidentally mark the wrong answer choice. Look over any you skipped and make an educated guess.

At the end, leave the test feeling confident. You've done your best, so don't waste time worrying about your performance or wishing you could change anything. Instead, celebrate the successful completion of this test. And finally, use this test to learn how to deal with anxiety even better next time.

Review Video: Test Anxiety
Visit mometrix.com/academy and enter code: 100340

Important Qualification

Not all anxiety is created equal. If your test anxiety is causing major issues in your life beyond the classroom or testing center, or if you are experiencing troubling physical symptoms related to your anxiety, it may be a sign of a serious physiological or psychological condition. If this sounds like your situation, we strongly encourage you to seek professional help.

Online Resources

Due to our efforts to try to keep this book to a manageable length, we've created a link that will give you access to all of your online resources:

mometrix.com/resources719/osatearsci108

It's Your Moment, Let's Celebrate It!

Share your story @mometrixtestpreparation